JAMES MADISON: DEFENDER OF THE AMERICAN REPUBLIC

(A VOLUME IN FIRST MEN, AMERICA'S PRESIDENTS SERIES)

OTHER BOOKS IN THE FIRST MEN, AMERICA'S PRESIDENTS SERIES

Barbara Bennett Peterson, Editor

Theodore Roosevelt: A Political Life
Tom Lansford
2004. ISBN 1-59033-990-8

Citizen Lincoln
Ward M. McAfee
2004. ISBN 1-59454-112-4

George Washington, America's Moral Exemplar
Barbara Bennet Peterson
2005. ISBN 1-59454-230-9

President James K. Polk: The Dark Horse President
Louise Mayo
2006. ISBN 1-59454-718-1

Franklin Delano Roosevelt, Preserver of Spirit and Hope
Barbara Bennett Peterson
2006. ISBN 1-60021-117-8

John Quincy Adams: Yankee Nationalist
Paul E. Teed
2006. ISBN 1-59454-797-1

President Herbert Hoover
Don W. Whisenhunt
2006. ISBN 1-60021-476-2

Chester Alan Arthur: The Life of a Gilded Age Politician and President
Gregory J. Dehler
2007. ISBN : 978-1-60021-079-2

William Henry Harrison: General and President
Mary Jane Child Queen
2007. ISBN 978-1-60021-407-3

Thomas Jefferson: A Public Life, A Private Life
David Kiracofe
2008. ISBN 978-1-60456-061-9

John Tyler: A Rare Career
Lyle Nelson
2008. ISBN-13: 978-1-60021-961-0

James Madison: Defender of the American Republic

(A Volume in First Men, America's Presidents Series)

Donald Dewey
and
Barbara Bennett Peterson

Nova Science Publishers, Inc.
New York

For permission to use material from this book please contact us:
Telephone 631-231-7269; Fax 631-231-8175
Web Site: http://www.novapublishers.com

LIBRARY OF CONGRESS CATALOGING-IN-PUBLICATION DATA

Available Upon Request

ISBN: 978-1-60456-858-5

Published by Nova Science Publishers, Inc. ✢ New York

Dedication

Gordon Freirich, Nathan Neville, Scott Dewey,
Lovers of History and my Hope for the Future,
And to Charlotte Dewey who made it all possible

Donald O. Dewey, PhD

My Family, My Friends,
My Colleagues, My University Students
All of whom have inspired my life writing

Barbara Bennett Peterson, PhD

CONTENTS

FOREWORD

President of the United States of America is an official title sought by many and won by only a few individuals. Most American presidents are of high merit and political acumen and reflected wisdom, leadership, and integrity. This series titled *First Men, America's Presidents* published by NOVA Science Publishers contains a book length biography of each president of the United States of America. Every book contains information on the president's early education, professional career, military service or political service prior to the presidency, interpretative discussion of both domestic and foreign policies during each presidency, and the conclusion of their political lives in public service. Every presidential biography in the Nova series has been written by a professional historian or political scientist well versed in the field of presidential scholarship The two major themes of this series are the character traits marking success in the presidency, and the changes in the office of the presidency through America's history. Character matters in all walks of life, but perhaps matters most within the character of the president of the United States.

The duties of the president of the United States are delegated through Article II of the Constitution of the United States of America, and from the successive laws passed by Congress over time. Each president takes the Oath of Affirmation. "I do solemnly swear (or affirm) that I will faithfully execute the Office of the President of the United States, and will to the best of my Ability, preserve, protect and defend the Constitution of the United States." The president's duties and responsibilities under the Constitution are to serve as "Commander in Chief of the Army and Navy of the United States, and the Militia of the several States, when called into actual Service of the United States." The president may invite the counsel and opinions of his various department heads upon any subject related to the execution of the duties of their offices, either in writing or orally as has become the custom within the president's Cabinet. The president "shall have the power to grant Reprieves and Pardons for Offenses against the United States, except in Cases of Impeachment." Every president has realized that each must administer through constitutional principles, as each was elected by the voting majority of the people to be their chief executive through the Electoral College. Each president of the United States "shall have Power, by and with the Advice and Consent of the Senate, to make Treaties, provided two thirds of the Senators present concur." As the president directs both the domestic and foreign activities of the government, he has the power to "nominate and by and with the Advice and Consent of the Senate....appoint Ambassadors, other public Ministers and Consuls, Judges of the Supreme Court, and all other Officers of the United States, whose Appointments are not herein otherwise provided for, and which shall be established by law." The president also receives foreign ambassadors and officials on behalf of the American people. The president "shall have the Power to fill up all Vacancies that may happen during the Recess of the Senate, by granting Commissions which shall expire at the End of their next Session." The president under the Constitution shall give Congress a State of the Union address every year to acquaint them with his policy agenda and plans for the future. Usually in this address to Congress he recommends "to their Consideration such Measures as he shall judge necessary and expedient." Above all, the president of the United States "shall take Care that the Laws be faithfully executed, and shall Commission all the Officers of the United States." A strong role for the president had been envisioned by the Founding Fathers who rejected the obsolete Articles of Confederation and replaced the framework of government with the Constitution of the United States. Article II of the Constitution outlining the powers of the presidency provided that the office of the president would be held by one individual. It provided the president with enumerated powers including the power of the veto, and stipulated that the president's election would be above the control of the Congress to ensure the separation of powers and the system of checks and balances. It stipulated that the president, vice president, and all civil officers of the United States *must govern in the name of the American people* lest they "be removed from Office on Impeachment for, and Conviction of Treason, Bribery, or other high Crimes and Misdemeanors."

From presidents George Washington through John Quincy Adams candidates for the presidency were selected in caucuses of senators and congressmen and then the state legislatures indirectly chose the president through the selection of Electors to the Electoral College. This system had worked for Washington, Adams, Jefferson, Madison and Monroe—they were statesmen who held wide appeal within Congress and the state legislatures and claimed to represent the people. But as demands for greater democracy in the election process were heard, the process was changed. In the outcome of the election of 1824, John Quincy Adams was chosen president by the Congressional House of Representatives under constitutional law after no candidate had received a majority of the electoral ballots in the Electoral College. Jackson, the candidate who had received the most popular votes was not chosen president and his supporters called for more direct popular participation and worked to introduce changes. Hence, the voting process was altered in the name of democracy. In the election of 1828 President Andrew Jackson triumphed after voting had been given directly to the people and removed from the state legislatures. Democracy further triumphed by the elimination of the congressional caucuses in naming presidential candidates and the holding of national political party conventions to name them instead, allowing greater voice and participation of the people. The institution of the party convention to nominate presidential candidates remains, although winners in various state primaries command party delegates to vote the choice of the people. The presidency, molded by the character and designs of each president, oversees command, administration, diplomacy, ceremony, legislation, and public opinion. The modern strength of the presidency is a reflection of the mighty power of the United States within a global world.

The majority of America's presidents have served for one four-year term or less as some died in office. Four presidents served out part of their predecessor's term and won subsequent re-election in their own right: Theodore Roosevelt, Calvin Coolidge, Harry S Truman, and Lyndon Baines Johnson. Only one president, Grover Cleveland, was elected to two discontinuous terms of office and thus was both the twenty-second and the twenty-fourth president of the United States. Several outstanding presidents have been elected to two four-year terms or more. They were: George Washington, Thomas Jefferson, James Madison, James Monroe, Andrew Jackson, Abraham Lincoln, Ulysses S. Grant, Grover Cleveland, William McKinley, Woodrow Wilson, Franklin D. Roosevelt, Dwight D. Eisenhower, Richard Nixon, Ronald Reagan, William Jefferson ("Bill") Clinton, and George W. Bush. Only one president, Franklin D. Roosevelt, was elected for a third and fourth term. Eight presidents have achieved their office as a result of being the vice-president of a preceding president who died in office or resigned: John Tyler, Millard Fillmore, Andrew Johnson, Chester Arthur, Theodore Roosevelt, Calvin Coolidge, Harry S. Truman, Lyndon Baines Johnson, and Gerald R. Ford. Additionally, John Adams, Thomas Jefferson, Martin Van Buren, Richard M. Nixon and George H.W. Bush also rose from the office of vice-president to president. Besides the vice-presidency as a stepping stone to the presidency, two thirds of the presidents elected had held congressional office earlier in their political careers. Twenty presidents had served as Governors of states or territories before being elected. They were: Thomas Jefferson (Virginia), James Monroe (Virginia), Andrew Jackson (Florida), Martin Van Buren (New York), William Henry Harrison (Indiana), John Tyler (Virginia), James K. Polk (Tennessee), Andrew Johnson (Tennessee), Rutherford B. Hayes (Ohio), Grover Cleveland (New York), William McKinley (Ohio), Theodore Roosevelt (New York), William Howard Taft (The Philippines), Woodrow Wilson (New Jersey), Calvin Coolidge (Massachusetts), Franklin D. Roosevelt (New York), Jimmy Carter (Georgia), Ronald Reagan (California), William Jefferson Clinton (Arkansas), and George W. Bush (Texas). Some states with larger voting populations and hence more electoral votes have seen their native sons rise to the presidency of the United States. The American presidents have come from both coasts, east and west, and from both the upper tier and the lower tier of states geographically, north and south. When elected, the president becomes the president of 'all the people', not just those of his political party. Since the president acts as America's commander in chief, the majority of the presidents of the United States have served in the U.S. military. George Washington, Andrew Jackson, William Henry Harrison, Zachary Taylor, Franklin Pierce, Ulysses S. Grant, Rutherford B. Hayes, James Garfield, Chester Arthur, Benjamin Harrison, and Dwight David Eisenhower served in the capacity of generals. James Monroe, John Tyler, Abraham Lincoln, William McKinley, Theodore Roosevelt, Harry Truman, John F. Kennedy, Lyndon Baines Johnson, Richard Nixon, Gerald R. Ford, Jimmy Carter, Ronald Reagan, George Herbert Walker Bush, and George W. Bush also served their country in military service at various ranks, and always with dedication. The youngest elected president was John F. Kennedy (1960) at forty-three. The youngest man to ever serve as president was Theodore Roosevelt who at forty-two assumed the office following William McKinley's assassination. The average age for an elected president was fifty-four. The oldest elected president was Ronald Reagan at sixty-nine (1980) and seventy-three (1984).[1]

One of the major features of American constitutional development has been the growth of the presidency both in power and prestige as well as in new Cabinet positions, departments and agencies under the control of the president. The Federal government has grown mightily in comparison with the states' governments since the inception of the Constitution. Increases in presidential powers have been occasioned by wars, depressions, foreign relations, and the agenda of the presidents themselves. Henry F. Graff, Emeritus Professor at

[1] David C. Whitney and Robin Vaughn Whitney, *The American President (*Garden City, New York: Doubleday, 1993), v-ix.

Columbia University, described the office of the president as "the most powerful office in the world" in *The Presidents*. The Executive Office of the President (EOP) was created during the administration of President Franklin D. Roosevelt upon passage by Congress of the Reorganization Act of 1939. The EOP originally included the White House Office (WHO), the Bureau of the Budget, the Office of Government Reports, the National Resources Planning Board, and the Liaison Office for Personnel Management. In addition, wrote Henry F. Graff, the 1939 Act provided that an "office for emergency management" may be formed "in the event of a national emergency, or threat of a national emergency."[2] Today the White House Office has become "the political as well as policy arm of the chief executive." The larger, all encompassing Executive Office of the President has expanded through time to include a myriad number of departments in addition to the first five listed above and the president is advised by nearly 60 active boards, committees and commissions. During and immediately after World War II the following additional departments within the purview of the EOP were organized: Committee for Congested Production Areas, 1943-1944; War Refugee Board, 1944-1945; Council of Economic Advisers, 1946-; National Security Council, 1947-, and National Security Resources Board, 1947-1953; During the Cold War, additions to the EOP were made adding the following departments: Telecommunications Adviser to the President, 1951-1953; Office of the Director for Mutual Security, 1951-1954; Office of Defense Mobilization, 1952-1958; President's Advisory Committee on Government Organization, 1953-1961; Operations Coordinating Board, 1953-1961; President's Board of Consultants on Foreign Intelligence Activities, 1956-1961; Office of Civil and Defense Mobilization, 1958-1962; and National Aeronautics and Space Council, 1958-1993. By the Sixties, some of the earlier departments organized in the 1939 to 1960 decades were allowed to close, with newer agencies with a new focus and expanded technology taking their place. These newer agencies included: President's Foreign Intelligence Advisory Board, 1961-1977; Office of Emergency Planning, 1962-1969; Office of Science and Technology, 1962-1973; Office of Economic Opportunity, 1964-1975; Office of Emergency Preparedness, 1965-1973, National Council on Marine Resources and Engineering Development, 1966-1971; Council on Environmental Quality, 1969-; Council for Urban Affairs, 1969-1970; and Office of Intergovernmental Relations, 1969-1973. By the mid-Seventies, once again there was a general reorganization with some of the earlier departments and offices being swept away and replaced by newer

---

[2] Henry F. Graff, Editor, *The Presidents* (New York: Charles Scribner's Sons, Simon & Schuster Macmillan, 2nd edition, 1996, Appendix C), 743-745.

agencies reflecting new presidential agendas. Many of the new agencies reflected the urgencies in domestic policies and included: the Domestic Council, 1970-1978; Office of Management and Budget, 1970-; Office of Telecommunications Policy, 1970-1977; Council on International Economic Policy, 1971-1977; Office of Consumer Affairs, 1971-1973; Special Action Office for Drug Abuse Prevention, 1971-1975; Federal Property Council, 1973-1977; Council on Economic Policy, 1973-1974; Energy Policy Office, 1973-1974; Council on Wage and Price Stability, 1974-1981; Energy Resource Council, 1974-1977; Office of Special Representative for Trade Negotiations, 1974-; Presidential Clemency Board, 1974-1975; Office of Science and Technology Policy, 1976-; Office of Administration, 1977-; and Domestic Policy Staff, 1978-1981. Many of the departments, councils and agencies organized as part of the Executive Office of the President by the late Seventies and early Eighties included: Office of Policy Development, 1981-; Office of the U.S. Trade Representative, 1981-; National Critical Materials Council, 1984-; Office of National Drug Control Policy, 1988-; National Economic Council, 1993-. By the 21st century the EOP continued several effective agencies started earlier: Council of Economic Advisers, 1946-; National Security Council, 1947-; Council on Environmental Quality 1964-; Office of Management and Budget 1970-; Office of Science and Technology Policy, 1976-; Office of Administration, 1977-; Office of the U.S. Trade Representative, 1981-; Office of Policy Development, 1981-; and the Office of National Drug Control Policy, 1988-. In addition to the White House Office of the President, the Office of the Vice President functions and is administered as part of the EOP.[3] At the turn of the millennium the department of Homeland Security, 2001-, was established by presidential executive order and administered by the Executive Office of the President that continues to be evolutionary in response to new issues, demands, and events.

Capable presidents have responded to America's changing needs and responsibilities by retooling their administrations to meet new crises, opportunities, and challenges. This series, *First Men, America's Presidents,* published by Nova, explains the personal and public life of each president of the United States. Their qualities of character and leadership are aptly interpreted and offer strong role models for all citizens. Presidential successes are recorded for posterity, as are the pitfalls that should be guarded against in the future. This series also explains the domestic reasons and world backdrop for the expansion of the Executive Office of the President. The president of the United States is

---

3 Henry F. Graff, Editor, *The Presidents* (New York: Charles Scribner's Sons, Simon & Schuster Macmillan, 3rd edition, 2002, Appendix), 743-747.

perhaps the most coveted position in the world and this series reveals the lives of all those successfully elected, how each performed as president, and how each is to be measured in history. The collective life stories of the presidents reveal the greatness that America represents in the world.

Dr. Barbara Bennett Peterson
First Men, America's Presidents Series, Nova Series Editor
Professor of History, Oregon State University (retired)
Emeritus Professor University of Hawaii
Former Adjunct Fellow East-West Center
Professor of History, California State University San Bernardino, Palm Desert

PREFACE

This book follows the life of James Madison, our 4th president, who at the tender age of twenty-five was thrust into significant politics as an elected member of the Virginia House of Burgesses. Even in his first venture into statesmanship. Madison took notes on constitutional deliberations, a practice that he would continue in the Federal Convention that proposed the United States Constitution and throughout much of his legislative career whether in Philadelphia, New York City, or Williamsburg, Virginia. Just as most of our knowledge of the framing of the U.S. Constitution is provided by Madison's painstaking notes of the Constitutional Convention of 1787, much of our knowledge of George Mason's many contributions to the Virginia Constitution of 1776 are also known through Madison's efforts.

His major personal contribution to that seminal state constitution is a brief but key phrase in the Virginia Declaration of Rights that would in many respects become a pattern for the Bill of Rights that Madison was later largely responsible for addition to the United States Constitution. His addition of a simple clause converted Mason's proposed language from religious toleration, where an official church would permit citizens to attend other churches, to religious freedom with its clear implication that it was one of the Rights of Man that were so important to that revolutionary generation. Throughout his career he remained committed to religious freedom and he is still considered one of its greatest contributors. During the brief time between his terms in Congress he would prevail in battles against the re-establishment of the Episcopal Church in Virginia and would win legislative approval for the Statute for Religious Freedom that Jefferson wrote and in which he took enormous pride, but which required the legislative management of James Madison to become law.

Madison is best and justifiably known as "Father of the Constitution" because of his heroic role in bringing together the Federal Convention in 1787, influencing its outcomes through the Virginia Plan, maintaining records of the debates, winning its ratification in the largest state and influencing several other states.

INTRODUCTION

Despite his notoriously diminutive physical stature, James Madison was a political and intellectual giant when he first became Secretary of State in 1801 and then President in 1809.

At the tender age of twenty-five Madison was thrust into significant politics as an elected member of the Virginia House of Burgesses. This legislature would soon convert itself into the convention that would enact the first independent constitution of any of the colonies that would survive into the Nineteenth Century. In May 1776 the convention directed Virginia delegates in the Continental Congress to introduce a resolution for American independence as well as authorization for the colonies to establish new governmental structures. Richard Henry Lee made the motion for independence that was approved on July 2. Two days later Congress approved the classic defense that was written by Thomas Jefferson. A positive vote was probably the still shy and reticent Madison's only impact on Virginia's initiative. It certainly accorded with his long-held conviction that such a decision was the responsibility of the central Congress rather than individual state legislatures or conventions.

Even in this first venture into statesmanship Madison took notes on constitutional deliberations, a practice that he would continue in the Federal Convention that proposed the United States Constitution and throughout much of his legislative career whether in Philadelphia, New York City, or Williamsburg, Virginia. Just as most of our knowledge of the framing of the U.S. Constitution is provided by Madison's painstaking notes of the Constitutional Convention of 1787, much of our knowledge of George Mason's many contributions to the Virginia Constitution of 1776 are also known through Madison's efforts.

His major personal contribution to that seminal state constitution is a brief but key phrase in the Virginia Declaration of Rights that would in many respects become a pattern for the Bill of Rights that Madison was later largely responsible for addition to the United States Constitution. His addition of a simple clause converted Mason's proposed language from religious *toleration*, where an official church would permit citizens to attend other churches, to religious *freedom* with its clear implication that it was one of the Rights of Man that were so important to that revolutionary generation. Throughout his career he remained committed to religious freedom and he is still considered one of its greatest contributors. During the brief time between his terms in Congress he would prevail in battles against the re-establishment of the Episcopal Church in Virginia and would win legislative approval for the Statute for Religious Freedom that Jefferson wrote and in which he took enormous pride, but which required the legislative management of James Madison to become law.

In the Continental Congress from 1780 to 1783 he fairly rapidly lost his shyness, although he never gained the commanding voice that would allow him to make the most of the change. Because of his years of study of government and his writing skill he quickly became chair of important committees, and he was the author of nearly all of the creative and thorough reports and legislation recommended by his committees. Particularly important were his successful efforts to maintain American control of the West as far as the Mississippi River, the attempt to establish responsible economic policies, and even the fruitless struggle to strengthen the Congress that was constrained by Articles of Confederation that had been intentionally made weak prior to his election.

Madison is best and justifiably known as "Father of the Constitution" because of his heroic role in bringing together the Federal Convention in 1787, influencing its outcomes through the Virginia Plan, maintaining records of the debates, and winning its ratification in the largest state and influencing several other states. When the new government came into being in 1789, Madison almost immediately became the unofficial leader of the first Congress that implemented the Constitution. As in earlier Congresses, he was principal author of major legislation that had been impossible to achieve under the earlier government. He was also the moving force for addition of the ten amendments to the Constitution that would be known as the Bill of Rights. Of almost equal importance was his role as friendly and creative liaison with President George Washington during his first administration.

Unfortunately this cooperation with administration waned as Congressman Madison and Secretary of State Jefferson strongly differed from the President in his frequent support for the economic programs proposed by Secretary of Treasury Alexander Hamilton. Gradually from 1792 to 1794 Madison became leader of the first opposition party. He described his and Jefferson's followers as

Republicans, although their infant party would become the forebear of the Democratic Party rather than the present-day Republican Party. They advocated limited government and state rights while Hamilton's influence was dominant Shortly after Madison left Congress for the last time in 1797, just as John Adams became President and Jefferson Vice President, he framed and defended Virginia legislation that implied state dominance. Meanwhile he led the successful campaign for Jefferson to succeed President Adams.

Like many another advocate of states' rights both Jefferson and Madison became less adamant when they assumed administrative responsibilities, Jefferson as President and Madison as Secretary of State in 1801. This is not hypocrisy, or at least it need not be. Governmental authority in the hands of people you trust does not appear nearly as ominous as it was when it was in the hands of opponents such as Hamilton and Adams and their allies. Even the foremost American voice of state sovereignty, John C. Calhoun, exerted surprising national authority when he was briefly Secretary of State in 1844-1845. Madison would play an active role in the vast Louisiana Purchase that doubled the size of the United States, and he later acquired parts of Florida. These acquisitions carried out Madison's commitment since 1780 to preserve the West as part of the American experiment in government. But to leaders of the former Federalist majority that had been supplanted by the Jefferson-Madison team this looked like administrative tyranny. His most striking "change of mind" was Madison's opposition to Hamilton's National Bank in 1791, yet as President in 1816 he would advocate and sign into law the Second Bank of the United States.

Suspicion of Great Britain and friendship for France were central to Madison's foreign and trade policy through most of his political career. He was firmly convinced that American commerce was so important to the former Mother Country that surely some tough negotiations would bring the British to a mutual understanding with their former colonists. This attitude influenced his diplomacy both as Secretary of State and as President. Failed efforts to force British retreat from what he regarded as bullying policies finally resulted in his request for a declaration of war in June 1812.

The war was welcomed largely by the West and South, where Republicans were dominant, but strongly opposed by the majority of New Englanders, whose intransigence would verge on treason. Crushing military defeats in 1812 were only partially offset by surprising naval victories against the world's greatest navy. The seizure and burning of Washington, D.C. in 1814 was the greatest blow and justified severe criticism of Madison's leadership. From that point Madison and the United States had colossal luck. The overthrow and capture of Napoleon in Europe caused the British finally to consent to negotiations in which an extraordinary diplomatic team achieved a fortunate peace—hardly a victory but at least not a defeat. In that same period President Madison and the United States were beneficiaries of a spectacular American victory by General Andrew Jackson at New Orleans. It came weeks after the peace agreement of Christmas 1815, but luckily it was weeks before news of peace arrived from Europe.

Thus the Americans could feel with satisfaction that they had indeed won their second war of independence, as they came to describe it. Madison and his hand-picked successor James Monroe profited from generations of cooperation as well as peace from their former British enemy. This allowed an extended period of American expansion and self-satisfaction until the ugly presence of slavery divided North and South. During his twenty years of retirement, spent entirely in Virginia and most of it very close to his Orange County home, he helped to establish the nation's first state university, attempted unsuccessfully to improve the Virginia constitution that he had frequently criticized since 1776, and even worked toward a "solution" to slavery by physical separation of the races. Most important was the devotion of much of his eighties to protection of his beloved Union from the first attacks that would be engendered in South Carolina and that would thirty-five years after Madison's death lead to Civil War.

Donald O. Dewey
Professor Emeritus of History
Dean Emeritus of Natural and Social Sciences
California State University, Los Angeles

Chapter 1

Statesman in Training

James Madison, Jr., fourth President of the United States but deservedly much better known as the Father of the Constitution, was born March 16, 1751, in King George County, Virginia, according to the Gregorian or New Style calendar that had been adopted in England and eventually made its way across the Atlantic to Virginia.[1] He was the first of three surviving sons and three surviving daughters of James and Nelly Conway Madison (among twelve total births). His siblings who survived beyond infancy were brothers Ambrose, Francis, and William, and sisters Nelly, Sarah, Frances Rose, and Elizabeth (who died at seven). James maintained the "Jr." in his signature, however significant the document, until his father's death in 1801. By then Junior was United States Secretary of State and had long since become THE James Madison so far as the nation was concerned. Of course the father did not call himself James Madison, Sr., but in early chapters he will often be so identified in order to distinguish between father and son.

Educational Opportunities

Jemmy Madison, as he was known throughout his youth and often (not always with friendly intent) well into his adult political career, profited from distinct advantages as the eldest son. Of course he became the master of the beautiful family plantation called Montpelier. He lived his entire life there, except for the many occasions when he was engaged in infinitely more important

---

[1] The Gregorian calendar was adopted in the American colonies in 1752. According to the Old Style or Julian calendar James Madison, Jr. was born on March 5, 1751.

business at New York City, Philadelphia, or Washington, D.C. Even more significant from the standpoint of his contributions to American history was the classical and scholarly education that he received and so clearly merited.

Young Madison attended a private school where he learned Latin and Greek and immersed himself in the writings of some of the greatest political and social thinkers of Seventeenth and Eighteenth Century Europe. Then, after studying at home with a tutor, he rounded out his education with two intensive years and a bachelor's degree from The College of New Jersey, which would be renamed Princeton University in 1796. Before he began his extraordinary political career, he returned to Montpelier to tutor those siblings who were old enough to profit from his guidance. Thus much of any educational advantage granted to them depended on the available time, commitment and teaching capacity of their older brother.

The exception was youngest brother William who was enrolled by his older brother at the Princeton Grammar School and later transferred to Hampden-Sidney Academy, which was closer to his Virginia home and whose President had been a Princeton classmate of James Madison. Willey eventually graduated with honors at The College of William and Mary, where their second-cousin, still another James Madison, was President. William was initiated into the nation's first chapter of Phi Beta Kappa, which was then a debating society. Reflecting the remarkable longevity of James Madison despite his frequent feelings of frail health, William was the only son other than James to survive their father who died in 1801. Two married daughters also lived into the nineteenth century, though one died only a year after their father. Francis, the second son died in 1800 and Ambrose, who had helped his father manage the estate, died in 1793. William and Nelly both lived a few years beyond their older brother. Thus only three of the children born to James and Nelly Madison survived beyond 1802.[2]

It is not possible to know if his parents recognized extraordinary talents in their young prince, or were merely giving special care to the youngster who was destined by seniority in those times to ascend to dominance and leadership of the family and most likely Orange County, Virginia. The two other brothers seem to have preferred plantation life to a life of scholarship, anyway, or at least they were reconciled to that position in life. Their father was a justice of the peace and before that one of the respected leaders of the recently established Orange County. His few surviving letters show that he was a competent writer, but he did not

---

[2] Ralph Ketcham, *James Madison: A Biography* (Charlottesville: University of Virginia Press, 1990), p. 370. The original volume was published in 1971. Robert S. Allen, "William Bradford" in Robert A. Rutland, *James Madison and the American Nation, 1751-1836, An Encyclopedia* (New York: Simon & Schuster, 1994), pp. 46-47.

leave us an assessment of his many offspring, not even the justly famous first-born.

Most of what we know of James Madison's youth comes from a brief autobiographical essay dictated to his stepson John Payne Todd in the last decade of his extremely long life. And even some of those details are challenged and successfully refuted by his master biographer, Irving Brant.[3] One thing that cannot be questioned is that, however they came to him, Madison made the most of his educational advantages. He became one of the great scholar Presidents of American history, ranking with his idol Thomas Jefferson and with Theodore Roosevelt and Woodrow Wilson.

LIFE AT MONTPELIER

Orange County and especially Montpelier were always major influences on Madison's development. The Madisons were among the first residents of the county named for King William of Orange, a Protestant hero of Great Britain's Glorious Revolution, when the county was separated from Virginia's Spotsylvania County. Jemmy Madison was born at the nearby home of his mother's family, but for the next eighty-six years he called Montpelier home, though it would be several years, perhaps as late as 1803, before it would be officially given that name. Even then Madison preferred the French spelling, "Montpellier."

James Madison, Sr., likewise lived a lifetime on the same fertile and rolling land, from about 1729 when he was six years old until his death in 1801. His father Ambrose Madison also lived there until his death in 1732. The steadily enlarging Madison estate was then managed by his widow Frances Taylor Madison (the future President's grandmother) for the next twelve years until her eldest son James was eighteen and ready to assume control. This extraordinary woman was also most likely the first mentor of future President Madison as well as the ancestor of a much younger and less scholarly but also wartime President, Zachary Taylor, who could have benefited from her good instruction. James, Sr., had taken charge of the plantation in the early 1760s when work began on the Montpelier mansion in which he and his son would live for the remainder of their lives—more than seven decades, until 1836, for the younger James Madison.

[3] Irving Brant *James Madison: The Virginia Revolutionist* (Indianapolis: Bobbs-Merrill, 1941), pp. 110-112. Because Brant's ground-breaking six-volume biography was published between 1941 and 1961 and since each volume was given an individual title they will be cited individually.

Until the mansion was habitable, he and his parents had lived in a small wooden structure about a half-mile from the building site. James, Jr. helped to move family belongings to his permanent home when he was about nine years old.

Jemmy Madison regarded his ancestors as "planters and among the respectable but not the most opulent class."[4] He traced his heritage back only to "John Maddison, ship's carpenter," who began acquiring Virginia land in 1653 as a "head right" bounty for transporting settlers to Virginia. Madison's lack of airs was offset by Virginia historians of the Nineteenth Century who professed to discover more satisfying roots among the nobility. The carpenter and his son, another John Maddison, rapidly extended their land holdings along the Mattapony River, eventually willing thousands of acres to the future President's grandfather Ambrose Madison, who would be part of the first generation to drop the extra "d" from his name. Ironically the archaic spelling would be dredged up throughout Madison's political career, especially by New England Federalists. Hence the name "Mr. Maddison's war" for the War of 1812. Ambrose Madison owned more than 5,000 acres when he died in 1732.

While Thomas Jefferson looked down to the east from his beloved Monticello, where he could keep an eye on Charlottesville and the University of Virginia, Madison's Montpelier faced the other direction to provide a magnificent view of the beautiful Blue Ridge only thirty miles distant. The building itself became considerably more magnificent in 1809 when Madison added extra quarters to accommodate his mother. It remains one of the handsomest Virginia estates but after his death it was closed to the public because it was a private home through the nineteenth and most of the twentieth century. When he became Secretary of State Madison enlarged Montpelier, adding one story wings to the basic two-story box. It was expanded much more in the 20th century when it was a duPont family mansion. It was donated as a historical landmark in 1984 and efforts are currently underway to restore it to its appearance at the time that the Madisons lived there. During the Madison years Montpelier was a frequent stopping place for the great and near great who traveled through western Virginia. On special occasions as many as a hundred friends and relatives visited James and Dolley Madison.

Tobacco culture and exportation, with most of the labor being done by slaves, were well established before young Jemmy's appearance at Montpelier. Like the other early Presidents, with the notable exception of the Adamses, Madison was able to devote his life to statesmanship and books because the home front on the tobacco plantation could be operated, though not always well, by hired white

---

[4] Ibid., p. 33.

overseers and slave labor. His father possessed eighty-eight slaves by the time the son became a national figure. In addition to his younger brothers and sisters and the large number of nearby relatives (mostly Taylors), many of his playmates were young slaves. The 29 slaves inherited by James Madison, Sr. in 1732 had increased to 118 in a half-century.

VIEWS OF SLAVERY

The younger Madison remained a slave owner throughout his long life, though he often expressed discomfort with this role. In 1780, for example, he was disgusted with a Virginia proposal to offer a slave as bounty for men who would enlist in the Continental Army for the duration, even though this was during the depths of the Revolutionary War when Virginia had finally become a major killing field. Struck by the inconsistency of using slavery as a reward in an alleged war for *independence*, he asked, "Would it not be as well to liberate and make soldiers at once of the blacks themselves, as to make them instruments for enlisting white Soldiers? It would certainly be more consonant to the principles of liberty, which ought never to be lost sight of in a contest for liberty?" Shortly afterwards, he willingly sustained a financial loss when his personal servant Billey was a runaway. Rather than return him to Virginia where he would be a bad influence, or transport him to the Caribbean which would be cruel punishment, "merely for coveting that liberty for which we have paid the price of so much blood, and have proclaimed so often to be the right, and worthy the pursuit, of every human being," Madison instead sold him in Philadelphia, where he would under Pennsylvania laws eventually gain that independence that he cherished.[5]

The improvement of agriculture and the study of American animals became a passion with him, partly inspired by his reverence for and teamwork with Thomas Jefferson, but also because of his early life on a Piedmont plantation. During his brief retirement from politics before his appointment as United States Secretary of State he would be elected president of the American Board of Agriculture.

---

[5] James Madison to Joseph Jones, November 28, 1780, William T. Hutchinson et al., eds., *The Papers of James Madison* (Chicago: University of Chicago, 1961----), II, p. 209.

SCHOOL DAYS IN VIRGINIA

Madison's education took a quantum leap when his grandmother died and he was sent in 1762 to Donald Robertson's school in nearby King and Queen County. He finally had the opportunity to read widely and deeply in the literature that had been denied him because of the few books, most of them religious and medical, available at Montpelier. As an adult he took steps to assure that he would never be deprived again. While he could never overtake Jefferson as a collector of books, he took full advantage of his friend's penchant for rummaging through bookstores by mailing a steady flow of requests during Jefferson's diplomatic mission to France.

In autobiographical notes written later in his presidency, Madison gave his Scottish teacher the ultimate praise: "All that I have been in life I owe largely to that man."[6] If Donald Robertson comes anywhere near deserving that praise, then it can justly be said that the entire nation was and is deeply in his debt. At the Robertson school Madison learned to read Latin and Greek and to speak French, though with so distinct a Scottish burr that French visitors could not recognize their language when spoken by him. He mastered logic, algebra, geometry and geography. Most important, he was finally able to read deeply and with comprehension political, economic and diplomatic literature, ranging from ancient Greece to seventeenth and eighteenth Century Europe. This was the beginning of his apprenticeship to become "Father" of the United States Constitution.

Like so many of his contemporaries he became addicted to the style of Joseph Addison, whose *Spectator* Madison regarded as the best essays "that had been peculiarly adapted to inculcate in youthful minds, just sentiments, an appetite for knowledge, and a taste for the improvement of the mind and manners, written for cherishing in young minds a desire of improvement, a taste for learning and a lively sense of the duties, the virtues and the proprieties of life."[7] Young Madison's worshipful insistence on "proper words in their proper places" engendered rare over-stated criticism even from his admiring biographer, Irving Brant: "Madison in all his life never contributed a striking aphorism to the language, nor a pungently quotable sentence."[8] Madison's careful and precise language never soared like that of his greatest friend and political ally Jefferson or his sometime ally but more often political foe Alexander Hamilton; perhaps it was not pungent, but never quotable? Hardly!

---

[6] Ketcham, *James Madison,* p. 21.

[7] Ibid., p. 41.

[8] Brant, *James Madison: Virginia Revolutionist,* p. 62.

In addition to some cousins from neighboring plantations, Madison was a classmate of John Taylor of Caroline, a more distant relation who would mature into a prominent Jeffersonian philosopher of state rights and whose turgid prose would make James Madison's language pungent beyond measure. John Tyler, father of the President of the same name, also attended the school shortly before Madison.

Between the Donald Robertson School and the College of New Jersey, at Princeton, James was one of three Madison boys and one girl (James plus Francis, Ambrose and Nelly) tutored at home by Thomas Martin, the new rector of the nearby Anglican Church, still another Scottish influence since Martin was Scotch-Irish. Thomas and his brother Alexander, who would later be Governor of North Carolina, had both been students at Princeton and very likely influenced their young student's decision to look northward for a college education.

FROM VIRGINIAN TO AMERICAN

James Madison's life as an American rather than a Virginian began in 1769 when he journeyed to Princeton to enroll at the College of New Jersey (now Princeton University). Leaving his western Virginia home behind for the first time had to be traumatic, but it opened new worlds for the eighteen-year old student. Other than tobacco traders along the neighboring rivers this was his first experience with a world beyond the Virginia piedmont. Even more revolutionary was the fact that he saw and associated with students from throughout the colonies—New York, the Carolinas and even Georgia, although most of the 115 students in the College and Grammar School were from New Jersey and the cosmopolitan Pennsylvania, especially Philadelphia. Some fellow-students would have lasting impact on his life.

Yet the fact that he was even there may provide evidence that he had already transcended his Virginia childhood. It was revolutionary, downright offensive to some, for a Virginian to buck the traces and matriculate anywhere but the College of William and Mary, down the York River in Williamsburg. In 1786 a pseudonymous writer in the *Virginia Gazette* grumbled, surely with Madison in mind, that "there is but one man educated out of the state, who either has risen, or promises to rise, much above a state of mediocrity."[9] The decision seems to have been his own, although his tutor Thomas Martin, an alumnus of Nassau Hall, very

9 Ibid., p. 20.

likely had influence. In fact the Martin brothers rode horseback with Madison and his slave Sawney from Virginia to New Jersey, to be sure that he arrived safely.

Early biographers argued that he headed north either because of his opposition to the Anglican dominance of William and Mary or his disapproval of the students' libertine penchant for drinking, gambling and horseracing—or perhaps all of the above. In his autobiographical notes written in old age, Madison states that it was instead New Jersey's healthier climate that had attracted him. Whether or not the religious freedom of the Middle States drew him to Princeton, it certainly helped to keep him there, because this was an issue that was important to him in his young life and that remained vital throughout his long political life. Baptists had not been tyrannized in Orange County as they were in Tidelands Virginia, but nevertheless the young Madison was appalled by their treatment in 1773 when Baptist preachers were punished for daring to preach without official approval. Although he remained an anti-establishment Anglican, his liberal views regarding Church and State issues made him a lifelong political hero to American Baptists.

ALREADY A WORKAHOLIC

This new student, who looked and seemed younger than his eighteen years until he began talking, had been well served by the Robertson-Martin team. He arrived at Princeton late in July and immediately initiated a course of independent study to prepare for the examinations taken by other freshmen in September. After examinations by the faculty, he was granted credit for his first year of college and therefore entered his first actual classes in September as a sophomore.[10] Then through an extraordinary regimen of reading and study, he was one of two students allowed to compress junior and senior years into a single year. He therefore graduated with the B. A. degree in September 1771, only a few weeks more than two years from the time of his arrival in New Jersey. Virginia and Republican partisan mythology contended that for months their wonder child slept only three hours per night, but Madison himself was surely closer to the truth when he wrote in his autobiography that there were *some* nights when his studies kept him from sleeping more than five hours. He hastened his formal education to help relieve financial strains at home. Excessive heat and then excessive rain came at just the wrong times in 1769, resulting in a dismal tobacco crop and complicating his father's ability to continue paying for his studies.

[10] Ibid., p. 28.

With degree in hand and not the slightest idea yet what to do with it, he nevertheless remained at Princeton until April 1772 reading under President John Witherspoon's guidance some of the history and public law that he cherished but could not squeeze into his busy student schedule. He also gained a smattering of the Hebrew language to advance his theological studies. Indeed his scholarship hardly lapsed even after his father insisted that he return home to tutor his brothers and sisters. It would be the theme of his life, man and boy, for decades. He became a dedicated book collector in 1773, as he studied law with special emphasis on religious freedom.

Since his dear friend William Bradford was preparing to become a lawyer, Madison picked his brain in December 1773 to learn the basics of legal studies. He had selected a worthy source for advice, because Billey Bradford would in 1794 succeed Edmund Randolph as the second United States Attorney General when Randolph replaced Thomas Jefferson as the second Secretary of State. Sadly his position in Washington's Cabinet would end the next year when he died at only 40. His father, also named William, had been since 1742 editor of a Philadelphia newspaper and was called the "patriot printer of 1776," a position that was enhanced as he managed a politically active coffee house. Another son later established another newspaper there.[11] Madison however had no intention of actually becoming a lawyer. Instead, these readings in "the principles and modes of government are too important to be disregarded by an inquisitive mind and I think are well worthy a critical examination by all students that have health and leisure."[12] Clearly he was preparing for a life in government, for a career in legislatures and conventions rather than the courtroom. He surely could not then have conceived of himself as Governor or President, even if he had somehow managed to envision the presidency that he helped to create in 1787, but a legislator? That is a different story.

The Perfect Place for James Madison

In its brief existence of a quarter century at the time of Madison's graduation, the College had known formidable presidents, starting with Jonathan Edwards, the famed theologian of the Great Awakening, as well as one of the most eminent American literary figures of the mid-Eighteenth Century. Aaron Burr, father of Madison's fellow student of the same name, was another prominent minister who

---

[11] *Webster's Biographical Dictionary* (Springfield, MA: G. & C. Merriam Co., 1959), pp. 183-184.

[12] Hutchinson, et al., eds., *The Papers of James Madison,* I, pp. 100-101.

succeeded to the presidency. The younger Aaron would sometimes be a burr under Madison's (and especially Jefferson's) saddle, but his impact was overall beneficial to Madison because he would play a major role in bringing the shy Madison and the outgoing widow Dolley Payne Todd together for a marriage in 1794. More than a century later, the Princeton presidency served as a springboard that brought still another presidential scholar, Governor Woodrow Wilson, to national prominence.

One of the most forceful and memorable presidents was Dr. John Witherspoon who arrived from Scotland only a year before James Madison arrived from Virginia. Contentious and exciting, he had fought hierarchies, both Presbyterian and Anglican, before becoming an American. Although he was essentially orthodox and conservative in his religious views, he was tried in Scotland for unorthodoxy because of a critique of church leadership that he had written while still a teen-ager. He was authoritarian in his own views and an intolerant opponent of Scottish liberals such as David Hume and Adam Smith, yet he was a radical when it came to American independence. Seven years after Madison first met him, Witherspoon was one of the signers of the Declaration of Independence. Madison heard Witherspoon's son James, who soon would be killed fighting for American freedom in 1777, vigorously support John Locke's justification of revolution against another British King in 1689. This whirlwind of contradictions influenced Madison's intellectual growth and, through him, the development of American thinking and history. Most important, Witherspoon was for Madison a model of religious freedom. Although the College was established to train Presbyterian clergy, Reverend Witherspoon presented religion philosophically rather than theologically in his classes. His role was crucial because students had frequent contact with the President since the faculty then consisted only of President Witherspoon and three tutors.

Dr. Witherspoon guided his students to intimate acquaintance with classic studies of government and the law of nations. All students learned the writings of Charles Montesquieu, Hugo Grotius, Samuel Pufendorf, and Emmerich Vattel, but Madison's independent thinking blended their ideas with his own, sometimes agreeing with the Scottish curmudgeon but often differing, circumspectly of course. During his deep and extensive reading of public law, he personally acquired the works of French and Scottish philosophers who were not tolerated by Witherspoon and were therefore excluded from the College library. When Madison became the creator of a Constitution in the 1780s and the defender of neutral rights against international bullies France and Great Britain during the first fifteen years of the Nineteenth Century, he could quote and expand on these authors chapter and verse, much more readily than he could have quoted

Scripture. Indeed they were his Scripture. In less than a decade Madison would meet his Princeton mentor in the Continental Congress, where he would again frequently differ with him.[13]

Historic Fellow Students

James Madison would in time become the best known of the bright and promising students with whom he lived at Nassau Hall, but he paled then in comparison with classmates who would gain early prominence but still fall well short of the Father of the Constitution. Hugh Henry Brackenridge and Philip Freneau would be foremost among successful American poets and writers. Aaron Burr would have a meteoric political career until his path encroached too much on that of Thomas Jefferson in 1801. Madison's best friend William Bradford won the oratory prize at graduation and would soon become Attorney General. Bradford's correspondence with Madison is one of the best sources of our knowledge of the quiet young Virginian. Student Gunning Bedford and tutor William C. Houston would serve with Madison and Witherspoon in the Federal Convention of 1787.

Every one of the twelve students who received their degree in September 1771 was honored for some achievement or another, with the sole exception of James Madison. He seems not to have participated in any fashion, not even by attendance. Worshipful early biographers have assumed that he was prevented from attending by illness resulting from the strain of his cloistered life of scholarship, but Irving Brant argues entirely persuasively that it was much more likely that Madison was prevented from playing any role because of excessive shyness and weakness of voice.[14] His weak voice and innate shyness dictated that life in the ministry or in the practice of law were impossible. The only life for him seemed to be quiet scholarship in the library or, could it be?, that of a scholar-statesman.

Although there was no doubt that Madison was a workaholic student, he was not an unsociable grind. His studies did not make James a dull boy. For more than a century his ribald poetic effusions in behalf of his friends in the American Whig Society were censored from history. He was fully engaged in verbal warfare between the Whigs and the Cliosophic Society, whom the Whigs unjustly branded as Tories simply because that was the worst epithet for the time. In a sense this

---

[13] Ketcham, *James Madison,* pp. 41-46; Brant, *James Madison: Virginia Revolutionist*, pp. 73-78.

[14] Brant, *James Madison: Virginia Revolutionist,* pp. 99-100.

was Madison's apprenticeship in the polemics of politics that he would encourage, at the birth of the Jeffersonian Democratic-Republican Party, especially by his schoolmate and fellow Whig, Philip Freneau. Madison's poetic jibes were read publicly, never by Madison himself of course, in the Princeton Prayer Hall of all places. These youthful sallies were excluded from his early_published works because surely they were too vulgar to have come from the pen of the future Father of the Constitution. His language is tame by the standards of the Twenty First Century, but his references to chamber pots, to asses (of the four-legged variety) and lice, to emasculation and to future Christian ministers among the Clio's who "whore and pimp and drink and swear/ Nor more the garb of Christian wear," was pretty strong stuff for his day. His writings were so thoroughly cleansed or buried by those who recorded his writings that efforts of his first biographer and close personal friend, William Cabell Rives, to humanize Madison were ridiculed. Henry Cabot Lodge, a Republican stalwart of more than a century later, knew Madison only through his published papers (many of them first edited by Rives himself) and insisted that Madison was "dry and serious to the last degree" and "in fact, utterly destitute of" humor or "strong and passionate temperament." Madison, he intoned, "seems never to have had any boyhood or youth."[15]

Madison's Whigs steadfastly opposed an Anglican bishop for the American colonies, as an initial step toward opposition to all things English, ironic since the first Bishop in the state of Virginia would be named James Madison and be a cousin to James Madison the statesman. Otherwise the Whigs did not outstrip the so-called Tories in their revolutionary spirit. The spirit at the College was highlighted at the commencement exercises that followed weeks after Madison's arrival. In September 1769 honorary degrees were awarded to John Hancock, John Dickinson and Joseph Galloway. Not all of them would remain heroes of the Revolution when the issue of American rights became more revolutionary, but at the time they were major leaders of the opposition to England. Madison boasted that these were the first degrees of their sort ever granted in America. The following summer students demonstrated when New York merchants violated non-importation agreements and their published justifications were burned ceremoniously at Princeton. In 1770 graduating students wore "American cloth" to express their opposition to England, a symbolic practice to which Madison, nearly always "the man in black," would often revert. The twin virtues of non-importation and American manufactures were frequent topics of discussion in the

[15] Henry Cabot Lodge, *Historical and Political Essays* cited in Brant, *James Madison: Virginia Revolutionist,* p. 90.

classroom as well as in the students' bedrooms—and later in Madison's political life. Some years later during the commencement program of September 1787, just as Madison would be completing his work on the proposed new Constitution, Princeton awarded him an honorary doctorate. He seems never to have called himself Dr. Madison, however.

MADISON'S FRAIL HEALTH

While he was tutoring his brothers and sisters in Latin, among many other subjects, Madison provided a vivid demonstration of the possibilities of the word "vale" (Latin for "farewell"). Their tutor first became something of a valetudinarian, one who always appeared ready to bid farewell due to presumed ill health. As early as November 9, 1772 young Madison bemoaned to his best friend William Bradford that he was "too dull and infirm now to look out for any extraordinary things in this world, for I think my sensations for many months past have intimated to me not to expect a long and healthy life, yet it may be better for me after some time tho I hardly dare expect it and therefore have little spirit and alacrity to set about any thing that is difficult in acquiring and useless in possessing after one has exchanged Time for Eternity."[16] Madison avoided the word "epilepsy," but he did later refer to "the falling illness" and Dolley Madison's brother wrote and then deleted the alarming word in a brief biography written shortly after the death of his famous brother-in-law. Bradford responded to this despair with what proved in the long run to be a brilliant prediction: "Persons of the weakest constitutions, by taking a proper care of themselves, often outlive those of the strongest." He reminded his distraught and hypochondriac correspondent of the poet Alexander Pope who also always insisted that he was at the threshold of another life, yet "lived longer than the generality of mankind do."[17] This could justly be called a succinct history of the recipient because James Madison lived on and on as the other members of the Federal Convention succumbed, until he was from 1829 to 1836 the sole remaining survivor of the fifty five men who participated in writing the United States Constitution. Throughout his eighty-six years Madison was notorious for his limited height, his frailness, for seeming to be a little old man long before he really was, and yet he long outlived the physical giants of his time. His "discouraging feebleness" has

---

[16] Hutchinson et al., eds., *The Papers of James Madison,* I, p. 75.

[17] March 1, 1773, ibid., I, p. 80.

been diagnosed now as epileptoid hysteria.[18] Yet the fears were sufficient that they kept Madison from the high seas and thus drastically limited his diplomatic career. Not even Thomas Jefferson could persuade Madison to visit him in France because of his fear of the personal physical consequences. He feared that his health may have been destroyed by his extraordinary schedule of studies that propelled him through the College of New Jersey in a mere two years. In an earlier letter, Bradford mentioned the early demise of Joseph Ross, the student who accompanied Madison on that two-year race.[19]

Fortunately, months later Jemmy Madison was able to write Bradford that his health was somewhat improved thanks to his doctor's wise counsel of "more exercise and less study."[20] He also took the first of many healing jaunts to Berkeley Warm Springs in what is now West Virginia. Despite his many fears he lived remarkably free from the contagions that took so many lives in the new nation. By 1774 he was well enough to escort his youngest student William Madison to the Princeton Graduate School and even to continue on from Philadelphia for a quick trip as far north as Albany, New York. Yet three decades later when Dolley Madison was in Philadelphia for medical attention to her own threatening ailment by famed Dr. Philip Physick, her greatest concern seemed to be for her husband's "old bilious complaint" because of "how delicate he is." [21]

---

[18] Brant, *James Madison: Virginia Revolutionist,* pp. 105-107.

[19] October 11, 1772, Hutchinson et al., eds., *The Papers of James Madison,* I, p. 73.

[20] April 28, 1773, ibid., I, p. 84.

[21] Ketcham, *James Madison,* pp. 445-446.

Chapter 2

LEARNING LEGISLATIVE MASTERY

Despite his enthusiastic patriotism for an America nation that did not yet officially exist, James Madison soon was forced to recognize that if he had a role to play it must be in legislative councils rather than the field of battle. Despite his youth and his shy personality he would soon become expert in his chosen field.

Madison's youthful letters demonstrate that he was already an American rather than an Englishman who happened to live across the Atlantic. He quietly favored independence well before it became a national article of faith following the publication of Thomas Paine's *Common Sense* in January 1776. He contended that Congress should take military action and in Orange County assisted in the recruitment of militia and the accumulation of food and supplies for them. His political career began in December 1774 when at the age of twenty three he was the youngest member elected to the Orange County Committee of Safety, with the responsibility of enforcing restraints on trade with Great Britain, even at the sacrifice of limiting their one money crop, tobacco. He briefly trained with the Orange County militia who were commanded by his father, who also chaired the Committee of Safety. Young Madison marched with the militia at least once and wrote with pride about his marksmanship with a rifle. Yet he was realistic enough to recognize that his slight stature and frail health made him an unlikely military hero. He could never compete with the rugged frontiersmen whom he greatly admired. Thus Madison would wage his revolution in legislative halls and council chambers—which was very fortunate for the future of the United States. Unfortunately his revolutionary zeal was then so ardent that his letters expressed views that belied the reputation for civil liberties for which he is so widely praised. He threatened tar and feathers as the proper reward for merchants who opposed restrictions of trade with the British, and he even gave too ready credence to rumors questioning Benjamin Franklin's patriotism. He sputtered that he never expected to hear that "Jeremiah's Doctrine that 'the heart of man is deceitful above all things and desperately wicked' was exemplified in the celebrated Dr. Franklin.... Indeed it seems to me that the bare suspicion of his guilt amounts very nearly to a proof of its reality."[1] Fortunately for his own reputation and that of Franklin he had matured by the time he arrived in Congress in 1780 where he would soon become one of Franklin's most steadfast advocates.

MADISON'S FIRST CONSTITUTION

In May 1776 James Madison graduated to the state level when he was elected to the Virginia Provincial Convention that would develop the first written constitution of an independent American state. Service in the Virginia capital of Williamsburg in 1776 approximated war duty, because the *colonial* government, as distinct from the state government, was confined to the nearby Royal vessels in the York River from which the Governor, Lord Dunmore, sometimes shelled his Virginia constituents. At twenty five, Madison was not even the youngest delegate because Edmund Randolph, his longtime friend and future political ally at state and national levels and in the Federal Convention of 1787, was three years younger.

The Virginia convention would assume major significance in the march to independence. Shortly after Madison's arrival on May 6, it instructed Virginia representatives in the Continental Congress to call for a vote for independence for the American states. Most Virginia leaders, not just the future nationalist Madison, were convinced that this was a decision for the Continental Congress rather than for individual states. The vote was unanimous, so Madison clearly voted for independence. Virginian Richard Henry Lee enhanced his national reputation by introducing the motion for independence and Virginian Thomas Jefferson was assigned the role of justifying it as the lead author of the Declaration of Independence. Jefferson would much rather have been in Williamsburg contributing to the Virginia constitution, on which Madison played a small role. Four decades later Madison wrote modestly and truthfully, to a grandson of George Mason that because Madison had in 1776 been "young and inexperienced I had of course but little agency in those proceedings."[2] Phrases

1 Ketcham, *James Madison,* pp. 63-65; James Madison to William Bradford, May 9, 1975 in Hutchinson et al., eds., *The Papers of James Madison,* I, p. 151.

2 Brant, *James Madison: Virginia Revolutionist,* p. 206.

like "little Madison" and "little Jemmy" would follow him all his days but his stature of five feet six inches was compounded by a slender and delicate frame and extreme shyness. In an age when tall men such as Washington and Jefferson dominated politics, as for that matter they still do, small men such as Madison and John Adams could easily be overshadowed unless they possessed an aggressive personality such as that of Adams. A recent biographer insists that Madison was five feet four inches rather than five-six and weighed only one hundred pounds.[3] Even Madison's eyes were slighted as "not of a bright blue." Randolph remarked that Madison's contributions consisted largely of muttered but highly pertinent asides heard only by those seated near him.[4] Because he and his family were well known by Convention President Edmund Pendleton, he was appointed to the Privileges and Elections Committee. This committee was important but it was so out-sized that it verged on being a committee of the whole because it included half of the members of the Convention.

Chairman George Mason had earlier regarded this committee as weak, though he really felt no need for assistance because most of the principles and even the language would be his own. A decade later Mason would be one of the three members of the Federal Convention who were still in Philadelphia in September 1787 but refused to sign the United States Constitution. Mason declined because the Convention refused to adopt his proposal for a United States Bill of Rights in its haste for adjournment. Justly revered as the unofficial scribe of the 1787 Convention, Madison began to learn this process by taking notes in 1776 that provide most of the limited knowledge that we have of Mason's first draft of the Declaration. Madison's crucial substantive contribution was his introduction of the words "are equally entitled to the free exercise of religion" in place of Mason's proposed language, "should enjoy the fullest toleration in the exercise of religion." Thus it was James Madison who first introduced religious freedom as a "natural right" rather than merely a concession by an established church.

Madison also tried unsuccessfully to insert a guarantee "that no man or class of men ought, on account of religion, to be invested with peculiar emoluments or privileges." Although this early attempt to end the establishment of the Anglican Church failed he would achieve this goal a decade later as a member of the Virginia House of Delegates. Thus the final section of the Declaration of Rights reads,

---

3 Gary Wills, *James Madison* (Lawrence: University of Kansas Press, 2007), pp. 3, 65.

4 Hugh Blair Grigsby, *The Virginia Convention of 1776* (Richmond, VA: J. W. Randolph, 1855), p. 36.

> "That Religion, or the duty which we owe to our Creator, and the manner of discharging it can be directed only by reason and conviction, not by force or violence, and therefore all men are equally entitled to the free exercise of religion, according to the dictates of conscience; and that it is the mutual duty of all to practice Christian forbearance, love and charity towards each other."[5]

Religious freedom was a major part of a life-long campaign for James Madison. Although he frequently attended Anglican services he was an unwavering opponent of the establishment of that church as the official church of Virginia, as it was in England. His disgust especially for official harassment of frontier Baptists caused him to yearn for the religious freedom of Pennsylvania. The Baptists, in turn, would provide him with a life-long base of political support.

While seeking constitutional revisions in June 1784, Madison would publicly scorn the Provincial Convention for writing and adopting a constitution without "due power from the people" and then in effect anointing itself as the first legislature under that very constitution. The very first words of his notes for a legislative speech advocating constitutional reform were "Convention of 1776, without due power from people," followed by objections such as: "4. power from people no where pretended" and "7. Convention make themselves branch of legislature."[6] Fortunately these principles did not prevent him from occupying his own seat when the Convention made itself the first House of Delegates in October 1776. When he sought re-election the next year, though, he learned a painful political lesson. He was defeated by Charles Porter, who followed the Virginia tradition of rewarding the voters with free whiskey. Porter was merely following the American tradition of rewarding his supporters and had the added advantage of operating a local tavern. Madison believed that the voters attributed his failure to ply them with drinks to pride rather than parsimony. Even though he never stooped to the practice of winning votes by "treating" his supporters, this was the only time that Madison ever lost an election.

Unhappy but Useful Executive Experience

Madison soon shifted from lawmaker to executive, to the limited extent that there was an executive in Virginia. In November 1777 "James Madison the Younger, of Orange" was elected to the Council of State, becoming one of eight

---

[5] Hutchinson et al., eds., *The Papers of James Madison,* I, pp. 172-175.

official advisors to the Governor, in place of the only member of the first Council who was not re-elected. He was sworn into office in January 1778 by Governor Patrick Henry. The position of Governor was thankless, so weak that it was sometimes mocked as nine governors. Council approval was required for any gubernatorial "action." Well into the Constitutional Convention of 1787 Madison was undecided whether the executive should be one man or a committee, but his experience with the Council of State left him convinced that the Virginia executive provided by the constitution of 1776 was a mistake. Madison's two years as advisor to Virginia governors marked the beginning of a long-time antagonism for his first Governor and a lifetime friendship and alliance with his second. He had known Patrick Henry previously and greatly admired him as an orator, but their working relationship gradually soured and never sweetened. Other than on American independence they concurred on few issues. Henry's voice so far transcended his pen in effectiveness that he welcomed Madison's readiness to write routine letters, yet he surely had Madison in mind when he was quoted by an anonymous writer as detesting "the projects of theorists and book worms."[7] Madison was not named as the target but the shoe fit his small foot better than those of all the other Councilors combined. Nevertheless he gained valuable experience in the writing of public papers, a task at which he would prove to be a master. A decade later Henry would be the most dangerous opponent of the United States Constitution which would be the great achievement of Madison's life. An enormous contrast was Madison's relationship with Thomas Jefferson, which became a mutual admiration society when Jefferson became Governor. They would be political allies and the best of friends for the next forty-five years, although Jefferson was eight years Madison's senior.

To his deep regret when Madison won re-election to the House of Delegates early in 1778 still without contributing to the inebriation of the constituents, he was ruled "ineligible of being elected" because he already held office in the Council of State, however unhappily. Ironically he was again supplanted by Charles Porter. Madison's role on the Council of State is difficult to determine because so many state records were destroyed in 1780 when British redcoats led by American turncoat Benedict Arnold rampaged through Virginia. It was also mercifully brief because on December 14, 1779, when he had already risen to fifth in seniority on the Council, he was elected to his cherished dream position in the Continental Congress, where he would serve until nearly the end of 1783.

---

[6] Ibid., VIII, pp. 75-79.

[7] Brant, *James Madison: Virginia Revolutionist*, p. 188.

Congressman Madison

James Madison was the youngest member of the Continental Congress when he arrived in Philadelphia on March 18, 1780, only two days after his 29th birthday. Despite his youth, his arrival marked a quantum leap in the quality of Virginia's delegation. This was a reflection less on Madison's standing and promise, for he was still a largely unknown asset, than on the dismal credentials and performance of his predecessors. The quality and especially the attendance record of Virginians in (and mostly out of) Congress was embarrassing to the state and distressing and depressing to General Washington. Washington pleaded without success for important Virginians to respond to the crisis. Madison was not well enough known to be on the list of worthies to whom Washington was appealing, but he was at least elected third after James Henry and Joseph Jones and ahead of John Walker. The Virginians stayed at the boarding house of Mrs. Mary House. Madison invariably roomed there when he was in Philadelphia. He would remain friendly with the House family and a grandson, Nicholas P. Trist, would long be Madison's political disciple and eventually ally in the 1830s.

Virginia had for months been without a vote because of the inadequacy and inattention of its delegation. Of sixteen different Virginians who were technically members of Congress during 1779, only Cyrus Griffin was on duty when the newcomers arrived. Too many others had resigned or simply failed to attend. Patrick Henry was foremost among those "Congressmen" who never bothered to leave Virginia. Soon Griffin, Henry and Walker were also gone and only Joseph Jones, a long-time friend of the Madison family, served at length with Madison.

The major exception to the dismal Virginia commitment to Congress was James Madison, although it must be added that Jones was a faithful and delegated colleague. Madison was delighted at the opportunity to advance to the national scene and pledged faithful participation. On December 16, 1779 he wrote to Speaker Benjamin Harrison: "Being notified that the General Assembly have honored me with a delegation to serve this commonwealth in general Congress, I beg the favor of you Sir to communicate to them my acceptance thereof, and my assurances that as far as fidelity and zeal can supply the place of abilities the interests of my Country shall be punctually promoted."[8] Fidelity and zeal would indeed sum up his entire career in Congress as well as in administration. He would be at his seat in Congress nearly every day for almost four years, the only exception being a brief visit to New Jersey that will be described at the end of this chapter. No one in Congress from any state achieved a comparable record. In

[8] Hutchinson, et al., eds., *The Papers of James Madison,* I, p. 319.

November 1782 he began the practice of compiling extensive notes on the activities of Congress that have often filled in the gaps of the official journals, just as his later notes would tell us much of what we know today about the Constitutional Convention of 1787.

COMMITTEE LEADERSHIP

More important, by the autumn of 1780 he would initiate a record of legislative leadership that he would never surrender, even though it would be seven months before he conquered his shyness sufficiently to engage in floor debate. He would hone the skills that he would for decades demonstrate as a masterful author of public papers. Increasingly he would chair the committees that dealt with highly controversial issues and write the reports that were required to win majorities.

Madison's future reputation was by no means obvious, though, during his first months in Congress. Martha Bland, the wife of Congressman Theodorick Bland who would join the Virginia delegation in August 1780, wrote that Madison was described as "clever in Congress but out of it he has nothing engaging or even bearable in his Manners—the most unsociable creature in Existance."[9] Her husband would never put it so bluntly, but he did everything he could to undercut Madison's position in Virginia. Even after a year's service, Madison's youth and shyness raised some eyebrows. A pompous new arrival in Congress, Thomas Rodney of Delaware, wrote in his diary in March 1781 that his young colleague was "just from the College, and possesses all the self conceit that is common to youth and inexperience in like cases—but it is unattended with that gracefulness and ease which some times makes even the impertinence of youth and inexperience agreeable or at least not offensive."[10] The French ambassador, Chevalier de la Luzerne, better assessed Madison's first congressional career (1780-1783) when he said he was "regarded as the man of the soundest judgment in Congress." Yet certainly he under-sold the extent of Madison's participation when he added that "He did not begin to take part in debate until he had been there two years and he speaks nearly always with fairness and wins the approval of his colleagues."[11]

---

[9] Ibid., II, p. 196.

[10] Ibid., II, pp. 13-14.

[11] Irving Brant, *James Madison: The Nationalist, 1780-1787* (Indianapolis: Bobbs-Merrill, 1948), p. 14.

Even before Madison claimed his seat in Congress Madison wrote to Governor Jefferson to bemoan the dire straits of the United States and its Congress. On the very day that Madison arrived in Philadelphia, Congress devalued Continental currency by forty to one, with a complex plan for the new currency to be issued by the individual states, though guaranteed by Congress, and with the unstated assumption that the interest (and most likely the principal!) would be paid by the still unsuspecting government of France. It is both regrettable and ironic that Madison was precluded from participation in these debates if, indeed, he *would* have spoken up this early. He had labored to write a lengthy essay on "Money" while he was snowed in at Montpelier, awaiting the break in the weather that would allow him to ride to Philadelphia. This precocious essay remained so relevant through the coming decade that he published it in December 1791 in Philip Freneau's *National Gazette* as a part of the Jeffersonian attack on Alexander Hamilton's monetary schemes.[12] In it he demonstrated his awareness that confidence by the public that their paper money must remain readily exchangeable was essential or the monetary system would not meet the needs of government or the people. This knowledge seemed lacking among most of his new colleagues. This homework and his obvious concern for fiscal responsibility may have been responsible for his first significant chairmanship—that of a committee dealing with the fiscal responsibility of the Quartermaster General. Here he gave early evidence that he was not always right, whatever his Nineteenth Century biographers might assert. This committee's hard-nosed response that the QMG was personally responsible for debts incurred by his subordinates led to the angry resignation of General Nathanael Greene. Fortunately Greene would soon become one of the major heroes of the American Revolution after Washington wisely gave his military career new direction by offering him command of the Carolina campaigns after Horatio Gates suffered overwhelming defeat and humiliating retreat at Camden, South Carolina.

Saving the West

Early and often during his years in the Congress, Madison demonstrated the nationalism that would characterize his political career at least until 1791 when he joined and sometimes led Thomas Jefferson in opposition to the nationalism of Alexander Hamilton. Virginia's imperial claims to the West made western lands and Mississippi navigation a state issue as well as a national issue, but Madison

[12] "Money," in Hutchinson, et al., eds., *The Papers of James Madison,* I, pp. 302-309.

remained steadfast for what France and Spain and many Americans considered excessive demands, even after his state lost interest. He led the effort in Congress to maintain an American West even after he had been abandoned by the Virginia House of Delegates and undercut by his fellow Virginia congressman, Theodorick Bland. Madison's first major assignment just six months after his arrival was as chairman of the committee that prepared a response to the request from John Jay, the American minister to Spain, for updated instructions regarding American claims to the West and the Mississippi River. The initial response on October 4, 1780, merely to reiterate the demands in the original instructions, was easy despite the lobbying of French diplomats who were intent on wooing Spanish military participation by enhancing Spanish prospects for expanded territory in what would someday be the American South.

As British troops rampaged almost at will through Virginia and the Carolinas late in 1780 and early in 1781, alarmed southerners joined the middle states in their eagerness to trade off American claims to the West and the Mississippi River for French and Spanish military support. Maryland, Pennsylvania and New Jersey who could make no legitimate claim to the West had always been quite content to trade off the claims of states such as Virginia that had been granted vast western empires by Royal charters. Just before fleeing Williamsburg with British redcoats at their heels, the Virginia legislature voted to rescind earlier instructions that Jay must not negotiate away control of the Mississippi. Finally Madison was compelled to write new instructions on February 15, 1781, authorizing Jay to retreat on navigation of the Mississippi if it was absolutely necessary to gain a military alliance with Spain. Fortunately he had sufficiently delayed the issue so that improved military prospects made it unnecessary for Jay to "purchase" a treaty with Spain. Jay responded with great pleasure and relief to the official communication then written by Madison in May. He notified Congress that I do not recollect to have ever received a letter that gave me more real pleasure.... It appearing to me that the communication...to this Court could not be better made than in the very words of this letter, which seemed exceedingly well calculated for the purpose, I recited them in a letter which I wrote two days afterwards to the minister.[13]

In June 1781 the West again became a pawn when Madison's college mentor John Witherspoon, by then a Congressman from landlocked New Jersey, cleverly but temporarily separated New England from the South by persuading Congress to authorize peace negotiators to concede the American claim for the west if necessary in exchange for the guarantee of New England fishing rights in the

[13] Ketcham, *James Madison,* p. 98.

North Atlantic. Correctly convinced that the attacks on western territorial claims were inspired by "self interest, prejudice, envy, jealousy and the intrigues of speculators" in the landless states that had negotiated private arrangements with Indian tribes, Madison again delayed a decision based on panic. Fortunately by the time those peace discussions became serious in 1782, after the triumph of General Washington with essential support from French troops and fleet at Yorktown, Virginia, the negotiators brilliantly led by Benjamin Franklin managed to win both control of the Mississippi River north of New Orleans and access to the northern fisheries.[14]

EFFORTS TO STRENGTHEN THE ARTICLES OF CONFEDERATION

The Articles of Confederation had been proposed in the summer of 1776 as a direct response to the vote in Congress for independence. The document was amended drastically in 1777 by Congressman Thomas Burke of North Carolina, primarily to weaken the limited national authorities that John Dickinson had included in the first draft. Then Congress waited until March 1781 for the thirteenth state to provide the unanimity that was required for even this weak document to be adopted. Maryland was for years the single holdout, inspired largely by the disparity of landless Maryland feeling dwarfed by its immediate neighbor, huge, populous and land-rich Virginia Giant Virginia's western claims by Royal charter included the present Kentucky, Ohio, Indiana, Illinois, Michigan, and Wisconsin as well as the present West Virginia which remained part of Virginia until the Civil War. The combination of British troops in Virginia and French pressure on Maryland finally forced a compromise. Virginia granted the territory north of the Ohio River to the United States as a national domain that would prove essential to its development and Maryland ratified the Articles, allowing them to become effective March 1, 1781, only six months before American victory at Yorktown forced the British finally to begin negotiations leading to peace. The Virginia cession required that these territories eventually become equal states within the Union and that slavery be disallowed north of the Ohio River. Madison remained in Philadelphia to persuade Congress to agree to this enormous gift, while his colleague Joseph Jones worked with the legislature in Williamsburg to persuade Virginia to make the offer.

[14]Ibid., pp. 95-100, 103.

When the United States finally had an official governmental structure to guide it, Madison almost immediately initiated efforts to strengthen this intentionally weakened government. To have done so by amendment prior to final ratification would have overthrown twelve ratifications already in hand, because the document would differ from that previously approved. Less than two weeks after the Articles were finally in effect, Madison pounced with the first of what would become many proposed constitutional amendments. His startling amendment attempted to provide more authority to Congress than Burke had taken away in 1777. He moved that "in case any one or more of the Confederated States shall refuse or neglect to abide by the determination of the United States in Congress assembled…the said…Congress assembled are fully authorized to employ the force of the United States as well by sea as by land to compel such State or States to fulfill their federal engagements…." Of course such a drastic amendment, which would require the unanimous consent of all states "not actually in the possession of the Enemy," was dead on arrival.

Rather than sulk over this disappointment, as a committee chairman Madison frequently experimented with the expansion through implied powers of the very weak Articles of Confederation. Legislation and nearly everything else depended heavily on the meaning of the first two sentences of Article 13: "Every state shall abide by the determinations of the united states in congress assembled, on all questions which by this confederation are submitted to them. And the Articles of this confederation shall be inviolably observed by every state…."[15] The Confederation Congress had been granted limited powers, to be sure, but Chairman Madison would frequently argue in documents emanating from his committees that "questions" that were correctly "submitted" to Congress *must* be "observed by every state." Madison would get a lot of mileage out of that language. It provided justification for the assertion of one committee that "a general and implied power is vested in the united states in congress assembled to carry into effect all the articles of the said confederation against any of the states which shall refuse or neglect to abide by such determinations, or shall otherwise violate any of the said articles." He asserted authority "to employ the force of the united states" to enforce trade restrictions and seize supplies needed by the Army. The phrase "sovereign and independent nation" increasingly crept into reports coming from committees led by Madison. A persistent struggle was over the interpretation of the majority required for congressional action. If it meant seven (a majority of the thirteen states) as some contended, then Congress would be

---

[15] Donald O. Dewey, *Union and Liberty: Documents in American Constitutionalism* (New York: McGraw-Hill, 1969), p. 27.

hamstrung because there were few occasions when all states were represented, and far too many when not even seven had voting representation. Because two representatives were required for a state's vote to be counted, some states went for long periods without a vote; and even when two were present they might vote differently and thereby negate their ballot.[16]

A decade later, Madison's teamwork with Jefferson in opposition to Alexander Hamilton's use of implied powers to justify a national bank would provide the classic arguments for strict interpretation of the Constitution. Yet in 1780 Madison supported —however uncomfortably—the first national bank. Although he regarded the Bank of North America as "pretty analogous in its principles to the Bank of England," he supported most of those principles, with the major exception of its charter from the government of the United States. When it finally became certain that the bank could not succeed without a federal charter he gave the charter an "acquiescing rather than an affirmative, vote."[17] This painful vote would have significant impact in 1791 when Secretary of Treasury Alexander Hamilton would persuade Congress and President Washington to utilize an implied power that Madison denied was present in the U.S. Constitution, to permit the chartering of another bank that would be "pretty analogous" to the Bank of England.

FISCAL LEADERSHIP

Madison arrived in Congress with deep concern regarding the fiscal stability—even survival—of the United States, and he devoted his greatest efforts in 1782-1783 to a ceaseless campaign to find some way for the Congress to meet its obligations, most notably long overdue payments to Continental troops and some return on the enormous loans provided by their French ally. Just like the Congress, Madison had been living on loans and gifts (mainly from his father) as American and Virginia "money", really just paper, plummeted from worth little to worthless. He was joined in Congress by Alexander Hamilton in November 1782 and the two rapidly became close allies working for increased authority for Congress, including even a taxing power. Hamilton stated it first but Madison soon responded in kind: He declared that "A requisition of Congress on the states

[16] Brant, *James Madison: Nationalist,* pp. 104-132. In this volume Brant breaks significant new ground in Madison biography by demonstrating and highlighting the extent of his subject's early nationalism.

[17] James Madison to Edmund Pendleton, January 8, 1782, Hutchinson, et al., eds., *The Papers of James Madison,* IV, pp. 22-23.

for money is as much a law to them as their revenue acts when passed are laws to their respective citizens."[18] But no state legislature, including that of Virginia, agreed. Lacking the power to tax, as well as lacking any power to enforce a tax even if it could levy one, Congress was reduced to continual *requests* for support from the states. Because most states were willing to respond to requisitions only if the other states met their obligations, any funds received by Congress were at best a pittance. There was always some state that could be pointed out as not paying its share.

The only realistic hope for Congress was a 5 per cent impost to be collected on goods imported into the United States. Eleven of the thirteen states had ratified a proposed impost by July 1782. Since Georgia was essentially a non-state then because of British control, it could be argued that the only holdout was Rhode Island, but that was always enough! The attitude of that smallest of states, one of the major ports into which those goods would pour, was ably expressed by its representative in Congress, David Howell, who urged that Rhode Island "grant your money like freemen, from time to time, bound only, as a sovereign and independent State, by your sentiments of Justice, of virtue and by your own SACRED HONOR."[19] In other words, do as before, providing no support to Congress. Poor Madison was on the road to Rhode Island with a small delegation of Congressmen to attempt to reason with the recalcitrant "Rogues Islanders" when the Virginia legislature happily responded to the Rhode Island invitation by rejecting the impost and ordering its representatives in Congress to oppose *any* tax. The timing was cruel, for Madison learned of his own state's abandonment of the impost on the day before Christmas. Madison violated these instructions as much as he dared. Yet Congress's only recourse was to continue sending its bills to Benjamin Franklin in hopes that the wily ambassador could continue to charm the French government to honor them.

By spring 1783 James Madison had become an unquestioned legislative leader, a spectacular advancement from the shy and quiet member who had arrived three years earlier. He chaired most of the committees on which he served and wrote many major reports, especially on foreign affairs and finance. Most important were his efforts to move the United States toward fiscal responsibility. Despite the orders from Virginia that no federal taxes be supported, Madison, Hamilton and John Rutledge of South Carolina were appointed to a committee to

[18] Ibid., VI, pp. 141-154.

[19] Rhode Island delegates to Governor William Greene, October 15, 1782, Edmund C. Burnett, ed., *Letters of Members of the Continental Congress,* 8 Volumes (Washington, D.C.: Carnegie Institution, 1921-1936), VI, pp. 502-507.

respond to justly bitter demands by the long-unpaid army. On March 6 he introduced a "general revenue" proposal that included an *impost* on trade, a *poll tax* and a *land tax*. After weeks of bitter and angry debate, Congress finally approved on April 18 a revenue plan with what it was hoped would be an inducement for every faction. It was approved by Congress, with only Rhode Island as usual opposed. New York's vote was divided, Madison believed, because Hamilton was hoping for something closer to his own ideas. It sought to achieve somewhat less than a million dollars from an impost on trade and half again more raised from the states by whatever means they should choose.[20]

Ten days later Congress unanimously approved Chairman Madison's powerful address to the states for their support for public credit. The "Address" was published in pamphlet form by Congress and reprinted in several states as well as in England; it is justly regarded as one of the outstanding products of the Confederation period. It was warmly praised by General Washington who saw it as America's one hope to avoid bankruptcy and perhaps mutiny. Washington would have been unaware of Madison's leadership because they were not yet acquainted but, for that matter, even Madison's own father was unaware of the authorship of the report. Madison (and thus Congress) argued powerfully that those who had made independence possible must finally be rewarded: the men in arms who were becoming increasingly rebellious; the great French ally who had been "rewarded" for the mountain of money, men and materiel that it had supplied only by demands for still more; and the many Americans who had provided loans and supplies often willingly but also often under duress. Madison even tried unsuccessfully to reimburse the expenditures of those states that had given most in the fight for freedom but was supported by no other state delegation. Ironically, Madison would lead the opposition a decade later to Hamilton's effort under the new Constitution to make the United States responsible for war debts of the states. Hamilton countered by using Madison's own arguments of 1783 against him, without branding it political "log-rolling" at its best, in order to attract more states to something approaching fiscal responsibility.[21]

Sadly no amount of logic and reason could persuade a nation that had gone to war in opposition to taxes imposed from some distant government to allow a good deal less distant government on this side of the Atlantic Ocean to impose taxes—especially when the terms of the Articles of Confederation enabled a single state to prevent any fundamental change. National honor could not begin to compete with local interest, and France could legitimately fear that its expenses and

[20] Hutchinson, et al., eds., *The Papers of James Madison,* VI, pp. 289-297.

[21] Ibid., VI, pp. 487-498.

exertions to achieve American independence might never be repaid. Meanwhile American troops verged on mutiny and sometimes crossed that line, refusing to be furloughed until they were paid and forcing the intimidated Congress to abandon Philadelphia and flee from its own army to Princeton.

Throughout this struggle for fiscal survival, Madison often had to fight to protect America's two principal personal financial resources from vicious attacks from within the Virginia delegation to Congress. The vindictive Arthur Lee and his followers, who too often included John Adams, waged continual warfare against Robert Morris, the Superintendent of Finance, and Benjamin Franklin, the American Minister to France, sometimes from a seat in Congress, sometimes from a seat in the Virginia legislature. Madison was frequently relegated to a minority in the Virginia delegation because of the teamwork of the waspish Lee and feckless Theodorick Bland.

Madison missed a congressional roll call for his very first time at the end of April, after an unequalled attendance of forty-two months, when he accompanied New York Congressman William Floyd and especially his daughter Kitty, whom he fervently believed was his fiancée, as far as New Jersey. Shocked soon to learn the impact that distance could have on a sixteen year old female heart, he tarried disconsolately in Congress until October 25. He labored then on two projects that would prove prophetic for him, though many years would pass before they bore fruit. Acutely missing the riches of Jefferson's personal library at Monticello, he argued strenuously for the establishment of a Library of Congress and even proposed a list of books essential to Congress. Congress could then scarcely afford a book, much less a library, but after Washington was burned by the British in the War of 1812, the Madison-Jefferson team would initiate the present Library of Congress which justly has two of its three principal buildings named for Thomas Jefferson and James Madison. He also initiated southern political finagling to move the capital of the United States permanently to the shores of the Potomac River, which was finally accomplished in 1800, the year before Madison became Secretary of State and nine years before he was inaugurated as President. Thus Madison would spend sixteen years in that southern outpost.

Chapter 3

"VACATION" IN VIRGINIA

James Madison arrived home at Montpelier early in December 1783 fully expecting to devote his unhappily unmarried life to reading and thinking, and even a bit of zoology, but he could not resist the pull of government and politics. Legislative sessions intruded on his scholarly reading for a total of eleven months during 1784, 1785 and 1786, and his activities there often continued his focus on his attempts to improve the performance of the Continental Congress. Whenever he and Thomas Jefferson could get together or corresponded in this period they discussed the books that would be needed for the Library of Congress that Madison felt was necessary for Congress, and the books that he would need in his own library for personal development. Those intellectual pleasures were too limited because Jefferson was back in Congress until 1785, when he departed for France as United States Minister. Madison craved books on government, especially on "the several confederations which have existed." Although their dream of a Library of Congress died for lack of funds, he would spend years devouring the books in his own and Jefferson's large library, as well as the large shipments of books that Jefferson would soon ship to him from Europe. This research would loom large in his personal deliberations and in discussion and debate in the Virginia House of Delegates and especially in the Federal Convention of 1787.[1]

Limited in access to desired reading material during the harsh winter of 1783-1784, he was otherwise occupied by visits from the many relatives whom he had not seen since his departure for Congress in March 1780, although even then social gatherings were frequently cut short so he could retreat to his library. He

---

[1] Ketcham, *James Madison,* pp. 140-141.

also busied himself with the study and measurement of Virginia wildlife, joining Jefferson in his patriotic venture of disproving the theories of the French naturalist Count George Louis Leclerc Buffon that American animals were physically inferior to those of Europe.

EXPLORING THE NORTH AND WEST

Every year during his Virginia interlude, Madison investigated parts of the northern states. In September 1784 he traveled farther north than he had previously ventured to learn more about the nation that he so persistently and creatively championed. He already knew Philadelphia and Princeton very well, but an invitation from his friend the Marquis de Lafayette to observe negotiations with the Iroquois Indians in upstate New York provided an opportunity to learn more regarding an important northern state and even to explore possibilities for a life other than the plantation South. He hoped that he might find a life where he need not depend on the social and political embarrassment of slave labor. Furthermore, Madison was an admirer of this heroic French friend to American liberty. From New York City they sailed painfully up the Hudson River to Albany. Eight days of battling adverse winds, rainstorms and frequent intestinal turmoil proved to Madison's satisfaction that he had been correct in his decision never to risk sailing the high seas. He fared better traveling west along the Mohawk River by carriage and horseback to Fort Schuyler (still generally known as Fort Stanwix) near the present city of Rome, where they spent more than a week. When the American negotiators were delayed, the small party even ventured eighteen miles farther west, through largely untracked wilderness, to the Oneida village where Lafayette was received with great honor and ceremony. Upon his return to Richmond in October the omnipresent Madison suffered the unique experience of paying a fine for his unexcused absence from the legislature. Ironically he actually missed very little legislative activity because so many of his peers were also absent and a quorum had been delayed.

The journey downstream to western civilization was much more comfortable and Madison obviously liked what he had seen because he was eager for another northern jaunt just the following year. He wrote Edmund Randolph on July 26, 1785, that he hoped to find "a decent and independent subsistence" where he might "depend as little as possible on the labor of slaves."[2] Shortly afterward his good friend James Monroe wrote from New York City to propose that Madison

[2] Hutchinson, et al., eds., *The Papers of James Madison,* VIII, pp. 327-328.

join him for a journey to view Indian negotiations even farther west in the Ohio Valley or "perhaps" for a "ramble" into New England. Especially intrigued by the latter, Madison hurried to Philadelphia in August, only to learn that Monroe had already departed without him. Disappointed, he turned back toward Virginia after briefly visiting the Congress in its new surroundings. He stopped at Mount Vernon to seek advice from Washington, an inveterate speculator on western lands, whether territory purchased in the Mohawk Valley would be a wise investment. After Monroe had viewed the United States as far west as the Mississippi River, he returned to Virginia as impressed as Madison had been by the economic prospects of the Mohawk Valley.

The next year the two future presidents became partners for the purchase of 900 acres near Fort Stanwix. Harsh economic times in Virginia compounded by even harsher weather kept them from investing as heavily as they would have wished. Madison even wrote unsuccessfully to Jefferson to seek investments from the presumably unlimited riches of France. In 1790 the younger Monroe became the first who was unable to continue financing their joint project so Madison bought his friend's share, offering him generous terms Six years later Madison, by then also strapped for money, sold the land at a modest profit rather than the riches that western land was supposed to bring. Thus ended his dream of escaping the plantation South, except for the several decades when he was in Philadelphia, New York, or Washington on important governmental affairs. In addition to this effort to find a life for himself in the West (admittedly the Mohawk Valley was geographically not far west of Montpelier, but it was much farther west culturally), Madison enthusiastically supported General Washington's creative and complex proposals to make the Potomac River a viable trade route from Virginia and Maryland to the trans-Appalachian West.

Frustrations of a Legislative Life in Virginia

In May 1784, four months before his trip to upstate New York, Madison had hurried back to his destined life of statesmanship. He again represented Orange County in the Virginia legislature in the new capital city of Richmond, which would at least provide for him a much healthier climate than Williamsburg. He was elected to the House of Delegates along with the same Charles Porter whose successful campaigning in 1777 had temporarily sidetracked Madison's first venture into state politics. This was a very different James Madison from the timid novice of 1776. His leadership was taken for granted even before he arrived in Richmond. He became chairman of the Commerce Committee and was disappointed by his failure to establish Norfolk as the seaport that would become the focus of the tobacco trade and thus keep foreign tobacco merchants from sailing up the Virginia rivers to negotiate with planters one-on-one. Much more successful, even though extremely frustrating, was his legislative leadership on governmental reform and religious freedom, both of which would be of special importance throughout his entire lifetime.

Assemblyman Patrick Henry at first met privately with Madison and former Congressman Joseph Jones and offered cooperation with them to meet the needs of the new nation. He even gave tacit approval to Madison's ambition to revise the state constitution on which they had collaborated in 1776. Unfortunately this was only a momentary truce. Henry began to counterattack once he was confronted with specific proposals. Constitutional revisions would be voted down and the constitution of 1776 would remain unchanged with all the flaws that offended Madison for another quarter century. When it came to support for the national government, Henry reprised his anti-tax arguments that had been so effective when the taxes came from across the Atlantic from 1765 to 1776, rather than more recent requisitions from Philadelphia or New York. His followers undermined Madison's recent efforts in Congress to provide fiscal stability and economic responsibility for the United States. They impeded payment of debts to American or British creditors, whatever the Congress or the peace treaty with Great Britain might mandate. Virginia refused to pay even a percentage of what it for years had owed to Congress. Henry postponed the payment even of local taxes for one year and planned to extend it for another year until in-kind payments, especially in tobacco, were adopted. Thus Virginia was not in a position to meet its obligations to Congress even if it had wanted to.

In fairness to Henry, it is quite likely that Madison would have been unable to gain the commitments that he needed even if Henry's voice had been in support of Madison's program. In a letter to Jefferson on October 3, 1785, Madison described goals that would alarm many state legislators. His call for "a recognition by the States of the authority of Congress to enforce payment of their respective quotas" and for "a grant to Congress of an adequate power over trade" came right out of the amendment to the Articles of Confederation that he had proposed in March 1783. It fell with a thud then in Congress and suffered similar fate in the House of Delegates. His assurance that "a single frigate under the orders of Congress could make it the interest of any one of the Atlantic States to pay its just Quota" was not assuring to the representatives of that particular Atlantic State.[3] Madison's lone fiscal triumph came in November 1786, after

[3] Ibid., VII, p. 374.

Henry had again become Governor so his voice no longer dominated the House of Delegates. Then Madison's powerful warning against paper money persuaded a large majority to refuse to "disgrace republican government in the eyes of mankind" by resisting the temptation to follow other states that were printing paper money that varied from little to no value. Yet Madison was realist enough to recognize that his victory would most likely be overturned when Henry returned to the legislature. He had no doubt that Henry was an "avowed patron of paper money." Madison, on the other hand, considered paper money not backed by specie "unjust, impolitic, destructive of public and private confidence."[4]

He had considerably more success in reforming the state legal code, to regularize legislation approved by the independent government since 1776. Early in the fall 1785 session he persuaded the House to schedule regular sessions for orderly review of 118 bills. At the end of the year thirty-six of them had been processed, but it was not continued the next year. The project was less than half completed but it did at least bring some regularity to a large portion of the legal code. Revision of the judicial system and penal code were more than he could manage. Perhaps this was because he was already beginning to think on a national scale, but he also encountered much greater resistance among the delegates to these reforms. By the end of 1785 members were impatient with Madison's forceful style (one even called him a dictator) and he, in turn, was tired of many of them. His experience with refractory state legislators helped to make him more willing to return to Congress. One major benefit for Madison's generally thankless task was that Jefferson's Statute for Religious Freedom had come up routinely and passed easily if not routinely.[5]

Religious Freedom Survives

Henry and Madison quickly became principal antagonists as Henry lent his powerful voice to the restoration of a state religious tax that Jefferson had succeeded in repealing in 1777. While the new tax would support religious teaching for all churches it was widely feared that it might become a foot in the doorway that might lead again to an established Episcopal church. The proposed religious assessment had been a dead issue until it was revived by Henry. He

---

[4] Ibid., IX, pp. 156-160; Gaillard Hunt, ed., *Writings of James Madison,* 9 Volumes (New York: G. P. Putnam's Sons, 1900-1910), II, pp. 279-280.

[5] Hutchinson, et al., eds., *The Papers of James Madison,* VIII, pp. 391-398; Jack N. Rakove, *James Madison and the Creation of the American Republic* (New York: Longman, 2002), pp. 41-42.

seemed certain to prevail until Madison's supporters adopted stalling tactics, waiting and perhaps praying for opposition petitions to arrive from the West, where Presbyterians, Baptists and Methodists were more prevalent. Jefferson then wrote Madison, probably not entirely in jest, in a numerical code that they shared: "While Mr. Henry lives another bad constitution would be formed & saddled forever on us. What we have to do I think is devoutly to pray for his death." Madison resorted to old fashioned politics rather than to religion. Instead of praying for deliverance he again turned his attention to advancing Henry to the governor's chair, sagely predicting to James Monroe that Henry would be easily elected "without competition or opposition" because his friends would accommodate his desire for the honor, while his opponents were equally enthusiastic about removing him from the House of Delegates.[6] Safely shunted away to one of the weakest offices in Virginia, or the United States for that matter, Henry's voice was largely muffled. Ironically the weakness of the executive, which was then a boon to Madison, was one of his major objections to the Virginia constitution of 1776, because it lacked an appropriate balance of powers. He considered it "the worst part of a bad Constitution. If he had been allowed to proceed with his proposed revision of the Constitution the Governor, the judiciary and the Virginia Senate would have been enhanced relative to the House of Delegates.[7]

Madison's anonymous "Memorial and Remonstrance against Religious Assessments"[8] was printed in the summer of 1785 and widely distributed to general applause. Still unexcelled as a defense of religious liberty, it was the most persuasive of many petitions with thousands of signatures that led to the defeat of the assessment. In firm control of the legislature after Henry was "kicked upstairs," Madison on October 31, 1785, pushed through with limited opposition and without amendments the Act for Establishing Religious Freedom that had languished in the House of Delegates since it was introduced by Jefferson in 1779. Jefferson was so proud of this legislation that he listed it as one of the three achievements (not including the presidency!) that he asked to have carved on his tombstone. In legislation as well as its Declaration of Rights Virginia had

---

6 December 8, 1784; and November 27, 1784 in Hutchinson, et al., eds., *The Papers of James Madison* VI, pp. 175, 177-180.

7 "Notes for a Speech Favoring Revision of the Virginia Constitution of 1776," June 1784, Ibid., VIII, pp. 75-82.

8 Ibid., VIII, pp. 295-306.

determined that "No man shall be compelled to frequent or support any religious worship, place, or ministry whatsoever."[9]

STEPS TOWARD A STRONGER NATIONAL GOVERNMENT

One of Madison's earliest goals when he returned to the House of Delegates in 1784 was the resolution of a century-long conflict over access to the Potomac River that flows between Virginia and Maryland. He surely could not have realized then that this would be a tiny first step toward the Federal Convention in which he would play such a key role three years later. Through administrative carelessness when the King of England apportioned what he could of the western hemisphere among English colonists, Maryland's boundary was the southern bank of the Potomac River, so Virginia was supposedly officially prevented from setting foot or, more important, ship in the river. Naturally the Virginians did not adhere to this restriction, so inter-colonial conflicts were sometimes followed by inter-state confrontations. In June 1784 Madison's motion to establish a Virginia commission to negotiate with Maryland commissioners "such liberal and equitable regulation concerning the [Potomac] river as may be mutually advantageous to the two states" was approved unanimously.[10] Madison was also selected as a commissioner with George Mason, Edmund Randolph and Alexander Henderson. Madison and Randolph missed the meeting nearly a year later because they were never notified. Governor Henry's failure to inform them most likely resulted from typical administrative carelessness rather than vindictiveness against Madison, since even George Mason only learned of the meeting when he was surprised as the Maryland delegation arrived at his door, expecting to meet there. It seems that all were surprised to learn that the meeting had been transferred at Washington's invitation to Mount Vernon, near Mason's Alexandria home. The absence of Madison and Randolph was not a problem because Mason and Henderson represented Virginia very well and won commercial advantages on the Potomac River, in return for comparable concessions to Maryland on Chesapeake Bay.

This success was followed by a proposal by a legislative committee, again chaired by Madison, that annual conferences be held to enhance economic cooperation among the states. On this issue Madison observed rather than led. The

---

9 Ibid., VIII, pp. 399-401; Donald O. Dewey, "Virginia Statute for Religious Freedom" in Rutland, *James Madison Encyclopedia,* pp. 428-429; Ketcham, *James Madison,* pp. 399-403.

10 Hutchinson, et al., eds., *The Papers of James Madison,* VIII, pp. 89-90.

motion to invite a conference in 1786 at Annapolis was presented by John Tyler. While Madison would have welcomed a convention attempting to correct the countless flaws in the Articles of Confederation, he considered this commercial program too small a first step, or perhaps no step at all. Even after he had agreed to attend the Annapolis Convention in September 1786, he remained too realistic as well as pessimistic to anticipate that "Many Gentlemen both within & without Congs. Wish to make this meeting subservient to a Plenipotentiary Convention for amending the Confederation. Tho' my wishes are in favor of such an event, yet I despair so much of its accomplishment at the present crisis that I do not extend my views beyond a Commercial Reform. To speak the truth I almost despair even of this."[11] Madison's "despair" was based in part on another threat to navigation of the Mississippi River that threatened from a new source. Foreign Secretary John Jay, who had performed to Madison's satisfaction when Madison was defending American claims to Mississippi navigation in 1780 and 1781, was in 1786 again engaged in alarming negotiations regarding that very subject. However disappointed Madison was that commercial reform was the stated goal of the Annapolis Convention, Jay's current_activities made it essential that Madison be there. While he was rather grudging in his attendance, he hoped that something more might develop—and it did.

Madison spent several days in New York City assessing the current Congress before arriving, as was his custom, among the first commissioners at Annapolis. A week later twelve commissioners finally convened; all of them were nationalists, from only five of the eight states that had selected a delegation (Virginia, Pennsylvania, New Jersey, Delaware, and New York). Three days later, on September 14, they adjourned with a recommendation that a new Convention be convened in Philadelphia in May 1787 to recommend to Congress "such further provisions as shall appear to them necessary to render the constitution of the federal government adequate to the exigencies of the Union."[12] Madison supported the sentiments of Alexander Hamilton's more pressing demands for change but pragmatically settled for less revolutionary and therefore less threatening language.

Back in Richmond, he took prompt action to assure that Virginia would lead in initiating the invitation to Philadelphia. The recommendations from Annapolis were approved unanimously in Virginia and Madison wrote the bill to implement the invitation. He immediately contacted George Washington to argue the absolute necessity that Washington lead the delegation. Washington begged off

---

[11] To Thomas Jefferson, August 12, 1786, Ibid., IX, p. 96.

[12] Dewey, *Union and Liberty,* pp. 30-31.

legitimately because of ill health and private affairs, and the embarrassment that these same conditions had been the justification for his refusal to preside in *May* and *in Philadelphia* at the meeting of the Society of the Cincinnati, the officers whom he had commanded in the war that had ended only three years earlier. Madison nevertheless joined the legislature in electing Washington. He then wrote first to apologize, followed by constant entreaties that Washington's attendance was crucial, in which he was joined by Governor Edmund Randolph. Fortunately Washington's old comrade in arms, General Henry Knox, who ranked second to Washington as leader of the Cincinnati, urged Washington to participate and carried the day.

Two current issues impinged heavily on Virginia's views regarding the need for a strengthened national government. News of the Shays Rebellion convinced many of the need for a stronger government to control the farmers who were then disrupting courts and tax collection in western Massachusetts. Accounts of the Shays uprising were so selectively distributed that other states were largely unaware that his followers were confronted with enormous taxes while the state and nation were both unable and unwilling to pay the many rebels who had fought for Massachusetts' independence. Daniel Shays, for instance, had fought in five battles in Massachusetts and New York from 1775 to 1777. Athough Madison thought that Massachusetts was overly zealous in its response to the Shays uprising, he also felt that a fellow state deserved support from the nation. Pulling Virginia in the opposite direction was Foreign Secretary John Jay's negotiations with Spanish Ambassador Diego de Gardoqui that considered trading off American claims to the navigation of the Mississippi River for a quarter-century in exchange for an assured market for New England fish in Catholic Spain. Madison was put in a position to blunt the second issue by writing and winning approval of instructions to himself (as a new member of Congress as of February 1787) and his colleagues to oppose any surrender of rights to the Mississippi River. He wrote Washington that this issue would lead to "destroying that confidence in the wisdom, justice and liberality of the federal councils which is so necessary at this crisis, to a proper enlargement of their authority; and finally, as tending to undermine our repose, our prosperity and our Union itself." He feared that if they lost on this issue, "the hopes of carrying this state into a proper federal system will be demolished" because Patrick Henry "who had been hitherto the champion of the federal cause, has become a cold advocate, and in the event of an actual sacrifice of the Mississippi by Congress will unquestionably go over to the opposite side."[13] Strong language indeed for the nationalistic Father of the

[13] December 7, 1786, Hutchinson, et al., eds., *The Papers of James Madison,* IX, pp. 199-200.

Constitution just five months before the Federal Convention was to convene. Unfortunately for Madison, Henry went into the opposition even though the Mississippi was saved.

However it was fortunate for Madison that Henry stayed away from the Federal Convention and the secrecy essential to compromises on the difficult issues was therefore preserved. Madison considered the threat to the Mississippi so dangerous that he rode directly from Richmond to New York City in a bitter January and February of 1787 to assume his seat in Congress. He was so eager to mount a defense against the Jay-Gardoqui negotiations that he did not even stop at home in Montpelier or to visit Monroe at Fredericksburg, Virginia. His lone brief visit was at Mount Vernon to consult with Washington. He arrived in Congress February 9, only three months before the Federal Convention that would be the highpoint of his life, where he was delighted to learn that the mad dash was unnecessary, because the northern states had begun to back away from the Jay plan.[14] Madison had been reinvigorated between 1783 and 1787 and was eager to re-enter political life. Emotions ran high for improving the newly independent nation through the scheduled Constitutional Convention in Philadelphia. Here Madison would mount his highest pinnacle.

[14] Ketcham, *James Madison,* p. 179.

Chapter 4

FATHER OF THE CONSTITUTION

James Madison's all-consuming commitment to the monumental project that he had done so much to set in motion for the summer of 1787 was evident from the moment of his arrival. With the obvious exception of delegates who lived in Philadelphia, he was the first delegate there. He arrived on May 3, eleven days *before* the scheduled date, a striking contrast from the vast majority of delegates, who instead arrived late. Ten days would pass before any other non-Philadelphian would check in, but that was a crucial arrival for George Washington was the one delegate, despite his massive silence, whose presence was even more critical than Madison's. Two more Virginia nationalists arrived by May 14, the date when the Convention was scheduled to begin. George Wythe, the first American professor of law, and Judge John Blair were joined within three days by Governor Edmund Randolph, George Mason and Dr. James McClurg to complete the Virginia delegation. Since Virginia and Pennsylvania had a quorum by May 14 they met briefly and adjourned to wait—and wait--for the stragglers. Delegates from those two populous states shared ideas and meals while waiting and laid the groundwork for a nationalist juggernaut when the Convention finally got down to business on May 25, when there were finally seven states (a majority of the thirteen) with a quorum. Until mid-June Madison and Pennsylvanian James Wilson were the dominant strategists and voices in what seemed likely to be a rapid and inevitable march towards the creation of a new and much stronger governmental framework.

REPORTING FOR DUTY

Madison not only preceded all the other delegates, he was also better prepared than any of them. He had studied previous confederations from ancient times right up to the Articles of Confederation which had been ratified only six years earlier, and which he was now determined to supplant. He had compiled more than forty pages of "Notes on Ancient and Modern Confederacies" a few months before his departure for the Annapolis convention. His descriptions of their strengths and weaknesses ended with sections on "vices" of the constitutions that usually emphasized the inadequacy of their central authority.[1] Then while he impatiently waited in Congress during the three months prior to his departure from New York for Philadelphia, a time when Congress seemed to be marking time, he wrote "The Vices of the Political System of the United States," which again contrasted the excessive power of the parts and the weaknesses of the Continental Congress. Here he organized his countless frustrations in Congress and in the Virginia legislature and thus came prepared with outlines for many of the positions and speeches that he would deliver during the summer of 1787. He headed for Philadelphia convinced that the national government must be "armed with a positive and complete authority in all cases where uniform measures are necessary" and that it must be armed further with "a negative, in all cases whatsoever on the legislative acts of the states." Before Madison, the emphasis of political theorists had been on protection of the people from kings and aristocrats. Madison's experience in the Virginia legislature had shown him that in America the legislative majority presented an even greater danger unless balanced powers were provided to protect the minority. Historian Jack N. Rakove argues perceptively that this document is "one of those rare documents in the history of political theory in which one can literally observe an original thinker forge his major discovery."[2]

In the month preceding the Convention, Madison vigorously expressed his ambitions in a long letter to Governor Edmund Randolph: "I hold it for a fundamental point that an individual independence of the States, is utterly irreconcilable with the idea of an aggregate sovereignty. I think at the same time that a consolidation of the States into one simple republic is not less unattainable than it would be inexpedient. Let it be tried then whether any middle ground can

1 Hutchinson, et al., eds., *The Papers of James Madison,* IX, pp. 3-24.

2 Ibid., IX, pp. 345-357; Rakove, *James Madison and the Creation of the* Constitution, p. 46. For an excellent overview and analysis of both the Constitutional Convention delegates and their designs for a new constitution and federal government see Carol Berkin, *A Brilliant Solution: Inventing the American Constitution* (New York: Harcourt, 2002).

be taken which will at once support a due supremacy of the national authority and leave in force the local authorities as far as they can be subordinately useful." A week later he advanced the same ideas to General Washington, though here his language was more circumspect.[3]

Beginning on May 17, when all seven Virginia delegates were present, they met regularly and were able to enter the Convention eight days later with what would for the first several weeks remain a unified position. Except for Washington, who stayed at Robert Morris's mansion at Morris's insistence, the Virginia delegates roomed at the boarding house of Mrs. Mary House, with whom Madison roomed throughout his years in Congress and whenever he was passing through Philadelphia. This Philadelphia home was only a block from the Pennsylvania Statehouse where the Convention met. Virginia acted almost as host of the Federal Convention. After all, it was the Virginia legislature that invited the other states to send delegates to meet in Philadelphia to remedy the failings of the Articles of Confederation. It was the largest state both numerically and geographically and, in its delegates' perception and perhaps in reality, the most important. Finally it was home to James Madison who had since 1780 devoted his political career to creating a responsible and effective federal Union. The first items of business, after the unanimous election of George Washington as president of the Convention and the establishment of procedural decisions such as the crucial requirement that secrecy be maintained regarding decisions and debates so that the Constitution could be presented as a completed document rather than a series of day-to-day decisions, was the presentation on May 29 of the Virginia Plan of Union.

Virginia Plan of Union

The Virginia Resolutions that dominated the early weeks of the Convention and in final analysis provided most of the structural framework for the Constitution that was eventually ratified, were introduced by Madison's close friend Governor Edmund Randolph and therefore is sometimes called the Randolph Plan. Randolph was quite appropriately the voice of the Virginia delegation because he was Governor and he was also a much more impressive orator than James Madison. Nevertheless the Virginia Plan is to a great extent the work of Madison. It reflects ideas that Madison had expressed in contemporary

---

[3] April 8 and April 16, 1787, Hutchinson, et al., eds., *The Papers of James Madison,* IX, pp. 368-371, 382-387.

letters to delegates Randolph and Washington, and its proposals are far more nationalistic than the often-timid Randolph would ever have written. Indeed, Madison was often required to advance with care in order not to increase his colleague's caution. Randolph apologized for his youth and limited political experience, "But, as the convention had originated from Virginia, and his colleagues supposed, that some proposition was expected from them, they had imposed this task on him."[4] It must be noted at this first quotation from Madison's extensive notes of the federal debates that speeches, including his own, are invariably stated in the third person, even though he sought and usually obtained the approval of delegates who delivered major speeches.

The first resolution called for the Articles of Confederation to be "corrected and enlarged" but the other resolutions proposed enlargements so dramatic as to belie the implication of this circumspect introduction that the Articles were being amended rather than supplanted. When this inconsistency was pointed out the next day, Randolph responded with three new resolutions, the most striking declaring "that a *national* Government (ought to be established) consisting of a *supreme* Legislative, Executive and Judiciary." This better accords with the remainder of the document, even though a motion to delete the words "supreme" and "national" failed by only a tied vote of four states to four. Irving Brant argues persuasively that these added resolutions did not represent quick thinking by Randolph but were instead the introduction to Madison's original proposal that had been briefly held back to satisfy Randolph's reservations.[5] With this amendment of the introductory resolution the document became a unified proposal rather than a series of anomalies.

A bicameral Congress "proportioned to the Quotas of contribution, or to the number of free inhabitants" would replace the former unicameral Congress where each state had an equal vote whatever its size or population. Members of the lower house would be selected by "the people of the several states" rather than by state legislatures and the first house would in turn select members of the other house. In addition to the limited legislative powers provided in the Articles, Congress would be able to "legislate in all cases to which the separate States are incompetent, or in which the harmony of the United States may be interrupted by the exercise of individual Legislation." There would be a separate executive and judiciary rather than the bare hints of separation of powers existing under the

---

[4] Max Farrand, ed., *The Records of the Federal Convention of 1787,* 4 Volumes, (New Haven: Yale University Press, 1911), I, p. 18. Madison's role as unofficial recorder of Convention deliberations is discussed at the end of this chapter.

[5] Hutchinson, et al., eds., *The Papers of James Madison,* X, pp. 12-18; Irving Brant, *James Madison: Father of the Constitution 1787* (Indianapolis: Bobbs-Merrill, 1959), p. 10.

Articles of Confederation. An amendment system would be developed which at least by implication did not require ratification by every state as was required in the Articles. And the new Constitution would be ratified by state conventions "expressly chosen by the people." Much of that plan is reflected in the Constitution that was submitted to Congress in September and thence to the states for ratification. A major exception was the resolution that Madison considered essential and that he continued to bring up frequently throughout the summer. He wanted Congress to have power "to negative all laws passed by the several States contravening in the opinion of the National Legislature the articles of Union; and to call forth the force of the Union ag[ain]st. any member of the Union failing to fulfill its duties under the articles thereof."[6]

MADISON'S LEADERSHIP

Madison was an active participant regarding most of the substantive issues raised in the Convention. The growth from the shy and quiet Virginia legislator of 1776 and Congressman of 1780 is highlighted in the notes of William Pierce of Georgia, the one delegate who rewarded us with character sketches of his fellow delegates. Pierce did not otherwise contribute significantly to the Convention, but his personality sketches vividly augment the substantive notes provided by others. Pierce wrote that

> "Mr. Maddison is a character who has long been in public life; and what is very remarkable every Person seems to acknowledge his greatness. He blends together the profound politician with the Scholar. In the management of every great question he evidently took the lead in the Convention, and tho' he cannot be called an Orator, he is a most agreeable, eloquent, and convincing Speaker. From a Spirit of industry and application which he possesses in a most eminent degree, he always comes forward the best informed Man of any point in debate. The affairs of the United States, he perhaps, has the most correct knowledge of, of any Man in the Union. He has been twice a Member of Congress, and was always thought one of the ablest Members that ever sat in that Council. Mr. Maddison is about 37 years of age, a Gentleman of great modesty,--with a remarkable sweet temper. He is easy and unreserved among his acquaintance, and has a most agreeable style of conversation."[7]

[6] Hutchinson, et al., eds., *The Papers of James Madison,* X, pp. 12-30.

Madison was a year younger than Pierce estimated, but this was not a significant issue in a Convention where twenty-seven per cent of the delegates were even younger than Madison and four were still in their twenties. In his brief paragraph on Madison the closest Pierce comes to criticism is that "he cannot be called an orator." In short, Madison seemed qualified to some day become "Father of the Constitution" whatever his age. Lest it be assumed that Pierce was a "Pollyanna" who could say ill of no one, he was very rough on some of his colleagues. He was critical of the only two delegates who received longer sketches than Madison's. Despite his brilliance, Gouverneur Morris of Pennsylvania "is fickle and inconstant,--never pursuing one train of reason,--or ever regular." It is surprising that he found Alexander Hamilton of New York "too feeble to be equal to the strain of oratory" and his manners "tinctured with stiffness, and sometimes with a degree of vanity that is highly disagreeable." He described Roger Sherman of Connecticut as "awkward, un-meaning, and unaccountably strange," as he spouted "vulgarisms" that made "everything that is connected with him grotesque and laughable." Rufus King of Massachusetts was faulted for "rudeness of manner." Sadly Pierce gives no picture of the only other future president who helped to create this new government—and the presidency. Under Pierce's microscope George Washington appears only as a list of past achievements followed by gratitude for his willingness in 1787 to be "virtuous and useful," with no real picture of him as a man. Of course as presiding officer Washington had less opportunity than others to show his style. The other giants of the Revolution who were there did not fare so well. Pierce observed John Dickinson especially closely because of his respect for his "Letters of a Farmer in Pennsylvania," but he "found him an indifferent Speaker. With an affected air of wisdom he labors to produce a trifle,--his language is irregular and incorrect,--his flourishes (for he attempts them), are like expiring flames, they just shew themselves and go out,--no traces are left on the mind to cheer or animate it." Even the sainted Benjamin Franklin "does not shine much in public Council,--he is no Speaker, nor does he seem to let politics engage his attention."[8] In fairness he might have added that Franklin at 81 was nearly two decades older than any other member.

By then Madison had even achieved international fame, thanks in large part to his friendly publicist in France, Thomas Jefferson. In the article on the United States in the famed French *Encyclopedie* (1786), Hector St. Jean de Crevecoeur, who would later visit and write much more about the United States, referred to

[7] Farrand, *Records of the Federal Convention of 1787,* III, pp. 94-95.

[8] Ibid., III, pp. 87-97.

"Mr. Maddison, who at the age of 30 astonished the new republics with his eloquence, his wisdom and his genius."[9] He surely learned his admiration of Madison from Jefferson, if not the spelling. Crevecoeur would soon become French counsel in New York City while Madison was again serving in Congress.

COMPROMISE BECOMES NECESSARY

Madison and James Wilson, Virginia and nationalism, prevailed in the early weeks of the Convention because they had the momentum and no successful opposition was mounted. Madison's powerful speech on July 6 for direct election of the House of Representatives was followed by a vote of 6 states to 2, a consistent majority for this House. In it he provided a preview of his famous argument in *Federalist* 10 that a large electorate was advantageous because it would assure varied interests that could not be dominated by a single faction or interest. By June 13 nearly all of the Virginia Plan had been approved. Early arrivals such as Roger Sherman and John Dickinson had ineffectively challenged the revisions demanded by the nationalists, but they were augmented by major reinforcements early in June. Lawyer Luther Martin replaced a nationalist Maryland delegate and would remain a political thorn to Madison for decades. More significant was the arrival from New Jersey of Governor William Livingston and especially William Paterson, the former attorney general. When he appeared on June 9, Paterson protested that members were violating their mandate to amend the Articles of Confederation rather than supplant them. On June 15 he introduced a New Jersey Plan of Union that was much less revolutionary than that of Virginia and most importantly called for state equality in the Senate, as had existed in the unicameral Confederation Congress. Following Madison's detailed refutation of the proposal on June 19, in which he emphasized that republican government must be based on representation of people rather than states, the New Jersey Plan was quickly defeated by seven states to three. But the issue just would not go away. A House and Senate based on population would be approved several times by the end of June, but the margin of the Senate vote kept narrowing.[10] Benjamin Franklin, the master of compromise, postponed the conflict by

---

[9] Brant, *James Madison: Father of the Constitution,* p. 56; Ketcham, *James Madison,* pp. 204-205.

[10] Farrand, *Records of the Federal Convention of 1787* , I, pp. 177-189; Hutchinson, et al., eds., *The Papers of James Madison,* X, pp. 4, 59-62; Donald O. Dewey, "William Paterson" in Rutland, *James Madison Encyclopedia,* pp. 333-334.

proposing an "equitable" basis for Senate representation, but eventually the meaning of that word had to be determined.

The absence of some states or tie votes in others frequently influenced votes as the New Jersey advocates crept toward their goal. For example New York lost its vote entirely when Robert Yates left permanently on July 9,[11] and New Hampshire never had any presence until July 23 when its delegates first appeared. In response to an alarmingly close five to four vote, Madison on June 30 took the dangerous step of introducing the issues of sectionalism and even slavery. He argued that significant differences between the states were really based on geographic interests (northern merchants vs. southern farmers) rather than on their relative size. He was the first to propose insertion in the Constitution of the three-fifths clause that already existed in the Articles of Confederation for the determination of fiscal requisitions. This would later be added to the Constitution, causing representation to be based on 60 per cent of slave population until this clause was made irrelevant by addition of the Thirteenth Amendment after the Civil War.[12]

The tone of the Convention shifted dramatically and permanently on July 2 when the advocates of state equality in the Senate achieved victory without ever gaining a majority vote. The motion for a proportional basis for Senate representation was defeated by a tie vote. This was only a temporary defeat because the arrival of a tardy Maryland member would again place the nationalists in the majority. Yet symbols are important, and the smaller states had finally achieved one with this momentary victory. Rather than renew the struggle later in the week, the members agreed by a vote of nine to two to establish a Grand Committee with one representative elected from each state. Their eagerness to compromise was obvious when Mason was elected rather than Madison for Virginia, Franklin rather than Wilson for Pennsylvania, and Elbridge Gerry rather than Rufus King for Massachusetts, while delegates such as William Paterson, Luther Martin, Gunning Bedford and Robert Yates were sent from their states to advocate equality of the states in the Senate.[13] The committee quickly reported on July 5 the compromise variously called "Federal," "Great," "Franklin" and "Connecticut," that provided for state equality in the Senate and proportional representation in the House, which would supposedly be the initiator of fiscal legislation. Despite the angry opposition of Madison, Wilson, Gouverneur Morris,

---

[11] Even when Hamilton returned in August, New York still had no vote because Governor Clinton had taken care to provide that his state could not vote unless two members were present.

[12] Hutchinson, et al., eds., *The Papers of James Madison,* X, pp. 88-92.

[13] Farrand, *Records of the Federal Convention of 1787,* I, pp. 510-516,

and Randolph, the Convention acquiesced and at last moved forward to other issues. When Randolph proposed that the Convention adjourn, Paterson countered that he would support a permanent adjournment. Instead there was a brief adjournment after which the subject of representation in the Senate was dropped.

MADISON AS COMPROMISER

Madison argued for and achieved a governmental framework based on compromise. He justified the secrecy of the Convention because it made possible a Constitution that could be supported by nearly every remaining participant, even though no one (including Madison) was delighted by every clause. The Convention would therefore be judged on a complete document rather than on a series of day-to-day votes and debates. Yet Madison himself was definitely not the best of compromisers. His views changed in the course of debates during sixteen long and hot Philadelphia weeks, but he had to retreat less often than most, because so much of the Virginia Plan survived in the completed document. When he did not prevail he held to his positions as long as possible, yet when defeat was certain he learned to live with it in order to maintain the favorable advances that had been achieved. He accepted equal representation of states in the Senate grudgingly and even bitterly. He continued to believe that "the lesser states must in every event yield to the predominant will" of the popular majority. For him popular election was essential to republican government. Madison still contended for a government that would "rest with solid foundation of the people." Paterson, leader of the states that insisted on equal representation, must have had Madison and Wilson in mind when he referred to the "sword and gallows" arguments of his opposition. Madison was an enthusiastic participant in a large state caucus to establish a separate union even after equality in the Senate had been conceded, but he lacked the support even of the Virginia delegation. This defeat was especially galling because he had envisioned the Senate as a body of philosophical elders, who would provide a check on the possible excesses of the U.S. House of Representatives as well as the state legislatures, rather than a political body based on conflicting state interests.[14] Yet the cessation of fears by the smaller states that they would be overwhelmed by the giants converted members who had formerly resisted any increase in the power of the central government into nationalists. Decades later Madison declared that "from the day when every doubt of the right of the smaller states to an equal vote in the Senate

---

[14] Hutchinson, et al., eds., *The Papers of James Madison,* X, pp. 55-61, 88-93, 100-102.

was quieted they…exceeded all others in zeal for granting powers to the general government."[15] Ironically, at this same point Madison changed too, becoming more cautious about granting these powers due to his, and Virginia's, defeat on the structure of the Senate.

Madison never surrendered on his insistence that Congress should be allowed to veto state legislation that impinged on central authorities. This had been approved without dissent back in May but discarded in mid-July. A few days before the Convention ended, he again introduced this issue and its insertion was rejected by six states to five. He continued to bemoan this defeat even after the Constitution had been submitted to the states. So far as the majority was concerned, though, addition of the Supreme Law clause in Article V of the Constitution obviated the need for Madison's cherished restraint on state legislatures.

THE EXECUTIVE DEPARTMENT

Madison's conception of the national executive assumes special significance because he was the only one of the Founding Fathers who would become President, other than the almost automatic George Washington. Article II of the Constitution was surely written with Washington clearly in mind because virtually everyone there, with the notable exception of Washington himself, assumed that he would be the first President and would therefore fill in the outlines and provide prudent precedents. His unanimous election as chairman of the Convention assured delegates that decorum would prevail and, more important, assured those excluded from the secret proceedings that nothing improper was likely to occur. But his position in the chair also assured that Washington's influence on substantive issues would be limited pretty much to his generally unknown votes in the Virginia delegation. He made only one substantive speech and that was as the Convention was ending in September. The Virginia Plan supported by both future Presidents proposed a National Executive "chosen by the National Legislature," without specifying whether it would be a committee or a single person, or the length of the term of office. It proposed ineligibility for a second term and a fixed salary that could not be increased or decreased during the single term of office, whatever length it might turn out to be. The executive proposed by the Virginians would also have acted with the National Judiciary to form a "Council of revision" that could reject acts of Congress and, in turn, review and sometimes overturn

---

[15] Historian George Bancroft cited in Brant, *James Madison: Father of the Constitution,* pp. 103-104.

vetoes by the Congress of state legislation. Madison had not given as much consideration to the executive branch as he did to the Congress. There is no evidence that this was because he too assumed that Washington would "fill in the blanks"; and even if he did it was not a subject that could be discussed in the caucus of Virginia delegates, with Washington present. In the newly independent states the legislatures were so dominant that Madison's principal focus was on protection of the executive and judiciary. And in the central government that they were replacing, the semblances of executive and judicial departments were feeble even relative to the toothless Confederation Congress. As a result of Virginia's indecision on this issue, James Wilson of Pennsylvania assumed leadership in the development of the executive and Madison regularly supported most of his initiatives. Most significantly, he consistently supported Wilson's proposal for a single President, rather than an executive committee, and that the position be filled by popular election. Wilson would two years later be rewarded for his leading Convention role by appointment as Supreme Court Justice, where he would serve until 1798.

The means of selecting the executive, the length of executive terms, and eligibility for the office were issues that were reconsidered and changed time and again throughout the steamy summer of 1787. Proposals for the length of presidential terms ranged from the absurd to a comparable absurdity at the other end of the scale (from one year to twenty-one years). Madison's position on these issues was determined by the method of selection. As a choice by the people became increasingly likely, Madison advocated relatively short terms that could be extended as long as the voting public desired. When he had earlier advocated election of the President by Congress, which it must be noted was not then based on state equality in the Senate, he favored one long term because he feared that the executive would curry favor with the legislature to remain in office. In Convention debates he consistently opposed legislative interference with executive functions. He opposed a proposal to suspend from office a President who had been impeached by the House of Representatives pending the Senate decision to uphold the impeachment. He also opposed a proposal to widen the grounds for impeachment by specifying "maladministration." History has demonstrated that "high crimes and misdemeanors" has been tricky enough as grounds for impeachment.[16]

Madison was on the Committee on Unfinished Parts, which resolved a number of controversial issues in the constitutional draft presented August 6 by the Committee of Detail. This committee proposed the basic structure of the

---

[16] Ibid., X, pp. 24-25, 103-105.

executive branch, including the Electoral College, although strangely that phrase appears nowhere in the Constitution. Individual roles cannot be determined because Madison did not keep meticulous notes of committee discussion, as he did of debates in the full Convention. However on July 19 he had hinted at a group of electors. Then on July 25 after a description of the dangers of undue influence if the Congress were to appoint the President, he noted the wisdom of a special group elected by the citizens to make this decision. However since this method "had been rejected so recently & by so great a majority that it probably would not be proposed anew," this left only "election by the people or by the qualified part of them, at large." He then described the difficulties for "the people" to choose a truly national figure because of the distances and differences of the states. In this context it is easy to picture Madison asking in the committee a few weeks later, "Well, after General Washington, then whom?" which might be followed by an argument to reconsider the previously rejected proposal for "electors."[17]

FOREBODINGS OF SECTIONALISM

Nationalism was by no means the only recurring theme in Madison's role in the Convention. He was prophetic in his arguments that the issues that really threatened the United States were those of North versus South, rather than large states versus small states. He continued his long-standing struggle to counterattack the inroads of land speculators, from those same small states who had just gained their equal rights in the Senate, and who then insisted that the landless states must also acquire equal rights to the West. Madison was more concerned for the West as a national domain than as an "empire" for Virginia, North Carolina and Georgia, but he was realist enough to know that if it became fair game for speculators whose claims were based on illegal negotiations with the Indians, the South would be much less supportive of a national union. The claims of the southern states were also based on questionable grounds, but at least they had Royal charters and nearly two centuries of time on their side.

Madison's most renowned contribution to the *Federalist* essays, No. 10, was advanced in Convention just as it had been hinted in Congress. Before Madison it was political gospel that democracy was limited to small units—city-states, town meetings, and the like. (His political mentor Thomas Jefferson had earlier proposed one hundred families as a proper basis of democratic government.)

17 Hutchinson, et al., eds., *The Papers of James Madison,* X, pp. 107-108, 115-117.

Madison, on the other hand, argued that the very size of the United States and its many conflicting economic interests would enable republican government to work on a large scale. The Convention epitomized his conception that political divisions were based on economic interests, for the delegates were highly committed to property rights—but they had widely differing views of the property they were committed to protect.

"Authorship" of the Constitution

Many of Madison's substantive offerings appear in the Constitution in the words of two nationalist Pennsylvanians. James Wilson was the dominant force on the Committee of Detail, on which the less forceful Edmund Randolph represented Virginia. Madison served on the Committee of Style and Arrangement elected on September 8 to fine-tune the document. The remarkably clear and succinct language of the United States Constitution, including the preamble, is largely the work of Gouverneur Morris. Madison wrote, "The finish given to the style and arrangement of the Constitution fairly belongs to the pen of Mr. Morris," adding that "A better choice could not have been made, as the performance of the task proved."[18] In the closing days of the Convention, Madison clarified and expanded the amendment process of Article V, establishing the Congressional role that has proven to be the method by which all twenty-seven constitutional amendments have been initiated. He also made one final effort to introduce a Congressional veto of state legislation. He supported unsuccessful efforts to require a three-fourths vote rather than two-thirds for Congress to override presidential vetoes. Other issues raised but rejected as unnecessary during the final week that would have had significant impact on Madison's later political life included rejection of Mason's proposal to add a Bill of Rights as unnecessary in a government of limited powers. This argument was justified by the listing of delegated powers to Congress in Article I, Section 8, in preference to the far more open-ended authority "to legislate in all cases to which the separate States are incompetent, or in which the harmony of the United States may be interrupted by the exercise of individual Legislation," that had been included in the sixth Virginia Resolution. The concept of enumerated powers was introduced by the Committee of Detail on August 6. Following that Madison spoke on several of the specific authorizations but did not specifically question the

[18] James Madison to Jared Sparks, April 8, 1831, Hunt, *Writings of James Madison,* IX, pp. 447-451.

decision to delegate specific powers to Congress.[19] Madison himself moved but failed to gain support for motions to allow Congress to build canals and to establish a national university. A proposal for constitutional power to grant charters of incorporation was also rejected. By then the members were simply too eager for adjournment to consider matters that would have merited their attention if they had surfaced earlier.

Madison and others attempted unsuccessfully to dissuade three members who were still present on September 17, including two Virginians, from refusing to sign the document. Randolph had moved for a new convention. It was seconded by Mason and supported by Elbridge Gerry of Massachusetts, who would be Madison's Vice President during his second term. Following its rejection by the unanimous vote of all states present, they were unwilling to sign their support of the Constitution. On the final day Franklin, in a charming speech read by Wilson, implored that members recognize that they, like Franklin himself, should not "think of themselves in possession of all truth, and that wherever others differ from them it is so far error." He added that "I agree to this Constitution with all its faults, if they are such; because I think a general Government necessary for us, and there is no form of Government but what may be a blessing to the people if well administered... It therefore astonishes me, Sir, to find this system approaching so near to perfection.... Thus I consent, Sir, to this Constitution because I expect no better, and because I am not sure, that it is not the best...." His admonition that members take pride in what was accomplished, rather than bemoan their occasional disappointments, surely struck a chord with Madison and Hamilton, who both were disappointed by the final product but who did more than any others to achieve its ratification. As recently as September 6, Madison had written Jefferson in numeric code that he suspected that "the plan should it be adopted will neither effectually answer its national object nor prevent the local mischiefs which every where excite disgust ag[ain]st the state governments."[20]

KEEPING THE RECORDS OF THE CONVENTION

Madison's contributions to the *creation* of the Constitution had ended. His contributions to its history, as well as its historiography, had just begun. Much of what we know about the birth of our governmental framework is due to his

[19] Hutchinson, et al., eds., *The Papers of James Madison,* X, pp. 16, 148-158.

[20] Farrand, *Records of the Federal Convention of 1787,* II, pp. 631-633, 641-643; Hutchinson, et al., eds., *The Papers of James Madison,* X, pp. 163-164.

certainty that something very important was afoot and that if its story was to be told it was up to him. He had been dismayed by the lack of knowledge regarding the ancient and medieval confederacies that he had recently studied. The decision to conduct a secret convention, combined with the limitations on—and of—Major William Jackson, the official secretary, made it certain that official records would tell little more than the important votes, if that. Madison would be the "court reporter" self-appointed to fill in the blanks. He had trained for this historic task by recording in his own shorthand debates in Congress for several years, as well as similar notes on the Virginia constitutional convention and the House of Delegates when he was there. At first the young Congressman listened more than he spoke, but by 1782 he had become adept at recording debate while participating in it actively. He continued to keep such notes when he was in the Virginia House of Delegates and was still doing the same during his brief time in Congress in 1787 before hastening to the Federal Convention. It is a sad commentary on the Confederation Congress that several times he wrote "Nothing worthy of posting," which he later revised to "Nothing posted." In the new Congress in 1789 and throughout the 1790s Madison was too busy to remain an unofficial secretary. Fortunately by then New York and Philadelphia newspapers provided a better record of the debates than had their predecessors. Madison's daunting project was useful not just to future generations but to immediate debates in which Madison had an advantage over other delegates because he had a more immediate recollection of prior actions of the Convention.

Decades later he wrote this description of his memorable role at Philadelphia:

> "In pursuance of the task I had assumed, I chose a seat in front of the presiding member…. I noted, in terms legible and in abbreviations and marks intelligible to myself, what was read from the chair or spoken by the members; and losing not a moment unnecessarily between the adjournment and reassembling of the convention, I was enabled to write out my notes during the session or within a few finishing days after its close…."
>
> "In the labor and correctness of this I was not a little aided by practice, and by a familiarity with the style and the train of observation and reasoning which characterized the principal speakers. It happened, also, that I was not absent a single day, nor more than a casual fraction of an hour in any day, so that I could not have lost a single speech unless a very short one."[21]

Eight other delegates wrote convention notes but only one other than Madison provided some thoroughness during his brief attendance. That was Robert Yates of New York who bitterly opposed what he was observing and left in frustration early in July. On the final day the delegates agreed to keep records private so decades would pass before any but a select few would have any detailed knowledge how their revered Constitution came into being. The barebones official journal, described by its editor Secretary of State John Quincy Adams as "no better than the daily minutes from which the regular journal ought to have been, but never was, made out," was not published until 1819, two years after Madison had left the presidency.[22] Yates's notes were published two years later, somewhat embarrassing Madison with the evidence of nationalism that seemed to splatter in the face of a statesman who was by then regarded as a patron saint of state sovereignty.

Madison nevertheless declined to publish his own notes while any members of the Convention were still living, then lived on and on after the others, seven years after the last to go before Madison. As a result Madison's notes of the debates were not published until 1840 when Congress finally appropriated the money, and many crucial decisions were made until then based on scanty information about the creation of the Constitution.

Another result was wide, and widely erroneous, speculation that Madison more than three decades later doctored his notes to hide his and his colleagues' nationalism.

After his retirement he pored over the records to make corrections that unfortunately led to a 20th century conspiracy theory that he had distorted the history of the Convention by inventing speeches and disguising issues to hide the Madisonian nationalism that had become an embarrassment to the state's rights theories of Jefferson and Madison that had become party doctrine during and after the 1790s. This theory is advanced in the first volume of William W. Crosskey's massive *Politics and the Constitution in the History of the United States,*[23] with the promise of evidence in forthcoming volumes, but the author and even his successor did not live to deliver on that promise. If they had, they would have been confronted by the embarrassing facts that Madison did not discard his Virginia Plan of Union, which provided the core of nationalist growth during the first month of the Convention, or his many nationalist speeches defending this plan. Furthermore, the ink and the paper and even the tiny and painful handwriting that arthritis and rheumatism imposed on the aged Madison argue

[21] Farrand, *Records of the Federal Convention of 1787,* III, p. 81; Hutchinson, et al., eds., *The Papers of James Madison,* X, pp. 6-9.

[22] Farrand, *Records of the Federal Convention of 1787,* I, p. xii.

[23] 3 Volumes, Chicago: University of Chicago Press, 1961-1985.

against the assertion that he drastically revised portions of the notes that he had written nearly four decades earlier. The public would not see these records until they were published in 1840 by the federal government, six years after Madison's death. Thus the great decisions of the John Marshall court, President Andrew Jackson's dismantling of the Bank of the United States (which had been formed with Madison's blessings), and the powerful debates of Senators Daniel Webster (Massachusetts) and Robert Y. Hayne (South Carolina) over the constitutionality of South Carolina's nullification of acts of Congress all occurred before accurate knowledge of the debates that led to the United States Constitution was available. This delay resulted from the failure of Congress to admit that this final legacy, which Madison believed would assure funds that would enable his widow to remain in their Orange County home, was worth what Madison believed. Sadly she was forced to sell Montpelier and live her final years in Washington, D.C., where she died in 1849.[24]

24 Donald O. Dewey, "Crosskey vs. Madison: James Madison and the United States Constitution," *Richmond Law Review,* XIX, (Winter 1985), pp. 435-446; Ketcham, *James Madison,* p. 661.

Chapter 5

VICTORY FOR THE CONSTITUTION

James Madison mistakenly believed that his labors for the Constitution were completed as he relaxed after the strenuous summer of 1787, because his constitutional principles directed that at this point the framers of the Constitution should step aside to allow "the people" to rule upon the framers' handwork through the ratification conventions that were to be elected in each state, as provided in the proposed Constitution. How wrong he was! Perfecting his notes of the Convention debates was soon interrupted by letters urging him to hasten to New York to reclaim his seat in Congress to assure a majority in the Virginia delegation's decision to forward the Constitution to the states. Next during his continuing congressional service Madison was drafted by Alexander Hamilton to participate in writing voluminous anonymous defenses of the document that Madison basically admired despite omissions that he considered tragic, and that Hamilton accepted grudgingly as at least a considerable improvement over the Articles of Confederation and as close to his ideal government as he could foresee in those times. The *Federalist Papers* were written by Hamilton and Madison, and to a very limited extent by John Jay, under the pseudonym "Publius." They were designed primarily to win ratification of the Constitution in New York where George Clinton, the state's governor and political boss from 1777 to 1795 and again from 1801 to 1804, was adamantly opposed to any change that might decrease his influence. Madison recognized, however, that they could be useful elsewhere and arranged for limited distribution in Virginia and other states that had not yet ratified the Constitution. Early in 1788 Virginia supporters of the Constitution begged him to hurry home to stand for election to the Virginia ratification convention of June 1788. He arrived just in time to earn Orange County's support and then ride on to Richmond to engage in one of the greatest and most significant political debates in American history—Patrick Henry the great American orator of the Revolutionary era against James Madison the constitutional thinker beyond compare.

When the eighteen members of Congress who had been on leave of absence to write a Constitution in Philadelphia hastened back to New York City, the supporters of the new Constitution had sufficient votes to forward the document to the state legislatures with a positive endorsement. But that would take time and stir up opposition debate even if it was sure to be overcome eventually by supportive debate and votes. To accommodate Pennsylvania's desire that the Constitution be forwarded promptly so that a state ratification convention could be called there prior to the imminent adjournment of the state legislature, Congress submitted the Constitution without expressing support or objections. The Pennsylvanians hoped to parlay an early approval of the Constitution into a decision to return the new government from New York to Philadelphia. Even before Madison arrived back in Congress, Richard Henry Lee of Virginia had already introduced what would be a continual argument by opponents of the new plan, insistence that a Bill of Rights must be added prior to ratification. Lee was one of the few prominent members of Congress who opposed the Constitution. Later he would write influential essays against it. Madison and his followers would discover in June 1788 that they were fortunate that Lee was in Congress rather than in the narrowly-divided Virginia ratification convention, where every vote was at a premium and he would have been a powerfully oratorical ally to Patrick Henry and George Mason.

Madison as Federalist

As soon as Madison arrived in New York he was drafted by Hamilton to participate in a major public relations campaign for the Constitution. Hamilton probably had already written the first essay of *The Federalist,* which introduced the plan for the project, because it appeared in a New York newspaper on October 27, only two weeks after his arrival. Fortunately for Madison, the morale and status and especially the attendance of Congress were so dismally low in 1787-1788 that his workload was significantly less than during his earlier service. *The Federalist* essays proved to be a much larger time commitment than he had anticipated when Hamilton recruited him to participate. Hamilton had originally envisioned four or five authors. Gouverneur Morris, who had been a significant contributor to the Constitution, declined an invitation and the efforts of William Duer, a former member of Congress and later known as "the prince of speculators" when he served as Hamilton's Assistant Secretary of the Treasury, did not meet Hamilton's or Madison's expectations, so then there were three. After writing only four early essays on foreign affairs, United States Foreign Secretary Jay's rheumatism forced him to withdraw and leave the project to Hamilton and Madison. On March 5, 1788, the day after Madison left for Virginia, Jay published *Federalist* No. 64 on the treaty powers of the Senate for his fifth and final offering. All eighty five essays would appear as a book in May 1788. This intensive study of the Constitution, which would remain a powerful guide to American government for more than two centuries, is the result of one of the most astonishing literary productions of all time. Madison wrote in a numeric code to Jefferson, one of very few friends to whom he revealed his role, that although the project was "carried on in concert, the writers are not mutually answerable for all the ideas of each other, there being seldom time for even a perusal of the pieces by any but the writer before they were wanted at the press, and sometimes hardly by the writer himself."[1] Hamilton and Madison cranked out thousands of words per week, missing only one newspaper deadline (during Christmas week) from late October 1787 through late May 1788. Madison had written twenty-nine essays by March 4 when he departed New York to seek election to the Virginia convention. Hamilton had written the same number by then, but following Madison's departure he wrote twenty-two more to complete the project with a total of eighty-five.

Madison's first contribution *Federalist* No. 10, the most famous, most studied, and sometimes most criticized of Publius's many justifications for a dramatic change in government, was printed on November 22. His frankness in acknowledging that economic self interest was at the core of political issues has caused him to be branded everything from a Marxist three decades before Karl Marx was born to one of the capitalists assumed by historian Charles A. Beard to have created a Constitution largely to protect private property.[2] The fact that private property was a major consideration of course did not mean that it was the only governmental concern, and certainly not property in public securities which was Beard's principal concern. Furthermore, government was designed to protect the poor from the rich, just as it was designed to protect the rich from the poor. Most significantly, No. 10 introduces the then revolutionary concept that large geographical size did not make representative government impossible. For Madison a great advantage of the American federal system was that when a

---

[1] August 10, 1788, Hutchinson, et al., eds., *The Papers of James Madison,* XI, pp. 225-227.

[2] Charles A. Beard, *An Economic Interpretation of the Constitution* (New York: Macmillan Co., 1913).

political experiment failed in one of the states, it need not affect the other states making up the United States. On the contrary, the sheer size of the United States and its national domain in the West assured that no single interest, economic or otherwise, could prevail because of the many competing interests. A wide diversity that prevented any one group from domination lessened the danger of a demagogue. (Thoughts of Patrick Henry may have crossed his mind at this point.) This was a dramatic advance in political theory, because until then it had been taken for granted that even a republican democracy could exist only in small governments—usually city states. For Madison the beauty of this large new republic was that the great number of elements or "factions" that it contained decreased the likelihood that any one of them could gain dominance and thus deprive citizens of their rights. He had argued this position in the Convention but in *Federalist* No. 10 it is for the first time fully developed. Eight days later in *Federalist* No.14 Madison again emphasized vast geography and challenged opponents of the Constitution to respond to his bold new theory.

Federalist No. 18 to 20 were an easy task because they drew heavily upon his "Notes on Ancient and Modern Confederacies," as well as notes provided by Hamilton. Next Madison published No. 37 to 58 between January 11 and February 20. Finally No. 62 and 63 by March 1 concluded his share of Publius as he left for Virginia. These essays are virtually a book within a book, heralding the strengths of this new republican government and the role of the new legislature in accomplishing them. Its recurring theme is that republican government must rest on the American people rather than the favored groups who dominate other nations. In *Federalist* No. 45 and 46 he asserted that the powers most important to the people remain within the states and the next twelve essays described the proper distribution of "limited" federal powers among the legislature, executive, and judiciary. (This highlights the extent to which Publius was more a political advocate than a political philosopher. Madison was making a virtue of state powers that survived in the new system, even though during the previous year he had been striving mightily to limit state authority.) His following essays focus heavily on checks and balances within Congress and between state and nation, even though the full explication of separation of powers awaited the final essays by Hamilton when he defended the executive and judiciary.

Who Wrote What?

The anonymity of *The Federalist* unfortunately led to a literary conflict that continued for more than a century between the two principal authors and their generations of adherents. An edition was published in 1802 for which Hamilton was believed to have personally assigned the authorship. Shortly before his death in an 1804 duel with Vice President Aaron Burr, Hamilton has been alleged to have left a list of authors with a fellow lawyer. If this story is correct, and it has been challenged, Hamilton claimed authorship of nearly 78 per cent of the essays. A "Jeffersonian Republican" edition was published in 1818, based on Madison's correction of Hamilton's assignment of authorship. It assigned Madison twenty-nine (rather than fourteen) and Hamilton fifty- one (rather than sixty-five). Succeeding editions often "voted" for Madison or Hamilton, depending on the politics of the editor, the publisher, or the times, while many begged the issue by listing both authors. This confusion was largely resolved in 1944 by Douglass Adair who demonstrated through historical methods that Madison's list was accurate and that Hamilton's resulted from faulty memory probably caused by the stress of his situation, as Madison had surmised at the outset, never assuming intentional falsehood by Hamilton. Madison obviously gave the issue closer attention than had Hamilton. Adair's results were confirmed by an extensive computer study of *The Federalist*.[3] The comprehensive edition that was edited in 1961 by Jacob Cooke, editor of many volumes of the definitive *Papers of Alexander Hamilton*, continues to list both names for nine of the challenged issues, to show that there had been a conflict, but with Madison named first and in larger type.[4] Hamilton's principal error seems to have been the assumption that Madison wrote *Federalist* No. 37 to 48 rather than 47 to 58, off by only one number but a very considerable number since it is in the "tens" column. This should have sounded alarms because of its assignment of No. 51, which is classical Madison in its description of republican government. The sad thing about this conflict is that Hamilton conceived the project, wrote both the beginning and concluding issues, and was author of a considerable majority of the essays, more than Madison and Jay combined. His precedence is unquestioned, but his errors caused undue confusion and may have made him appear greedy. Because the essays were handset in type as soon as they arrived at the newspaper office, and the editors of course had no way of knowing they were dealing with what would one day be a classic whose original manuscripts would some day be valuable, there was no reason to preserve them. This hectic method of publication

---

3 Douglass Adair, "The Disputed Authorship of the Federalist Papers," *William and Mary Quarterly*, 3rd Series, I, pp. 97-122, 235-264; Frederick Mosteller and Daniel P. Wallace, *Inference and Disputed Authorship: The Federalist* (Reading, MA: Addison-Wesley, 1964).

4 Jacob Cooke, ed., *The Federalist* (Middleton, CT: Wesleyan University Press, 1961) presents the issue of disputed authorship in great detail, pp. xix-xxx. This volume and Ketcham, *James Madison*, pp. 239-248 are sources for this and the preceding section on *The Federalist*.

made it entirely believable that Hamilton would in a state of stress prior to a life-ending duel, or even without such spectacular stress, recall that he had begun writing on a given topic but not recall that an essay may have come in from Madison and been sent directly to press before his own work was finished.

MADISON VERSUS PATRICK HENRY

Madison finally succumbed to the pleading of Washington and others early in March and departed for Virginia after the publication of his final Publius essay. He arrived in Orange County the day before he would present a speech supporting the Constitution and stand for election to the ratification convention. Madison was most likely also the author of anonymous advocacy for the Constitution in a Virginia newspaper. Shortly after the Constitution was submitted to Congress he had anticipated a severe struggle in Virginia. He knew what to expect from Henry and his followers but was disheartened to see that men whom he respected were also in opposition. On October 30, 1787 he wrote Archibald Stuart that he was "truly sorry to find so many respectable names on your list of adversaries to the Federal Constitution. The diversity of opinions on so interesting a subject, among men of equal integrity & discernment, is at once a melancholy proof of the infallibility of the human judgment…."[5] In the midst of his responsibilities as Congressman and Publius, Madison was sending a steady stream of letters to his allies, especially Washington; to adversaries who might yet be salvaged such as Randolph, Monroe, and his cousin Bishop James Madison; and to Jefferson who remained in doubt because of the lack of a bill of rights. By the time Madison left Congress he could lessen his correspondence with Rufus King and Tench Coxe because by then Massachusetts and Pennsylvania had ratified the Constitution. Delaware and New Jersey also ratified quickly and unanimously thanks to their achievement of equality in the Senate. Before the Virginia convention, Maryland and Connecticut had also ratified. However the vote in Massachusetts was painfully close and New Hampshire had avoided rejection only by adjourning to seek further advice from constituents. In any event, even if all the other states had ratified Virginia would have been crucial because of its size and population and its presumed influence on the Carolinas.

Madison arrived home just a day before the election on March 24. There he delivered the only out-of-doors "stump speech" in his career. He won the election and had the pleasure of gaining more votes than Charles Porter who had handed

---

[5] Hutchinson, et al., eds., *The Papers of James Madison,* X, p. 232.

Madison his only electoral defeat in 1777. Madison arrived at Richmond on June 3, 1788, a day late because most delegates arrived on schedule, an uncommon event in Virginia politics, and in such numbers that the convention was forced to move to larger quarters. Delegates had to adhere to a tight schedule because a large number of them were also members of the state legislature which would meet late in that same month. He was encouraged to learn that his close friend and long-time political ally Edmund Pendleton had already been elected presiding officer. The battle for Virginia was joined on June 4, when rhetorical giant Patrick Henry launched his lengthy attack on the famous first three words of the Constitution: What justification was there for the words "We the people"? Then in his assault on tax policy the other opposition leader, George Mason, next preceded Henry in laying waste to Mason's own insistence that the delegates proceed in orderly fashion through the Constitution rather than leaping back and forth from issue to issue. This seemed an invitation to Henry to spend all of the next day berating the entire document and threatening secession by the southern area of the state, which he controlled, from Virginia as well as from the United States if necessary: "I declare that if twelve states and a half had adopted it, I would with manly firmness and in spite of an erring world reject it." The historian of that convention estimates that Henry's speech that day covered seven hours; it fills twenty pages of the convention journal.[6] Henry's oratory that day and through much of the remainder of the month until adjournment on June 25 is a dramatic personification of Cecelia Kenyon's brilliant summary of anti-federalist arguments: "All in all, a terrible prospect, the Pope as President, operating from a base in Peking, superintending a series of hangings without benefit of clergy! Or worse!"[7]

To borrow the comparison made by Irving Brant in the title of his first chapter on the Virginia convention, when "Goliath" Henry finally paused, "David" Madison on July 6 could finally strike back. Despite a quiet manner that sometimes eluded the convention secretary, Madison coolly and calmly responded to Henry's dire warnings. He referred continuously to "the people" who would have the good sense to choose virtuous and wise men as legislators as the key to successful republican government. He delivered a long and powerful refutation,

---

[6] Hugh Blair Grigsby, *The History of the Virginia Federal Convention of 1788,* 2 Volumes (New York; Da Capo Press, 1969), I, pp. 118-119; Jonathan Elliot, ed., *Debates in the Several State Conventions on the Adoption of the Federal Constitution*, 5 Volumes (Philadelphia: Lippincott, 1836-1845), III, pp. 434-64.

[7] Cecelia Kenyon, "Men of Little Faith: The Anti-Federalists on the Nature of Republican Government," *William and Mary Quarterly*, 3rd series, XII (1955), p. 18.

lecturing Henry and his followers on the history of representative government in America and the western the world. He chided Henry for the inconsistency of his defense of a system in which "a trifling minority" could impede the important needs of twelve other states. Clearly regarding Rhode Island a lost cause, he challenged Henry: "Would the honorable gentleman agree to continue the most radical defects in the old system, because the petty state of Rhode Island would not agree to remove them?"[8] His suspicion proved painfully accurate because Rhode Island would not join the United States until two years after the Constitution had been ratified by the required nine states, and a year after North Carolina, became the twelfth state to ratify. In general, however, his strategy was to keep to the high road, demonstrating flaws in Henry's logic but leaving the attacking to his allies.

By mid-June the Convention had not technically advanced beyond Article I, Section 2, because of Henry's flights of fear and fancy throughout the document. The fearsome powers of Congress would not even appear until Section 8! Amid fears that the new government in New York or Philadelphia would overtax Virginia, would turn over the West to speculators from Maryland and Pennsylvania, and would force Virginians to pay their debts to Great Britain, the famed "voice" of the American revolution even praised the King of England and declared that the British government was less dangerous than the executive and legislature proposed by Madison and Co. Such scattered assaults on countless clauses contributed to eventual victory by supporters of the Constitution. Anti-federalists attacked everything but differed among themselves on what they would favor instead. The federalists, on the other hand, were united in the single goal of ratification of the document in their hands, because they were positive that they could demonstrate that a different government created after the political attacks of 1788 would certainly be worse. Madison began to fear though that they might never get to utilize this strategic advantage, even as he reeled off the ineffectiveness of the existing government with great, if quiet, gusto. He not only distributed the first volume of *The Federalist* to key Virginians, he also delivered great portions of it orally.[9] He presented memorable arguments on the power to

---

8 Hutchinson, et al., eds., *The Papers of James Madison,* XI, pp. 71-78 and especially pp. 80-81.

9 The federalists and anti-federalists existed to determine a single issue, the ratification of the Constitution. Because they were not real political parties, we follow the wise practice of Ralph Ketcham in using lower case at this point. This helps to clarify Madison's role in 1787-1788. He was then clearly a *federalist* but certainly no *Federalist* after the establishment of political parties.

levy direct taxes, on American rights to the Mississippi River under the new Constitution, and on judicial powers.[10]

Madison's speech on June 23 led directly to the defeat of Henry's final effort. on the last day on which debate was allowed, to require approval of forty amendments prior to ratification. This would in effect hold up the Union until a new national convention considered them and, worse yet, each state considered them in detail. He characterized Henry's demands as "a bill of rights which contains twenty amendments and twenty other alterations, some of which are improper and inadmissible." After highlighting the inconsistency within Henry's demands, Madison's final words were that their approval would present "an extreme risk of perpetual disunion." The eight uncommitted voters that would determine Virginia's presence in the Union, all living west of the Appalachian Mountains but east of Kentucky, were influenced by Madison's arguments and provided the votes to defeat Henry 88 to 80.[11] George Wythe's motion to ratify the Constitution was then quickly approved 89 to 79. Two days later the federalists agreed to forward amendments but only as *suggestions,* for the new Congress to consider later.

While Madison was by far the best informed of any delegate there, he was by no means a lone voice. The multiple defections of Governor Edmund Randolph were crucial to both sides because he was an effective orator. At first Randolph favored the events at Philadelphia, but later he grew timid and refused to sign the Constitution as the Convention adjourned. He was therefore relied on by opposition leaders. Then when he wavered once again just prior to the Virginia ratification convention it was an enormous blow to the opponents. Randolph not only withheld the offer from New York Governor George Clinton to join Virginia in demanding a new Convention, he now spoke powerfully in support of a Constitution that was, however flawed, superior to anything likely to emanate from the amending convention that he previously had advocated. Obviously Madison's flood of letters to Randolph had their effect. Even before the Virginians convened on June 3, Madison was confident that Randolph had recognized the futility of achieving an improved document in the circumstances. George Mason would bitterly call Randolph a young Benedict Arnold during the remaining four years that Mason lived. George Nicholas, John Marshall and Edmund Pendleton, plus George Wythe and John Blair from the Philadelphia Convention, would also make major contributions at Richmond, and of course Chairman Pendleton was a great asset. George Washington also played a crucial

---

[10] Hutchinson, et al., eds., *The Papers of James Madison,* XI, pp. 71-78, 107-139, 158-165.

[11] Ibid., XI, pp. 174-177.

role behind the scenes, through personal letters to influential friends and the none-too-subtle hints regarding his opinions that were cited in debate by Madison and Randolph. This teamwork was crucial because for several days Madison suffered illness that impaired his efforts. However he was sufficiently healthy to hurry directly to New York to resume his seat in Congress, bypassing Montpelier but not Mount Vernon and Philadelphia, just as he had immediately after the decision at Richmond in the winter of 1786-1787 to request the Federal Convention.

But What About a Bill of Rights?

Madison's fathering of the United States Bill of Rights was one of many important actions as a member of the first Congress under the Constitution. Yet these amendments were so integral to the completion of the Constitution, not just its ratification, that they are presented as a conclusion to his role as Constitution-maker rather than as an introduction to his also spectacular career as leader of the first United States Congress that he had helped to create and the new political party system that he would soon develop. George Mason had decried the absence of protection of individual rights shortly before the Convention ended. When the delegates refused to concur at that late stage he joined Randolph and Elbridge Gerry of Massachusetts in refusing (each for somewhat different reasons) to sign the Constitution. Mason published his objections early in October, the first essay to oppose the Constitution. Richard Henry Lee of Virginia had also moved for the addition of a Bill of Rights when the Constitution was received in Congress. Although Lee's motion was stricken from the journals the issue just would not go away.

Madison however agreed with his nationalist allies James Wilson and Alexander Hamilton that the addition of a Bill of Rights was unnecessary, though he did not find it as threatening as they did. Hamilton stated this view with his customary succinctness within lengthy *Federalist* 84: "Why declare that things shall not be done which there is no power to do?"[12] Wilson said much the same thing at infinitely greater length in the Pennsylvania ratification convention. It is ironic that Hamilton, who would later prove so adept at locating implied powers within the Constitution, would seem so concerned that a declaration of rights might *extend* the powers of the central government. Before election to the convention Madison was in the odd position of having to defend himself from

---

[12] Cooke, *The Federalist,* p. 579.

criticism from his customary Baptist allies for the absence of a guarantee of religious freedom in the Constitution.

Madison's more nuanced acceptance of a Bill of Rights was written a few months after the convention:

> "My own opinion has always been in favor of a bill of rights; provided it be so framed as not to imply powers not meant to be included in the enumeration. At the same time I have never thought the omission a material defect, nor been anxious to supply it even by *subsequent* amendment, for any reason other than that it is anxiously desired by others."[13]

Despite the risk that a list of "thou shalt nots" might be twisted into governmental authorities that might otherwise never have been considered, he was realist enough to recognize that they were needed in order to broaden support for the Constitution. Thus Madison and his allies argued in convention for immediate ratification while assuring members that amendments would follow. This strategy had earlier achieved ratification in Massachusetts, another state that was narrowly divided, and it became the pattern for most of the following states. Henry, on the other hand, counted on the new convention that would be called to consider the forty amendments that he and Mason proposed would instead become so deadlocked that the Constitution would be permanently buried there. At the end of the Virginia convention, Randolph warned that "If in this situation we reject the Constitution the Union will be dissolved, the dogs of war will break loose, and anarchy and discord will complete the ruin of this country."[14] Henry's proposal for a Bill of Rights prior to ratification failed by eight votes among a total of 168, and the Constitution was approved the next day by ten votes. Henry said he would not take an oath to support the new government but would at least submit to it. In Madison's final speech Madison conceded that he would not oppose useful amendments, so long as they were not dangerous, but that they must follow ratification rather than precede (and therefore delay) acceptance of the document.[15] He had to become more specific when he competed for the seat in Congress from which he hoped to secure those carefully framed amendments. Orange County had been packed into a congressional district that Henry counted on to be anti-Constitution and anti-Madison. When the voters were told that Madison would never deliver on the promised amendments, he assured a Baptist

---

13 James Madison to Edmund Randolph, October 17, 1788, Hutchinson, et al., eds., *The Papers of James Madison,* VIII, pp. 195-200.

14 Grigsby, *Virginia Federal Convention of 1788,* I, p. 325.

15 Elliot, *Debates in the State Conventions,* III, pp. 629-630.

minister that he would support amendments. He did not feel it necessary to add that it would include protection of religious freedom. Madison was campaigning for a seat in the new Congress to the limited extent that he allowed himself: "It is my sincere opinion that the constitution ought to be revised, and that the first Congress meeting under it, ought to prepare and recommend to the States for ratification, the most satisfactory Provisions for all essential rights."[16]

Two veterans of the constitutional battles, each in unique positions of influence forced this resolution on a refractory (and admittedly very busy) First Congress. In the first inaugural address, on April 30, 1789, President Washington admonished Congress to give priority to constitutional amendments. That was no surprise to Madison, who had drafted the message at Washington's request. Four days later Madison announced that he would propose amendments to the House of Representatives in June. His announcement trumped by one day the introduction by another congressman of Virginia's proposal for a new convention and hence a new Constitution. Virginia's proposal and a similar one from New York were rejected by Congress because nine states would be required in order to initiate a new constitutional convention. Madison reviewed the many proposals submitted by the various state conventions, with heavy emphasis on those from Virginia, and submitted a series of amendments to the House of Representatives on June 8. They were designed "to limit and quantify the powers of Government by excepting out of the grant of power those cases in which the Government ought not to act, or to act only in a particular mode."[17]

Most of his proposals survived in the ten amendments that were ratified in 1791 and became known as the Bill of Rights. Of course he placed major emphasis on religious freedom which, in committee, was combined with freedom of speech (a Madison oversight) to form the heart of the First Amendment, which is in turn the heart of the Bill of Rights. The Ninth Amendment was his solution to fears that listing of what Congress could not do might be used to extend its authority to rights that were not listed. The proposal that he considered the most potentially valuable was rejected by the House: "No State shall violate the equal rights of conscience, or the freedom of the press, or the trial by jury in criminal cases, because it is proper that every government should be disarmed of powers

---

[16] James Madison to George Eve, January 2, 1789, Hutchinson, et al., eds., *The Papers of James Madison,* XI, pp. 404-405.

[17] Hutchinson, et al., eds., *The Papers of James Madison,* XII, pp. 57-59, 196-209, 339-346; For the working relationship between President George Washington and James Madison in the first Congressional sessions see Barbara Bennett Peterson, *George Washington, America's Moral Exemplar* (New York: Nova Science Publishers, 2005), pp. 177-179.

which trench upon those particular rights"[18] This would have been a major variance from the remainder of the Bill of Rights, which restricted only the central government until well into the Twentieth Century when the Supreme Court utilized the Fourteenth Amendment gradually to extend most of these protections to all levels of government.

The congressional response, or really non-response, was shocking and enlightening considering the attention the lack of a Bill of Rights had received throughout 1788. The supporters of the Constitution were impatient with Madison's persistence, as they were busily filling in gaps in the governmental outline they had just received. The Anti-federalists who had so adamantly demanded amendments were no more helpful.

They preferred to be in a position to say "I told you so!" when those who won the Constitution violated their promises. After six weeks Madison, in his own words, "begged the House" to indulge him by considering his proposals. They were finally submitted to a committee whose chairman also protested that Congress was too busy to deal with amendments. Fortunately Madison was also placed on that committee. It reported seventeen amendments within a week, but then Madison was required once again to "beg" on August 13 for the House to do something with the report. The amendments were finally approved and sent to the Senate but not until after the rejection of Madison's wish that they be blended into the Constitution, rather than tacked on at the end.

Ten of the twelve amendments that survived the Senate's trimming were ratified by the required nine states by December 1791 and have been known since as the Bill of Rights. Three states ratified them in 1789, six more the next year. Madison's own state of Virginia stalled for so long because of Patrick Henry's continued influence that its ratification, which provided the required three-fourths majority came after a new state, Vermont, had already ratified.[19] An eleventh amendment from the original twelve has been added to the Constitution more than two hundred years after being submitted to the states and is properly known only as the Twenty-Seventh Amendment, because a restriction on congressional salaries hardly merits inclusion with the Bill of Rights.[20]

---

18 Ibid., p. 208.

19 Ironically the ratification became unanimous during the sesquicentennial of the Bill of Rights when Massachusetts, Connecticut and Georgia became aware that they had neglected to ratify the ten amendments once they had been added to the Constitution. They submitted belated ratifications in 1939. Donald O. Dewey, "Vote of Confidence for the Bill of Rights," *American Journal of Legal History,* VII, pp. 137-141.

20 Robert S. Miller and Donald O. Dewey, "The Congressional Salary Amendment," *Glendale Law Review,* X (1991), pp. 98-109.

Since Madison was drawn so hesitantly into this issue, one must ask if he was off base when he insisted that the amendments were unnecessary. The Bill of Rights had limited impact for more than a century! The authorities of the central government did not extend into most of the areas protected by these amendments. The notable exception would be First Amendment rights of speech and press that became vulnerable in wartime. Otherwise the Bill of Rights has reached its status of reverence largely in the Twentieth Century when the Supreme Court, especially under the guidance of Chief Justice Earl Warren and Associate Justice Hugo L. Black, extended more and more of these limitations to the state governments. It is significant that the very first book on the Bill of Rights was not published until 1955. It is especially fitting that it was written by Robert Rutland, who decades later became senior editor of *The Papers of James Madison* at the University of Virginia and author of a number of other books on Madison.

Chapter 6

Implementing the Constitution

James Madison hastened back to his seat in Congress to deliver formal notice of Virginia's ratification of the Constitution. This made a new United States under a new Constitution a certainty, and Madison intended to play a major role in shaping that nation. Shortly before Virginia entered the Union, New Hampshire had become the ninth state to ratify. This was all that was required technically, but the inclusion of the tenth state assured that the three largest and most influential states, Virginia, Pennsylvania, and Massachusetts, were included in the Union. New York soon followed grudgingly, after an unsuccessful attempt to ratify while asserting its right to secede if the Constitution was not perfected with satisfactory amendments. Significantly, it was to James Madison that Alexander Hamilton submitted Governor George Clinton's proposal for a provisional ratification. Madison replied that his "opinion is that a reservation of a right to withdraw if amendments be not decided on ...within a certain time is a conditional ratification, that it does not make N. York a member of the new Union and consequently that she would not be received on that plan....The Constitution requires an adoption *in toto* and forever."[1] The North Carolina convention, which had overwhelmingly rejected the Constitution in 1788, would be dramatically changed in membership and would vote overwhelmingly in favor in 1789. Little Rhode Island would finally enter ungraciously in 1790 to become the thirteenth state, not long before Vermont, which had long been a colonial battleground between New York and New Hampshire, became the fourteenth state.

---

[1] July 20, 1788, Hutchinson, et al., eds., *The Papers of James Madison,* XI, p. 189.

ELECTION TO THE FIRST CONGRESS

Madison wrote Governor Randolph that "I mean not to decline an agency in launching the new Govt.," adding that he despised electioneering and hoped to be able to avoid it.[2] He sought election to Congress, but Patrick Henry used his immense influence in the legislature to deprive Madison of any choice in the matter. He superintended Madison's re-election to the dying Congress to keep him out of Virginia during the transition, and then did his utmost to keep him out of the Congress yet unborn. During the election of senators, Madison's close friend General Henry Lee (widely known as Lighthorse Harry Lee and much later as the father of General Robert E. Lee) wrote Madison that "Mr. Henry on the floor exclaimed against your political character, and pronounced you unworthy of the confidence of the people in the station of senator. That your election would terminate in producing rivulets of blood throughout the land."[3] Because for more than a century state legislatures, rather than the people, elected U.S. Senators, Virginia was the only state to have anti-federalists in both of its Senate seats in the First Congress. Henry's continued dominance of the state legislature assured that his allies Richard Henry Lee and William Grayson received 98 and 86 votes to Madison's 77. Despite Washington's encouragement that he should become a senator, Madison professed that he preferred a seat in the House of Representatives because there he would represent the people rather than the states. His "preference" may well have been strongly influenced by the certainty that Henry would choose the senators and Madison certainly would not be chosen.

Henry could not have the same influence on how the people would vote, but he could and did control how they would be divided into congressional districts. Madison's Orange County was therefore grouped with five other counties, most significantly Spotsylvania County to assure a strong opponent (James Monroe who had opposed the Constitution), and large Amherst County which could be relied upon to vote against Madison. Madison and the electorate again upset Henry's strategy. Madison and Monroe traveled together from county to county to continue debating the new Constitution. Madison wrote that their friendship did not suffer "the slightest diminution" from this conflict, at least not on his part.[4] Twenty years later, a presidential election would severely diminish that friendship and require Jefferson's personal intervention to restore communication between the two future Presidents and his allies. Monroe was on the short end of both

[2] October 17, 1788, ibid., XI, pp. 304-305.

[3] November 19, 1788, ibid., XI, pp. 356-357.

[4] To Edmund Randolph, March 29, 1788, ibid., XI, pp. 356-357.

electoral counts. Madison was elected to the first Congress by a sizeable margin, with Monroe winning only Amherst County by impressive numbers and more narrowly his own Spotsylvania County.

Madison assumed his cherished seat in the House of Representatives early in April 1789 and rapidly assumed an unofficial position of leadership. He was surrounded by supporters of the Constitution. He was one of eight participants in the Federal Convention who were among the fifty-nine Representatives in 1789, and there were another nine in the first Senate. Slightly more than thirty per cent of the fifty five Convention participants were in the First Congress and, of course, the percentage of those who participated actively in writing the Constitution was considerably higher. Despite Henry's efforts, seven of ten Virginia Representatives were supporters of the Constitution. Although Frederick Muhlenberg of Pennsylvania was the first Speaker of the House, Madison would be the principal "talker." Judging from the journals, Madison spoke twice as much as any other member. He seemed intent on becoming the spokesman of the constitutional government, just as he had been of the Constitution itself. Fisher Ames from Massachusetts would later become Madison's life-long political foe, but in 1789 he described him as the "first man" in the House because of his "sound judgment, which perceives truth with great clearness...and a thorough master of almost every public question that can arise."[5]

When the Senate finally achieved a quorum on April 7, electoral votes could at last be counted and election predictions were validated as George Washington was elected President, again unanimously. John Adams resented being elected Vice President by only a plurality rather than a majority.[6] Presidential electors had been selected in January 1789, they voted the following month, and the results were supposed to be determined by Congress in March. Representative Madison wrote the message notifying Washington and Vice President John Adams of their election, initiating one of the most fascinating one-way correspondences in American history. Washington had asked Madison to draft his first inaugural address. They discussed it at Mount Vernon on Madison's way to New York, where the First Congress would convene. When the first inaugural address was delivered on April 30, Madison was assigned to write the response of the House of Representatives, addressing Washington as "President of the United States"

---

5 Ibid., XII, p. 53.

6 Ironically Governor George Clinton of New York was so strong a second that this leader of the opposition to the Constitution would very likely have been the first Vice President if his state had not refused to cast its electoral votes. Madison was unhappy with Adams' election because he feared that he was too aristocratic and "monarchical," a view that would continue through Adams' presidency.

rather than as "His Highness the President of the United States and Protector of their Liberties," the title that was preferred by Vice President Adams and the Senate. Next Madison was asked by the President to write the executive response to the House and Senate messages. Washington was sufficiently aware of Madison's literary style that he surely recognized Madison's dual role. Historian Robert Rutland comments on the irony that "in the opening series of exchanges between the president and Congress, JM was in dialogue with himself."[7] There is no evidence whether either was amused by this unique correspondence. Fortunately this orgy of formalities ended there and Madison could get on to the business of legislation and Washington the business of administration. Madison continued this ghost writing relationship for several years, although the growth of partisan politics gradually shifted the role to Alexander Hamilton. As a prime example, Madison wrote the first draft of Washington's second inaugural address of March 1793, but it was forwarded to the Secretary of the Treasury for revisions where it became far more Hamiltonian than Madisonian. Ralph Ketcham describes Madison's role in the first administration as Washington's "aide, grand vizier, and prime minister," second only to Washington himself.[8]

Leadership in Congress Again

In the early months of the first Congress, Madison spoke more often than the combined total of the two next most prominent members—and nearly always on important matters, for this new government had much catching up to do after the Confederation Congress had marked time for months, some would say years, while waiting for the new government. Only two days after Congress finally achieved a quorum, he took it upon himself to establish the executive branch of government, which had been left somewhat vague in the Constitution because of confidence that Washington would establish safe and responsible precedents. How it must have pained Patrick Henry as he learned of Madison's role in proposing the legislation that established departments of Foreign Affairs (soon changed to the State Department), Treasury, and War; and next he was asked by Washington for advice on both administrative and judicial appointments. Madison withstood mild opposition in Congress to establishment of a Secretary of the Treasury rather than a Treasury Board. Before appointments were made to any of these positions, in May and June he prevailed in his first constitutional debates, persuading an

[7] Hutchinson, et al., eds., *The Papers of James Madison,* XII, pp. 120-121.

[8] Ketcham, *James Madison,* p. 287.

argumentative House to adopt his proposal to grant the President sole authority to *remove* officials whom he had appointed. Some contended that because senators performed the constitutional function of providing "advice and consent" regarding appointments, their consent should also be required for dismissals. Madison insisted that Senate interference would be just a first step toward overpowering the executive. This victory was important to Washington and all of his successors. More than forty years later an aged Madison was defending President Andrew Jackson from Senate attacks for his removal of a Secretary of the Treasury.[9]

Today we would say that Washington used a litmus test in his appointments. He was determined to appoint officers whom he could rely on to support the new Constitution and Madison was the best possible source for that advice. Regarding his recent and present ally and future adversary, Madison wrote to Jefferson in a number code that Hamilton "is perhaps best qualified" as Secretary of Treasury and "on that account would be preferred by those who know him personally."[10] Madison was relieved by John Jay's preference to be Chief Justice of the Supreme Court because this left the way open for his dearest friend Jefferson to become Secretary of State. Senator William Maclay, a Pennsylvania anti-federalist who would be a supporter of Madison's later opposition to Hamilton, grumbled in July 1789 that Madison "already affects to govern" the President.[11] Washington appointed three members of the Federal Convention among the five Associate Justices joining Jay on the Supreme Court, James Wilson, John Blair, and John Rutledge, although Rutledge declined in favor of a South Carolina judicial position. Two more, William Paterson and Oliver Ellsworth as Chief Justice, would be added by President Adams. Authors of *The Federalist* assumed leadership in all three branches of the new government, Madison in Congress, Hamilton in the Treasury, and Jay in the Supreme Court.

ECONOMIC STRUGGLES

Madison's extensive study of monetary systems and valiant but fruitless efforts to establish a viable fiscal structure and revenue in the previous government assured that economic reform would be high on his agenda. Even

---

9 Hutchinson, et al., eds., *The Papers of James Madison,* XII, pp. 55-57; pp. 170-174, 232-239, 244-246; 354-256.

10 Ibid., May 17, 1789, XII, pp. 185-186.

11 Brant, James Madison: Father of the Constitution, p. 281.

before his administrative proposals he offered legislation that would control external commerce to generate vital revenue from imported goods. The three per cent impost on importations that was the heart of Madison's proposed amendment to the Articles of Confederation was an obvious starting point, with the addition of differing rates on a number of largely luxury importations. It had not been adopted in 1783 because it never had the support of all thirteen states at the same time, yet it had received general approval. He was also willing to accept higher tariffs for some imported goods to provide temporary support to help American manufactures become more competitive. This brought on conflicts among areas that wanted special help for their own economy. These were generally resolved in cooperative fashion, though New Englanders continually demanded lower tariffs on the sugar and molasses that were essential to their rum industry. By June 1789 the United States finally had a legitimate revenue base.

Madison also wanted to support American shipping by assessing tonnage rates of only nine cents on American ships, thirty cents on ships of nations with whom there were commercial treaties (notably France), and fifty cents on nations that refused such a treaty. His main goal was to force the British to negotiate with their former colonies, in particular to open trade to the British West Indies, or if that failed to punish them for being obstinate. He also favored a national tax on whiskey, a tax that five years later would become a large barrel of contention between the Federalists who collected the tax and the western Pennsylvania segment of the new political opposition that was organized and led by Madison. Based on Madison's early economic programs Alexander Hamilton anticipated that his teamwork with Madison would continue into the new government, although he and other New Yorkers were already concerned about Madison's presumed pro-French leanings.

As with nearly all significant legislation during 1789, direction to the Secretary of the Treasury to submit a plan for "adequate provision for support of the public credit" was moved by Madison. Hamilton quickly sent a cordial request for Madison's ideas and Madison responded in similar vein, concluding his letter with "affection and regards."[12] Hamilton responded to this welcome directive with the same enormous energy, organization, skill and speed that he had devoted to *The Federalist.* His ambitious public credit program introduced in January 1790 would lead to the first friction between Madison and Hamilton. All agreed that the United States must meet its financial obligations as it entered the world scene, but

[12] October 12 and November 19, 1789, Hutchinson, et al., eds., *The Papers of James Madison,* XII, pp. 435-436, 449-451. The only significant exception to Madison's leadership was the Judiciary Act of 1789 that was originated by the Senate. The structure of the judiciary in the Constitution was even less detailed than that of the executive.

after guaranteeing the foreign debt there were differences regarding just who else were deserving creditors. Commitments to the soldiers, contractors and farmers who had contributed to the victory and been paid in six per cent certificates was widely accepted. Yet many of these certificates had not really been worth their declared value even when first issued, and they had declined further as Americans lost confidence in their government's ability to meet its obligations. Madison argued without success that the holder of a note at the day of reckoning in 1791, even if he was a speculator who might have acquired it only recently, should be paid the highest value the note had ever attained in the open market, while the remainder should go to the original recipient. Innocent parties between the first and final creditor would be slighted but absolute equity was not possible. Madison was disgusted by the sight of speculators with insider information scouring the country for these certificates long before those in the hinterland could learn of the "bonanza." Hamilton prevailed in his insistence that only the current holder be reimbursed.

Despite eventual though grudging acquiescence in the funding proposal, Madison could not accept Hamilton's proposal that the United States should also assume debts that had been incurred by individual state in their struggle for independence. Since Madison had favored federal payment of such debts by Congress in 1783, Hamilton was surprised by the defection of his former congressional partner. Perceived unfairness became a heated issue because several states, including Virginia, felt that they had made more progress than others in retiring their war debts. Pent-up demand for tobacco had helped to extinguish some of Virginia's war debt. And those same northern speculators were already gathering evidence of this promising new investment. Madison managed to block assumption of state debts in the House for four months until Hamilton persuaded him and Jefferson to find some Virginia congressional votes for assumption in return for something that was even more important to them. Since 1783 Madison had worked with Washington's enthusiastic approval to establish their Potomac River as the home of the new government. This was not entirely because of concerns for his home state. He also felt that this would tie the western territories more closely to the United States. Throughout the summer of 1789 Madison had used his parliamentary skills to prevent Philadelphia from gaining dominance. An arrival in his youth from the West Indies, Hamilton was quite willing to trade away the claims of his adopted New York home for a capital near Washington's home on the Potomac, in order to increase the economic influence of the new nation. Hamilton acquired a few more votes from Pennsylvania by allowing the seat of the federal government to move to Philadelphia for a decade, pending creation of the new city of Washington in what would become the District of

Columbia, then straddling the Potomac in both Maryland and Virginia. Madison in turn provided two votes from Virginia, pointedly not his own, to provide a majority for assumption. During the next decade Pennsylvanians would do everything possible to assure that the new city would never be developed.[13]

> The dispute with Hamilton expanded in December 1790 when Hamilton presented his proposal for a national bank patterned after the Bank of England. His reports to Congress became a classic program of political economy, when it was completed by a plan to provide government support for the development of manufacturing. Hamilton would harness the economy to serve the government, which would reciprocate by serving the economy. You must have capitalists to have capitalism and Hamilton was determined to have capitalism. A key part of the program was for the debt to be maintained long-term rather than quickly paid off, so it could become the backbone of the American economy. He contended, generally correctly, that the certificates in recognition of the debt would provide the negotiable paper money that would encourage wealthy Americans to invest in the new government. Madison instead wanted liquidation of the debt as early as possible.

THE GREAT CONSTITUTIONAL DEBATE

Congress and Madison would spend much of 1791 disputing the Bank of the United States, which Hamilton considered necessary to serve the economic needs of the fledgling government. Madison believed though that it would even better serve the selfish interests of the northern speculators who were already profiting from funding and assumption. The perceived impact of this monopoly led to a rapid increase in the value of public securities because they were required as a significant part of the payment by those clamoring to invest in this latest "good deal." For Madison the bank posed a special constitutional problem because he had proposed in the Convention that Congress be specifically authorized to establish corporations, which was rejected in the rush to adjournment. In 1780, his first year in a much more tightly constrained Congress, he justified support for an earlier national bank because it was a "child of necessity."[14] He wanted to avoid similar constitutional qualms in the new government by making such power explicit in the Constitution. Since this was rejected in 1787, he could not agree that it was there four years later, lurking within the "necessary and proper" clause, as Hamilton contended. Although the bank was rapidly approved by acclamation in the Senate, Madison spent an entire day February 4, 1791, challenging its constitutionality. This was the first truly major constitutional debate in the House. Madison's *Federalist* No. 44 was a close approach to Hamilton's expansive

---

[13] Hutchinson, et al., eds., *The Papers of James Madison,* XII, pp. 59-62.

[14] See Chapter 2.

interpretation of the Constitution's "elastic clause." Yet in 1791 he insisted that "the essential characteristic of the government as composed of limited and enumerated powers would be destroyed" by such a reading. This address would be the first of many occasions when he would cite the views of state ratification conventions as prime authority regarding constitutionality.[15] He readily admitted the value of banks throughout America but not a monopoly bank in Philadelphia. A national bank would be a convenience but was not to him "necessary and proper." When he was outvoted by nearly two to one, Madison met with Washington to urge him to veto the Bank.

Washington shared Madison's concerns regarding constitutionality, though not his intensity. After all he had presided over the Convention at which Madison had attempted to remove any doubt by including authority to establish corporations among the enumerated powers of Congress in Article I, Section 8. Washington asked Jefferson, Randolph, and Hamilton to write their views. Randolph's opposition was brief. Jefferson consulted closely with Madison and submitted an argument that while not extensive is still regarded as the classic exposition of strict or limited interpretation of the Constitution. Hamilton provided a massive counter-attack that remains the classic brief for a broad or expansive interpretation. During the ten days in which the President must either approve or veto the legislation, he gave hope to the opponents by asking Madison to draft a potential veto message. Madison quickly responded but on February 15, the final day for approval, Washington sided with Hamilton and approved the legislation.[16]

Madison and Jefferson soon began edging toward the formation of an opposition political party. The intense competition among Hamiltonian capitalists, usually called "stock jobbers" by Madison, for shares of the Bank of the United States caused them to be sold out entirely on the first day that they were offered for sale. Madison was especially offended to see members of Congress clamoring to gain stock. This confirmed to his satisfaction that the national bank was an *unnecessary* and *improper* exercise of congressional power and therefore a threat to republican government. Ironically this view would change during the Bank's final days in 1811 when his responsibilities as President and soon Commander in Chief made the national bank look necessary after all in time of war. Madison did gain one economic/constitutional victory over Hamilton. The Report on

15 Speech on the Bank Bill, February 2, 1791, Hutchinson et al., eds., XII, pp. 376, 370-380. On February 11 he used comparable language in a possible veto message written at Washington's request, ibid., p. 395.

16 Ibid., XIII, pp. 372-387, 395.

Manufactures was rejected during the first week of February 1792 following vigorous debate in the House.[17]

After happy and productive years as President Washington's principal advisor, Madison's opposition to Hamilton's economic policies led him to establish a political following that as early as 1792 would be interpreted by Washington himself as an *opposition* party. Madison and Jefferson yearned to remain faithful to Washington but found it more difficult as Washington was increasingly persuaded by Hamilton's arguments.

WHO'S REPUBLICAN PARTY?

There is a perennial argument whether the United States is a democratic republic or a republican democracy. It may never be resolved because there is truth in both of these political principles. The United States is a democracy because it is based largely on public consent, much more than it was in Madison's time. It is a republic because that popular consent is expressed through elected representatives in Congress and in the White House. Since these basic principles of government are so highly regarded, it is not surprising that political parties benefit by claiming them as their own. During the first years of government under the new Constitution some even linked the two to describe the new-born opposition to the dominant Federalist Party as Democratic-Republicans or Republican-Democrats. Yet when Madison who was the leader of the first opposition to Hamilton's policies finally gave his following a party name in writing it was "Republican." He consistently used this name for the remainder of his life, as did their charismatic leader Thomas Jefferson. Reaching for consensus in his first inaugural address in 1801, Jefferson tried to assure the defeated opponents that "We are all republicans, we are all federalists." Political organizations that effectively aroused support for Jefferson's politics were known as the Democratic-Republican Societies, but this became a term to be avoided when even the sainted Washington criticized them as a dangerous faction in 1796. Presidents Jefferson, Madison, and Monroe all ran as Republicans and the four candidates for President in 1824 all described themselves as members of this party. By 1828 Andrew Jackson's supporters evolved from the Jeffersonian-Madisonian Republicans and called themselves Democrats. John Quincy Adams and Henry Clay campaigned as National Republicans in 1818 and 1832. This party would evolve into the Whig party by 1834 and was eventually largely

---

[17] Brant, *James Madison: Father of the Constitution,* p. 348.

supplanted in 1854 by the modern Republican Party by 1854 of Lincoln. Thus the party of Jefferson and Madison evolved into the modern Democratic Party of Jackson. Their party has been referred to by many historians as the Democratic-Republican Party even though Jefferson and Madison invariably called themselves "Republicans."

There was no conflict over party names so long as the Federalists survived. The Federalists, however, were so wounded by their unpatriotic conduct in the War of 1812 that they offered ineffective opposition to James Monroe's candidacy to succeed Madison in 1816 and no candidate at all in 1820. Because Monroe was then re-elected with only one electoral vote cast against him, his second term is called the "Era of Good Feelings." This is a troublesome phrase since the era was instead dominated by battling Republicans (John Quincy Adams, Andrew Jackson, William H. Crawford, and Henry Clay) all seeking to succeed Monroe. In 1828 Adams, the son of the second Federalist president, campaigned as a National Republican.[18] When Jackson received more popular votes as well as electoral votes, but still was defeated by Adams in the House of Representatives, Jackson led his followers into the Democratic Party that defeated Adams in 1828. The Democratic Party still celebrates Jefferson and Jackson, augmented by Franklin D. Roosevelt, as its patron saints. The principal opposition to the Democratic Party in succeeding elections called themselves Whigs because their target was "King Andrew I." They borrowed the name from English critics of King George III during the American Revolution. The leading voice and often candidate of the Whigs was Henry Clay, one of the Republicans of 1824. The Whigs remained a major party until 1856 when they were replaced by the new Republican Party that was created by northern opponents of slavery, and the Republicans became one of the two major parties almost at birth. Thus the modern Republican Party is not the heir of Madison's and Jefferson's (Democratic) Republican Party. It bears economic links to the long-dead Federalist Party but was created in 1854 from a coalition of Whigs, abolitionist Democrats, and a variety of "third parties," some of them even more specifically abolitionist parties, that were formed in the interim between the Jeffersonian Republican dominance of the 1820s and the dominance of the new Republican Party during and after the Civil War. This new party called itself the Grand Old Party (GOP) soon after the

[18] The fluctuation of political parties in their infancy is highlighted by the career of Adams, who was elected as a Federalist senator from Massachusetts, but soon supported Jefferson's and Madison's policies when New England Federalists became more extreme in their oppositionism. Madison, who had been preeminent as a federalist during the framing and adoption of the Constitution, had a difficult time conceding the title to Hamilton's followers.

end of the Civil War, even though it was a half-century younger than the Republican Party (Democratic-Republican) of Madison, Jefferson, and Monroe.

Political Manager

Madison really had what it takes to become a party manager. He had an abiding appreciation for the representative government that he had so recently helped to create.

He had been a master of political strategy throughout his long legislative career. He had a keen analytical mind and presented political arguments with great thoroughness and precision, especially in writing. His party, still a faction in the minds of Hamilton and Washington, was called the Madisonians before they became the Democratic-Republicans, and very soon the Jeffersonians or Republicans. Madison had everything that was needed for party leadership except for the charisma that forced Thomas Jefferson soon to move somewhat unwillingly to the top.

One of the earliest major steps was the creation of an opposition press within the administration. Madison had for months attempted to persuade his college friend and poet Philip Freneau to bring his journalistic talents to Philadelphia. Only three days after Washington signed the bill authorizing the National Bank, Freneau was hired by Jefferson as a clerk to translate foreign documents for the State Department. He could augment his annual salary of $250 by meeting the official publication needs of the State Department, if he should happen also to establish a newspaper. He did just that and his *National Gazette* was soon waging political warfare against John Fenno's *Gazette of the United States*. Both warring Gazettes operated within the Washington administration because Fenno's journal profited much more than Freneau's from the more munificent publication contracts of Treasury Secretary Alexander Hamilton, as well as the U.S. Senate, which was also controlled by Federalists.

Madison provided ample ammunition for the Gazette Wars. From December 1791 to the following April, he published a series of thirteen anonymous essays in the *National Gazette.* Before venturing fully into politics Madison's "Population and Emigration" anticipated by seven years the warnings of English economist Thomas R. Malthus that mankind was destined for poverty because of the inevitable over-population of the world, and that emigration offered at most a temporary respite. The many essays that followed became increasingly political, setting forth the program of what would soon be properly recognized as an opposition party. Recurring themes are the virtues of republican governments that

Americans had demonstrated for Europe; public opinion as the justification for governmental action, including the decision to go to war *and* the responsibility of the warring generation to pay its own bills; the Constitution's exquisite balance between state and national powers and legislative, executive and judicial powers; the adverse effect of wide disparities in wealth; the unique virtues of the small "yeoman farmers;" and, pointedly, the justification for political parties. The later issues became more overtly political, with titles such as "Parties," "The Union: Who Are Its Real Friends," "A Candid State of Parties," and "Who Are the Best Keepers of the People's Liberties?" The last of these powerful articles contrasted "the Republican party, as it may be termed" with what he described as the "Anti-Republican party." These two essays have been described by Irving Brant as the "political christening of the Republican Party."[19] Even when he finally conceded that he was speaking for a political *party*, as well as a philosophy, Madison still would not concede the name "Federalist" to his opponents. He had so recently borne that name with pride in the struggle to win the Constitution that for the present he would not yield that or any field to Hamilton.

HAMILTON VS. MADISON; ENGLAND VS. FRANCE

Even before this fairly direct assault on his policies, Hamilton described Madison as a political enemy committed to driving him from office. In May 1792 he wrote an extremely long letter to Virginian Edward Carrington, pouring out his resentments against Madison, apparently hoping to organize Virginians to turn against Madison and Jefferson. Although the letter fills fifteen pages of Hamilton's published papers, Madison's name was mentioned passionately on nearly every page. Carrington was economically and philosophically attuned to Hamilton. Yet he was also a close personal friend of Madison and even indebted to him for his position as United States marshal for Virginia, so it is hard to imagine that knowledge of this letter would not reach its target. The impetuous Hamilton may even have been intentionally throwing down the gauntlet to a gadfly. Hamilton declared that he became Secretary of the Treasury "under a full

---

19 Hutchinson, et al., eds., *The Papers of James Madison,* XIV, pp. 370-372, 426-427; Brant, *James Madison: Father of the Constitution,* p. 348. For a full discussion of the Federalist and Republican (Democratic-Republican) parties see the editors' introductory comments on "Jefferson and Hamilton: The Struggle for Democracy in America" in Andrew S. Berky and James P. Shenton, editors, *The Historians History of the United State* (New York: G.P. Putnam's Sons, 1966), I, p. 363; and Donald O. Dewey, "Democratic-Republican Societies" in Rutland, *James Madison Encyclopedia,* pp. 111-112.

persuasion that from familiarity of thinking, conspiring with personal good will, I should have the firm support of Mr. Madison in the general course of my administration." He added that otherwise his knowledge of the difficulties of the position and "the powers of Mr. Madison" would have persuaded him to decline the appointment. He complained that Madison was "at the head of a faction decidedly hostile to me and my administration." He wanted to believe that Jefferson had seduced Madison but had to admit that, on the contrary, Jefferson had aligned with anti-administration views taken by Madison even before Jefferson's return from France. He considered Madison and Jefferson "at the head of a faction decidedly hostile to me and my administration, and actuated by views…subversive of the principles of good government, and dangerous to the union, peace and happiness of the Country." Hamilton promised that henceforth he would openly treat Madison as "a political enemy" and he certainly kept that promise.[20]

Disapproval of Hamilton's economic policies led rapidly to political opposition. The war between France and Great Britain that erupted four years after the French Revolution made the political rift irrevocable. For the remainder of Madison's political career, neutral American vessels and seamen were victimized whenever these world powers were at war. In 1793 this issue was heightened by Hamilton's admiration for English institutions, both political and economic, by Jefferson's and Madison's equal admiration for the French and their Revolution, and by Madison's continuing suspicion of Great Britain. Madison was thrilled at a distance by the French uprising, while Jefferson was in France to revel first hand as the government of America's great ally became republican. He had returned to the United States before the French Revolution turned violent in January 1793, beginning with the beheading of the King, and he never could quite believe what others observed and relayed. In August 1792 Madison was listed as the second among eighteen world figures honored as "Citizen of the French Republic." Tom Paine was the first one named, and Hamilton and Washington were farther down on the list though neither accepted the "honor." Madison was so offended when President Washington proclaimed in the Neutrality Proclamation on April 22, 1793, that the United States would not be drawn into the new war between their old French ally and their old British enemy, that he was

[20] May 26, 1792, Harold Syrett, et al, eds., *The Papers of Alexander Hamilton* (New York: Columbia University Press, 1966), XI, pp. 426-441.

unconcerned that acceptance of honorary citizenship might be interpreted as a flouting of Washington's policy of neutrality.[21]

Madison regarded the President's "unfortunate error" as a wound to "National honor, by seeming to disregard the stipulated duties to France. It wounds the popular feelings by a seeming indifference to the cause of liberty. And it seems to violate the forms & spirit of the Constitution by making the executive Magistrate the organ of the disposition, the duty and the interest of the Nation in relation to war and peace—subjects appropriated to other departments of the government."[22] In his view, the executive that he had been so concerned in 1787 about protecting from the legislature was now intruding on the war powers of Congress. Hamilton and Madison were drawn into yet another series of newspaper essays in which the American statesmen hid behind Roman pseudonyms while authorship was obvious to many. Hamilton's eight *Pacificus* essays justified the determination of war and peace as an executive authority, whether it was granted explicitly in the Constitution or not. He even went beyond Washington's words to insist that the proclamation had negated the wartime alliance with France; it certainly weakened those ties but Washington had taken pains to avoid saying so. Jefferson implored Madison, "For God's sake, my dear sir, take up your pen, select the most striking heresies and cut him to pieces in the face of the public. There is nobody else who can and will enter the lists with him."[23] The first sentence of Madison's five *Helvidius* essays demonstrated the heightened level of partisanship by asserting that *Pacificus* could be appreciated only by "the foreigners and degenerate citizens among us, who hate our republican government and the French Revolution." He went on to disparage Hamilton's "extraordinary doctrine that the powers of making war and treaties, are in their nature executive." While the Constitution assigns a role to the executive in such matters, he argued that Congress's role was much more significant, even citing *Federalist* No. 75 as authority, although without exposing Hamilton as the author. He accused *Pacificus* of inventing implied powers within Article II of the Constitution.[24]

Washington leaned less heavily on Madison for political advice after the partisan journalistic conflicts, but their friendship survived. He favored Madison

---

[21] Hutchinson, et al., eds., *The Papers of James Madison,* XIV, p. 381; Brant, *James Madison: Father of the Constitution*, p. 374; Barbara Bennett Peterson, *George Washington, America's Moral Exemplar* (New York: Nova Science Publishers, 2005), pp. 218-220 explains President Washington's views on neutrality and provides the Neutrality Proclamation.

[22] James Madison to Thomas Jefferson, June 19, 1793, Hutchinson, et al., eds., *The Papers of James Madison,* XV, p. 33.

[23] July 7, 1793, ibid., XV, p. 43.

[24] August 24, 1793, ibid., XV, pp. 65-73.

as Secretary of State when Jefferson retired on the last day of 1793 but Madison preferred to remain in Congress. He there led another major drive, again unsuccessful, for trade policy that would punish the British for their unwillingness to establish treaty relations with the United States and reward the French for being so much more agreeable. Because the British sold much more to the United States than they purchased, while the trade balance with France contrasted handsomely in the opposite direction, he was positive, as too often would be the case, that the threat of the loss of American markets would bring the British to terms. Imposing heavy tariffs on British goods in British vessels was then and would long remain Madison's dream. It would not be achieved despite comparable efforts every time France and England were again at war. A decade later he would argue that an embargo on American trade would impose peace on the rest of the world, and perhaps liberty along with it. The imposition of trade barriers and offering of trade incentives would be the consistent Jefferson-Madison solution to safeguard neutral shipping against the warring major powers of their day. Madison held the floor in the House for days and published an extremely lengthy monograph entitled *Political Observations*, but to no avail.[25]

Confronting the Jay Treaty

More dangerous conflict with Great Britain resumed late in 1793 when more than 200 American merchant ships were seized in the West Indies by the British as they were again waging war against France. Washington sent Chief Justice John Jay to England to negotiate for better treatment of American shipping. Madison distrusted Jay's judgment but at least Hamilton, who craved the assignment and who wrote Jay's instructions, was not selected. A series of French successes convinced Madison that the British would be compelled to offer generous terms to gain American friendship. He wrote that "it will be scandalous, if we do not under present circumstances, get all that we have a right to demand."[26] On the contrary, Jay obtained much *less* than was anticipated, in large part because Hamilton was so eager to maintain the trade and good relations of the British that were so essential to his economic programs that he deprived Jay of his principal negotiating point by leaking to a British official that the United States would under no circumstances enter the "Armed Neutrality" then being considered in Europe. Jay's only real gain was a British promise to vacate the

[25] April 20, 1795, ibid., XV, pp. 511-533.

[26] To Jefferson, January 11, 1795, ibid., XV, p. 441.

Northwest outposts, although this had also been promised but not delivered a decade earlier in the treaty ending the Revolutionary War.

Their only concession on the West Indies trade was more insulting than gratifying. And for the first of many times the British flatly refused to cease the impressment of American seamen and forced enlistment in the Royal Navy. The Jay Treaty in effect granted "most favored nation" status to Great Britain without significant British concessions. This was not yet known to Madison in February 1795 but he suspected "that Jay has been betrayed by his anxiety to couple us with England, and to avoid returning home with his finger in his mouth. It is apparent that those most likely to be in the secret of the affair, do not assume an air of triumph"[27] Madison was asked but again refused to sail to France to attempt to mollify objections to what the French with just cause would interpret as favoritism toward their enemy by their supposed American ally. Instead he remained in Congress to wage what would be his final battle as an opposition leader, against the treaty that Jay brought back from England in 1794. Monroe was sent in Madison's place but had scant success in charming the French.

How to oppose a treaty that was rumored and widely assumed to be a failure but that was kept secret until it was leaked by a Republican Senator after its approval was a quandary for Madison. The President had been as disappointed as others that Jay had not won more concessions but after a lengthy delay he took the unique position of submitting the treaty to the Senate *in secret.* In line with his recent proclamation of neutrality, Washington well understood that his weak infant nation must go to extreme lengths if necessary to maintain peace. Even the Federalist-dominated Senate showed its dismay when it ratified the treaty by the absolute minimum vote, exactly two-thirds. When Hamilton utilized insider information to produce *Camillus* essays to defend the treaty, Jefferson again attempted to shame Madison to respond in the press but Madison agreed only to a circular letter.[28] He resolved instead to hamstring the treaty by persuading the House of Representatives to refuse to provide supportive legislation, especially needed funding. Washington's tart refusal to provide diplomatic instructions demanded by the House, observing that the House had no role in treaty negotiations unless its goal was impeachment of the President, took the wind out of the Republican sails. After the President further asserted that a House role in treaties was specifically rejected by the Federal Convention, Madison was challenged by Federalists to disprove the President's contention by producing his own Convention notes. Then he was chided for not complying. Madison's

27 James Madison to Thomas Jefferson, February 15, 1795, ibid., XV, p. 473.

28 August 23, 1795, ibid., XVI, pp. 56-58.

majority soon slipped away, in response to respect for Washington and fears of war with England. He had learned the painful lesson that a President who is unbending in defense of "executive privilege" could survive the dissatisfactions of a House majority so long as the Senate stood fast with the President. He complained that Washington's "absolute refusal" to provide the diplomatic instructions that were requested by the House was "as unexpected as the tone and tenor of the message are improper and indelicate." He considered this response as Washington's greatest error. Only two years earlier he had regarded Washington's attempt to blame the Democratic-Republican Societies for the Whiskey Rebellion, when he referred in his annual message to "certain self-created societies," as the "greatest political error of his life." Washington and Hamilton had then led federal troops to western Pennsylvania to quell protests against federal taxes on whiskey, which were resisted because it was so much easier for farmers to get their corn to market in liquid form.[29]

Getting Along with President Adams

During his last year in Congress Madison also led the movement to win the presidency for Jefferson and when that failed to persuade him to settle for the vice presidency when Adams prevailed by a scant three electoral votes. While Madison was laboring for Jefferson as President in 1796, the reluctant "candidate" told others that he hoped that Madison would somehow be elected, and he even wrote a letter to Adams implying that he would be pleased if Adams would prevail. Fortunately for the Republican opposition, this letter was sent to the "party boss" to deliver to Adams if it seemed appropriate. Madison deemed it highly inappropriate and declined to forward it. In an earlier letter Jefferson wrote to Madison that "I pray you and authorize you fully to solicit in my behalf that Mr. Adams may be preferred to me. He has always been my senior from the commencement of our public life, and the expression of the public will being equal, this circumstance ought to give him the preference."[30]

---

[29] To Thomas Jefferson, April 4, 1796, and to James Monroe, December 4, 1794, ibid., XVI, p. 286, XV, p. 406. This presidential power was demonstrated in 2007-2008 when a Republican President who lost *both* houses of Congress in 2006, and who had spectacularly low public support, could impose his will during two "lame duck" years so long as the Democratic majority in the Senate was slim and the Republican minority risked siding with him on positions that the public seemed to have summarily rejected.

[30] Jefferson to Adams, December 28, 1796 (never sent) and to James Madison, December 17; James Madison to Thomas Jefferson, December 19, 1796 and January 22, 1797, Hutchinson, et al., eds., *The Papers of James Madison,* XVI, pp. 152-153, 431-432.

Madison took care to avoid meetings with Jefferson to deny him the opportunity to refuse nomination and election. Before ratification of the Twelfth Amendment of the Constitution, the candidate who received the second largest electoral vote became President, whatever his party, so Jefferson became Vice President to President Adams, the titular leader of the opposition party. He described himself as a member of the legislature rather than the administration, because of his constitutional role as president of the Senate, a position that Vice President Richard Cheney would briefly espouse more than two centuries later. Adams was elected with only two electoral votes south of the Potomac River, while Jefferson received only five votes north of that dividing line. Thus the accuracy of Madison's warning in the Federal Convention that the real conflict within the Union would be between North and South rather than between large and small states was proven much earlier than he would have wished.

With Jefferson in Philadelphia to protect his party's interests in 1797, Madison could finally retire to a life as gentleman farmer, believing unrealistically that it was a permanent withdrawal from politics at the relatively young age of 46. 1788 would be the first since he departed for college in 1769 when he would spend an entire year in Virginia, and he would not leave again until he became Secretary of State in 1801. He was finally able to begin the long-delayed remodeling of Montpelier and bring his recent bride to their Virginia home. Dolley Payne Todd had become a widow in 1793 when her Lawyer-husband John Todd courageously remained in Philadelphia through the disastrous yellow fever epidemic to care for the countless dead and dying. Todd also lost both of his parents but had sent Dolley with her two sons to a safer rural setting. The next year, Madison approached her through his college friend and political ally, Aaron Burr, who was also a friend of the young widow who then lived near him in Philadelphia. Dolley wrote with excitement that "the great little Madison has asked to be brought to see me this evening." On September 15, 1794, she wrote that "in the course of this day I give my hand to the man of all others I most admire."[31] Their mutual love and respect continued until his death in 1836 and she added joy and gracious style to the presidential mansion for sixteen years, through the terms of Presidents Jefferson, a widower, and Madison. She was born in Virginia and related to Patrick Henry, but the family had lived in Philadelphia since she was fifteen. She was one of several family members formally expelled from the Quaker church because they found the "plain" life uncomfortable. Her highly sociable presence made life in Washington, D.C. tolerable when it was

---

[31] Paul M. Zall, *Dolley Madison* (New York: Nova History Publications, 2001), pp. 13-29; Brant, *James Madison: Father of the Constitution,* pp. 406-410.

basically a wilderness. She was specifically expelled for marrying a non-Quaker. Eleven years earlier Madison had been crushed when his fiancée Catherine (Kitty) Floyd, the young daughter of a fellow Congressman, threw him over for a medical student who was closer to her own age. Ironically, Catherine Clarkson became a widow just as Dolley Madison was entering a second term as Madison's, and America's, First Lady.

Madison actually managed to avoid political office for most of the final years of the eighteenth century. He declined certain election as Governor of Virginia and even rejected a return to the state legislature until necessity called in 1799. He would have rejected still another appointment as minister to France if President Adams had followed through on his first intent. Even Hamilton supported Madison's appointment to a trio of diplomats seeking to convince France that the United States had not fallen totally under England's sway. His lifetime friendship for France would ease the reception for the delegates and, besides, he would be in a minority if the other two representatives were strategically selected. The issue was moot because Adams retreated when Treasury Secretary Oliver Wolcott threatened that the entire Cabinet would resign if Madison was appointed. How much happier Adams' one administration might have been if he had called Wolcott's bluff, *and* if Madison had accepted. Then Adams might no longer have been victimized by the second-rate cabinet that he had inherited from Washington and that was faithful to their party boss, Hamilton, rather than to their titular leader, the President.

Madison even played an unconscious role in the preparation of Washington's justly famous Farewell Address, as he too left government in 1797. Even though he had joined Jefferson and Hamilton in persuading the unwilling Washington that survival of the Union depended on his serving a second term, Madison had drafted a tentative farewell four years earlier at Washington's request.[32] Despite the political rancor that so pained Washington throughout his second administration, Washington intended to use much of the 1792 draft and even to refer to Madison in a footnote. Hamilton was allowed to revise the message considerably and get rid of that politically embarrassing footnote. Bits of Madison's draft in Washington's hand are in autograph collections because when historian Jared Sparks was editing the papers of George Washington decades later he felt the unsent address insignificant and cut it into pieces to satisfy persistent collectors pressed him for some writing by the sainted Washington.

---

[32] Republicans supported the candidacy of George Clinton for President, though he was viewed unofficially only as an opponent to Adams, not to Washington.

The Adams administration was a time when Republican leaders could be grateful to be at home rather than in the new capital city. French resentment against the Jay Treaty finally led to retaliatory seizures of American ships carrying British goods in 1796, just as Adams was being elected. Thus his administration continually seemed at the verge of war. French attacks surely helped Adams' candidacy but it assured turmoil for his presidency. The negotiations in which he wished Madison to participate foundered when bungling French subordinates demanded a bribe to smooth the way toward negotiations with Foreign Minister Talleyrand (which led to what was called the XYZ affair to disguise the anonymous French agents). This soon led to a quasi-war with France on the high seas and threatened full-scale war as an army was organized. It was technically led by the aging Washington, but his second-in-command was really in charge and was itching to show his valor against France and hopefully even against troublesome Virginians. Most Federalists were eager for war but fortunately the major exception was President Adams who again demonstrated the influence of the presidency. He risked his political career for peace, responding to hints from the French Directory after military defeats in Europe that they would welcome new negotiations. Over the objection of his Cabinet, nearly all of whom were covertly subservient to Hamilton, he sent a second diplomatic delegation that negotiated the Peace Treaty of 1800. He wanted the waging of peace to be carved on his tombstone but the 1800 electorate did not reward him for his political sacrifice. To Madison, Adams was the personification of aristocracy and Anglicism. Ralph Ketcham wittily remarks that "Removed from the scene, and unaffected by responsibilities felt only in the capital, Madison spent four years 'viewing with alarm'."[33] And Madison regularly expressed this alarm with language as harsh for Adams as for the greater foe Hamilton.

The Virginia and Kentucky Resolutions

By May 1798 Madison was convinced that the President was more in need of restraint than of the protections that he had once felt were required against rampant legislatures. He wrote Jefferson that "The management of foreign relations appears to be the most susceptible of abuse, of all the trusts committed to a Government, because they can be concealed or disclosed, or disclosed in such parts & in such times as will best suit particular views; and because the body of

[33] Ketcham, *James Madison,* p. 391.

the people are less capable of judging and are more under the influence of prejudices...."[34]

This was written only days before the Vice President would send him news of domestic legislation proceeding rapidly through Congress in response to deteriorating relations with France. The Alien and Sedition Acts authorized the removal of "dangerous" aliens and criminal action against citizens accused of conspiring against the administration or of defaming the government, the Congress or the President in writing or by public speaking. A related Naturalization Act extended the length of time required to achieve citizenship. Madison's first comment on the Alien Act described it as a "monster that must for ever disgrace its parents,"[35] but the Sedition Act became the greater threat as high-handed Federalist judges acted against Republican editors and even a Republican member of Congress. Even Madison and Jefferson became cautious in their correspondence because they regarded themselves as potential targets and they did not trust the postal service that was dominated by Federalist appointees. Thus Citizen Madison and Vice President Jefferson acted in secrecy with their Resolutions against the Alien and Sedition Acts, which were introduced in the Kentucky and Virginia legislatures by surrogates. They may have discussed a preliminary response early in June when Jefferson stopped at Montpelier. Then in mid-October Madison visited Monticello to view Jefferson's draft of what would become the Kentucky Resolutions. In November Madison wrote the Virginia Resolutions, which were adopted by the houses of the General Assembly in December by votes of 100-63 and 14-3. If there were other personal meetings their tracks were well covered. These documents forcefully disputed the constitutionality of the hated acts, though Madison's protested other excesses of central authority as well. The Virginia Resolutions were introduced by John Taylor of Caroline and Madison's authorship was concealed until 1809.

Characteristically, Jefferson's language for Kentucky was more flamboyant and political, while Madison's language for Virginia was more cautious and constitutional. Whereas Jefferson declared the authority of a *single* state to declare unconstitutional laws that had been adopted by Congress "altogether void and of no effect," Madison consistently argued for action by the *states* and invited others to join Virginia. Some of Jefferson's tone was inserted in the Virginia Resolutions without Madison's knowledge but the words "not law, but utterly null, void, and of no effect" were deleted before the document was approved exactly as Madison

---

[34] May 17, 1798, Hutchinson, et al., eds., *The Papers of James Madison,* XVII, p. 132.

[35] James Madison to Thomas Jefferson, May 20, 1798, Hutchinson, et al., eds., *The Papers of James Madison,* XVII, pp. 133-134.

had originally written it. Jefferson wrote that extremist legislation could even "drive these states into revolution & blood." On the other hand Madison's first two resolutions commit Virginia "to maintain and defend the constitution" and "a warm attachment to the Union of the States." He invited the other states to concur with Virginia in declaring the Alien and Sedition Acts unconstitutional and to cooperate "in maintaining unimpaired the authorities, rights and liberties reserved to the states respectively or to the people." To preserve the Constitution and the Union, these states were "duty bound to interpose" themselves between Congress and the people when the legislature exceeds its authority.[36]

Learning that Patrick Henry had succumbed to pleas from Washington that he return to the Virginia legislature to attack the Virginia Resolutions, Madison consented to election for one more political battle with his long-time political foe. This conflict never materialized because Henry died in June 1799, six months before the legislature convened in 1799. By then, though, there was ample evidence that those states that even bothered to respond to the Virginia Resolutions were entirely unconvinced. Seven states, all northern except for Delaware, responded that the Supreme Court was the appropriate authority to decide issues of constitutionality. What an invitation to Virginian John Marshall who would soon be Chief Justice and would establish this very point in *Marbury v. Madison* (1803). Some states even retorted that the Alien and Sedition Acts were themselves clearly constitutional. Jefferson, Madison and Monroe met to decide how to respond. Since Madison would be in the House of Delegates and he was their "work horse" anyway the task was quickly assigned to him. Jefferson wanted him to threaten that Kentucky and Virginia would abandon the Union "rather than give up the rights of self government."

Of course Madison would have nothing to do with that. He labored through December to produce a point-by-point discussion of the resolutions followed by refutation of the comments of the opposing states. It is most significant for its allegation, never stated directly in the Virginia Resolutions, that the Alien and Sedition Acts were "palpable and alarming infractions of the Constitution." The Report was adamant that American laws were "destitute of every authority for restraining the licentiousness of the press." It would be 130 years before the U.S. Supreme Court would grant the level of protection of freedom of speech and press that Madison found in the First Amendment. The Report was introduced in the House on December 23 and approved by a vote of 60 to 40 on January 7 after five days of debate. The Senate soon followed with a 15-6 vote. The Virginia Resolutions fill only two pages of Madison's published papers, while the Report

---

[36] Ibid., XVII, pp. 188-191.

consumes 43 pages. It was published as a pamphlet and received great applause in Virginia, but elsewhere it was largely ignored, even though Historian Ralph Ketcham justly describes it as Madison's "most important statement of the principles that should guide republican governments in protecting civil liberties during a national crisis."[37]

The Virginia and Kentucky Resolutions would sometimes be an embarrassment to Madison and Jefferson when they demonstrated a desire actually to govern in the next two decades, rather than allow the states to dominate. True believers of the states' rights doctrine of 1798, calling themselves Old Republicans, would turn against Presidents Jefferson and Madison, and even Monroe, when they varied from the implications of their opposition to the Alien and Sedition Acts. Their principal spokesmen were John Taylor of Caroline and John Randolph of Roanoke. From 1828 to 1833 when John C. Calhoun would assert South Carolina's constitutional right to *nullify* an act of Congress, Madison spent countless hours refuting claims that Jefferson was the grandfather of nullification. Although he was generally successful in distancing Jefferson and Kentucky from the nullification crisis of his waning years, of course he could not anticipate the use that would be made of his word "interpose" during the Southern resistance to school integration in and after the 1954 Brown vs. Board of Education decision that ruled against school segregation.

These documents were very much a part of the Jefferson presidential campaign to which Madison turned his attention through the remainder of 1800. They are not just a defense of states' rights, but also campaign documents focused on the election of Jefferson as President. With Jefferson replacing Adams and bringing with him a

Republican Congress the despised legislation would die a quick and quiet death. In this they were entirely successful. The offending legislation thus died with John Adams's presidency.

---

[37] Ibid., VII, pp. 304-306; the Resolutions are on pp. 188-190, the Report on pp. 307-350; Leonard W. Levy, "Virginia Report of 1799-1800" in Rutland, *James Madison Encyclopedia,* p. 428; Ketcham, *James Madison,* pp. 399-403.

Chapter 7

SECRETARY OF STATE

In the Constitutional Convention of 1787, James Madison contributed to the development of the American presidency. After the ratification of the Constitution, he next played a key role in establishing both the powers and limitations on the executive, as leader of the House of Representatives and personal counselor to President Washington in his crucial first administration. It could fairly be argued with his return to government leadership in 1801 after an extremely brief "retirement" as a Virginia planter, that Madison, with major assistance from President Jefferson, next established the political training ground for Presidents. It was Thomas Jefferson who really established the two-term limitation for the office; he was even receptive to a constitutional amendment for that purpose. Washington had not desired even one term, much less two, though he is invariably cited as the great exemplar of term limits. John Adams would have loved a second term and perhaps more, but the voters (and Jefferson) denied him that honor. Jefferson, on the other hand, had the health, relative youth, and still sufficient popular support that he could have served a third term if he had wished. He lived through the remainder of the "Virginia Dynasty"—Madison's two terms and two more for James Monroe. By the same token it was Madison who established the office of Secretary of State as the avenue to the White House. Jefferson, to be sure, had been Secretary of State as well as Vice President, but he advanced directly from the latter office just as had Adams before him. Midway through Madison's first term as President, James Monroe, who was drawn into a pointless presidential campaign against Madison in 1808, was urged by a realist advisor to mend fences with the President and accept the "presidential ermine" already linked to the Secretary of State.

PATHWAY TO THE PRESIDENCY

The embarrassing tie vote between Jefferson and Aaron Burr, which resulted in 1801 because electors still voted for their two first choices without regard for party affiliation, led quickly to the proposal and ratification of the Twelfth Amendment of the United States Constitution in September 1804, just in time for Jefferson's second election. The old system permitted, even encouraged, election of a Vice President from a different party from that of the President (comparable to Governor-Lieutenant Governor pairings in many current state governments). Before the Twelfth Amendment provided a clear distinction between candidates for President and Vice President, the latter office was filled by national figures: John Adams, Thomas Jefferson, and Aaron Burr. After the Twelfth Amendment the office was usually filled by regional figures designed to balance the ticket and far too often by political hacks. Martin Van Buren was Vice President when he succeeded Andrew Jackson but he had also been Secretary of State in Jackson's first term; he was going to be rewarded for his personal loyalty to Jackson, whatever office he might hold when Jackson retired. After Van Buren no former Vice President became President without climbing over the body of a fallen predecessor until Richard Nixon was elected in 1968, defeating the incumbent Vice President, Hubert Humphrey. Since then three Vice Presidents have been nominated as President by the major parties and one of them, George H. W. Bush, was elected in 1988.

In the twelve decades between Van Buren's single term and Nixon's first nomination, no Vice President who had not become President by succession had even received the nomination of the Republican or Democratic parties. Countless incumbents disparaged that position but it was perhaps most effectively put in its place by Theodore Roosevelt who said "The more I have thought it over, the more I have felt that I would a great deal rather be anything, say a professor of history, than vice president. He even considered studying for a law degree during his brief tenure as Vice President prior to the assassination of William McKinley.[1] Through the relatively orderly era before Jacksonian democracy, Secretary of State Madison succeeded Jefferson, Secretary of State James Monroe succeeded

---

[1] L. Edward Purcell, ed., *The Vice Presidents: A Biographical Dictionary* (New York: Facts on File, 1998), pp. 231 and 296. See also Elliott A. Rosen's essay in Timothy Walch, ed., *At the President's Side: The Vice Presidency in the Twentieth Century* (Columbia: University of Missouri Press, 1997), pp. 45-53, for a critical view of the Vice Presidency as a stepping stone to the Presidency. During periods of partisan strife former Vice Presidents were occasionally nominated as third party candidates. Van Buren, Millard Fillmore, and Theodore Roosevelt had

Madison, Secretary of State John Quincy Adams succeeded Monroe, and Secretary of State Henry Clay certainly believed that he had assured his succession until he and Adams were consumed by the tornado of Jacksonian Democracy. As was so often the case in the political life of James Madison, Jefferson played a huge role behind the scenes, just as Madison had in Jefferson's political career. Jefferson kept Aaron Burr at arm's length because of his failure to step gracefully aside and facilitate Jefferson's advancement to the executive mansion when Jefferson and Burr were tied in the electoral vote. Next he arranged for Burr to be replaced as Vice President in Jefferson's second administration by Burr's New York political enemy George Clinton. It was surely assumed that Clinton could not be a credible competitor against Madison in 1808. After Clinton continued in office during Madison's first term, he even mounted an abortive campaign against Madison in 1812, although by then he had advanced from inability to senility.

Madison had been the major political manager of Jefferson's campaign for the presidency, unsuccessfully in 1796 but later resulting in Jefferson's "Revolution of 1800." In those days presidential candidates were expected merely to await the honor and it would have been considered bad taste for Jefferson, or later Madison, to solicit or campaign for that honor. Some of their colleagues even regretted the constitutional restriction that prevented the nomination of both Virginians. Ironically, Madison contributed to the indecisive election that would require the U.S. House of Representatives to break a tie in electoral votes between Jefferson and Burr. In 1799 Madison finally succumbed to the entreaties of Jefferson and many others that he terminate his brief retirement and accept election again to the Virginia House of Delegates. There he wrote the state's powerful defense of his own Virginia Resolutions, which had been approved the previous year, with Madison kept as much behind the scene as could be arranged by his political allies. As the presidential election of 1800 approached he presented the motion for a general ticket for the presidential election. Although it was approved by a mere five votes, this decision led to the most populous state casting all of its electoral votes for Jefferson *and* for Burr, even though every Virginia elector, and many others, understood that he was voting for Burr as Vice President. In 1796 when Virginia's electors were selected by district elections, two votes went to Adams rather than Jefferson. This must not happen again. Virginia was not the first state to take this momentous step toward winner-take-all presidential elections, which remains in the 21st Century the pattern for 48 of our

all held the presidency, so John C. Breckinridge in 1860 was the only early Vice President to move directly to a presidential nomination.

50 states; the other states fell rapidly into line once the largest state showed the way.[2]

As one of Virginia's presidential electors, Madison cast votes for both Jefferson and Burr, but only after considering whether he should throw aside a Burr vote to assure that an inadvertent tie in the electoral vote not result from the party discipline that he had done so much to establish. As the senior member of his party he must have been asked by other electors how to proceed. Adams had prevailed by only three electoral votes in 1796, so Republicans were more worried about votes for Adams than for Burr. Through extensive correspondence with political allies in other states he had no doubt that the election of 1800 would be extremely close (by eight votes this time rather than the three by which Adams had prevailed over Jefferson), even though the new President would dramatically call it the "Revolution of 1800." It was understood that Burr's supporters had arranged to have a northern vote cast for someone else, so if Virginia started doing the same it could drastically affect the outcome. John Adams or even Charles Cotesworth Pinckney from South Carolina, Adams' running-mate, might slip into the second office. Ironically the resulting tie between Jefferson and Burr was accomplished to a major degree by Burr himself, who managed the votes of New York City so astutely that his state's votes that had gone to Adams in 1796 went instead to Jefferson (and Burr!) in 1800. Burr had justly felt betrayed in 1796 when so many of Jefferson's Virginia votes went to other southerners rather than to his official New York running-mate. Thus Jefferson's (and Madison's) state must show good faith with Burr and he could be counted on to reciprocate. Surely Madison's college friend Burr (the son and namesake of a prominent minister and president of Madison's beloved College of New Jersey, even if he also was the preeminent professional political operator of early American history) could be relied on to prevent a tie.[3] Madison had labored mightily for party discipline through the 1790s but he little realized how successful he had been. Even if Burr somehow gained an equal electoral vote, Madison was confident that Jefferson would prevail in the House of Representatives. He could not conceive that even a "lame duck" Federalist House would dare to smuggle a pretender into the presidency. However, Burr failed to step graciously out of Jefferson's way and left the nation uncertain for weeks who would become President. Burr was never forgiven by the new President or by his Secretary of State. There can be no

[2] The two exceptions are Nebraska and Maine.

[3] Burr's reputation as a political manager was such that Gore Vidal's *Burr: A Novel* (New York: Random House, 1973) introduces "the little magician" Martin Van Buren, the political manager of the next generation, as Burr's fictional illegitimate son.

question that Madison would have been Jefferson's preeminent choice as his successor, but achievement of that desire might have been more complicated if Aaron Burr had not lost credibility with leading Republican statesmen.

While Madison was the new President's first choice for a major administrative appointment, he was the last to assume his official responsibilities. He remained at home in Virginia for nearly two months after Jefferson's inauguration because of his obligations as family leader and heir to the family estate when James Madison, Sr., died late in February, 1801. In addition, the new Secretary of State was ill through much of this period. Attorney General Levi Lincoln of Massachusetts served in both offices until Madison arrived on May 1. The Madisons roomed with the President for several weeks before renting a house two blocks from the future "White House." This was good training for Dolley Madison, who would serve for eight years as the social director for the widowed President Jefferson.

Diplomatic Mr. Madison

The first Republican administration inherited two peaceful years from the final Federalist administration. In 1800 Adams ended the quasi-war with France as well as lingering obligations from the Treaty of 1783. In September 1801, just six months after Jefferson's inauguration, France and England achieved a temporary truce that would continue only until May 1803 when Napoleon resumed his campaign to dominate Europe. Although Madison was a late arrival at the State Department, he had been heavily involved in American diplomacy for more than two prior decades, chairing important committees shortly after his arrival in Congress in 1780. In this role he penned key reports and instructions that maintained American claims to the Mississippi River. Had he been less successful in preventing the bartering away of this most important part of the nation's western boundary, the greatest achievement of Jefferson's presidency, the Louisiana Purchase, would not have been possible. Considering the seventeen large volumes of correspondence, reports and legislation that he had written before becoming Secretary of State it is humbling to recognize that never until then did Madison have clerical help. He inherited eight clerks from the Adams administration, most of them committed Federalists. Whatever their politics, their help was fortunate because the Secretary of State was then responsible for an oppressive quantity of responsibilities beyond his most important duties as director of foreign relations and major advisor to the President. He would soon be apologizing to correspondents that the administrative workload deprived him of the pleasure of writing personal letters [4]

The extraordinary teamwork of President Jefferson and Secretary Madison, augmented splendidly in economic matters by Treasury Secretary Albert Gallatin, often makes it difficult to determine with certainty the precise role of any one of them. Of course President Jefferson had the final word and the final responsibility but the decades of mutual respect and close consultation between Madison and Jefferson found them acting very often as one. Madison shared in the huge diplomatic successes of the first Jefferson administration as well as the frustration and disappointment of the second. Irving Brant, Madison's major biographer, grumbles early in his volume on Madison's career from 1801 to 1809 that too many diplomatic historians "don't even mention that Jefferson had a Secretary of State." As he describes the intense but extremely lucky negotiations of the first administration, Brant cites the President's need for someone "to keep his speculations from running away with his policies." With the assistance of Madison's analytical mind and strategic skill, "these two set the course and held the steering oar together" in domestic policy as well as international affairs. After nearly a hundred pages of dredging the diplomatic sparring that resulted in the fortuitous Louisiana Purchase that doubled the size of the United States and opened still more of the North American continent to American expansion, Brant complains that everything that "leads in the direction of pre-eminence" for Madison has to be "dug out of the records."[5] In fairness to Jefferson, he did not create the problem. A few weeks after he turned over the presidency to Madison, he wrote, "as to the merit of the result of our measures against England, mr. Madison is justly entitled to his full share of it, as he is of all the measures of my administration. Our principles were the same, & we never differed sensibly in the application of them. I am glad therefore that my enemies, & hope that my friends will do him justice as to this & all our other measures."[6] Brant frequently argues that Jefferson co-opted Madison's ideas while presenting them as his own—certainly not the only American President to do so.

If Jefferson and Madison aimed to confuse French diplomats in America with a "nice cop, tough cop" performance, their aim was perfect. This is best reflected in the correspondence of Chargé d'Affaires Louis Pichon, who was a key figure in

---

[4] Ketcham, *James Madison,* p. 410.

[5] Irving Brant, *James Madison: Secretary of State, 1801-1809* (Indianapolis: Bobbs-Merrill, 1950), pp. 47-58.

[6] To Wilson C. Nicholas, May 25, 1809, J. Jefferson Looney, ed., *Papers of Thomas Jefferson: Retirement Series* (Princeton: Princeton University Press, 2004), I, p. 224; Brant, *James Madison: Secretary of State,* p. 482.

making it possible for the United States to acquire from France the enormous Louisiana Purchase that would by itself have made Jefferson's presidency a success. Luckily the daring Pichon had the courage to caution Foreign Minister Charles Maurice Talleyrand regarding the danger of pushing the Americans too far. Madison convinced Pichon that the survival of French ambitions on the island of Santo Domingo (San Dominique when it was a French colony) would depend on the friendship of America, even if France succeeded in putting down the slave uprising led by General Toussaint L'Ouverture. As a statesman whose constituents had always been slave owners who lived in terror of such an insurrection, Madison could hardly resist French efforts to regain control, until he saw that it would become the basis of a return to the North American continent, which France had abandoned in the Treaty of Versailles at the end of the American Revolutionary War. Madison was personally committed to peace, yet he subtly advanced effective threats that the United States would inevitably be allied with Great Britain if France placed itself between American westerners and the Gulf of Mexico. He warned that when France next went to war with Great Britain, New Orleans would be at the mercy of American land forces pouring down the Mississippi River, who would cooperate with the British fleet if necessary. Pichon reported that he was encouraged by comments of the President regarding San Dominique but that those of the Secretary of State were discouraging. Madison's diplomats were directed to warn their counterparts in Europe that to western Americans the Mississippi River was "the Hudson, the Delaware, the Potomac and all the navigable rivers of the atlantic States formed into one stream."[7] Clearly Madison was laying the groundwork for Jefferson's justly famous warning that any powerful nation in control of the mouth of the Mississippi River would be a natural enemy of the United States that would force a U.S. marriage to the British fleet. Such warnings did not apply to Spain which had long controlled the lower Mississippi and the Gulf Coast including Florida, but Spain was rumored then to be in the process of ceding Louisiana to France. Because Spain was then weak and steadily declining it was in the American interest that the Mississippi remain in Spanish control until it was ripe for seizure or purchase at the convenience of the United States. Pichon admitted great difficulty in responding to Madison's threats to seize New Orleans if France took control. His perceptive warnings of growing American irritation with French intrusions in the Americas were unwelcome to Talleyrand and especially to his master, Napoleon Bonaparte, who was already firmly committed to developing

[7] For example, James Madison to Charles Pinckney, U.S. minister to Spain, November 27, 1802, Hunt, *Writings of James Madison*, VI, pp. 461-464.

the trans-Mississippi west as a granary for the valuable sugar island of San Dominique, which he envisioned as the economic and political base of a new French empire in the western hemisphere.

DOUBLING THE UNITED STATES

History smiled on Jefferson, assuring him ranking among presidential giants. It was on his (and Madison's) watch on April 11, 1803, after the loss of most of an army and his own brother-in-law who commanded it, that the mercurial First Consul conceded his failure to quell slave uprisings in Santo Domingo and offered to sell to the United States the Louisiana Territory that he had just reclaimed from Spain largely because of his soon to be broken promise to protect Spain's many other colonies from American intrusion. He thereby gathered financial resources for the next stage of his warfare with England and hopefully purchased American friendship, at what was to him the petty expense of betraying his Spanish ally. He cynically justified this abrupt shift when he declared, "They ask me only for one city of Louisiana, but I regard the entire colony as already lost, and it seems to me that in the hands of this new-born power, it will be more useful to the policy and even to the commerce of France, than if I should try to retain it."[8] American minister Robert R. Livingston proceeded as rapidly as he dared, in hopes of completing arrangements before the arrival of James Monroe who had been appointed a special envoy to France when Spain revealed its plans to close New Orleans to American goods. Monroe arrived just as Napoleon surprised Livingston by offering all of Louisiana, from the Mississippi River to the Rocky Mountains rather than just New Orleans, which they were authorized to purchase. Fortunately they risked exceeding their instructions and negotiated the Louisiana Purchase on April 29 for fifteen million dollars, extending U.S. boundaries to the Rocky Mountains. In less than a month France and England were again at war and American shipping would soon be vulnerable to attacks from both belligerents, but the American flag would be raised over New Orleans on December 20, 1803.[9]

Madison was much less worried than the President about the constitutionality of doubling the size of the United States by this huge purchase from France. Jefferson fairly early agreed that broad construction of the Constitution justified the acquisition of the vast new territory by treaty but he continued to worry that

---

[8] Cited in Brant, *James Madison: Secretary of State,* p. 125.

[9] Ketcham, *James Madison,* pp. 418-422.

statehood for the new territory and citizenship for its inhabitants, both guaranteed by the treaty, could be accomplished only by a constitutional amendment. When Napoleon demonstrated impatience at the delay Jefferson even considered somehow amending the Constitution in secrecy. Fortunately this dreadful precedent, far more serious than Washington's secretive transmission of the Jay Treaty to the Senate in 1795, was avoided when Jefferson finally acquiesced with satisfaction and relief to the arguments of his advisors, led by Gallatin but enthusiastically abetted by Madison, that an amendment was unnecessary. Ironically it was only the minority Federalists, who had advocated an expansive Constitution in the 1790s under Hamilton, who continued to demand that this vast acquisition could not be accomplished without amendment of the Constitution.

Although they had already gained more from France than they could ever have dreamed when they sought to buy New Orleans, Jefferson and Madison were typically American in wanting still more. Having at last gained control of the entire Mississippi River, they next turned to the need for other rivers flowing into the Gulf of Mexico, especially into Mobile Bay. He directed Livingston to seek agreement from France that the purchase of Louisiana "as it was and is" included West Florida. Because French claims had once extended to the Perdido River, this would have added those southern parts of the states of Alabama and Mississippi that extend to the Gulf of Mexico. The Perdido River forms part of the border between the states of Florida and Alabama.[10]

Unfortunately for Madison, Napoleon was unwilling to betray his Spanish ally even further, at least not publicly. After all, he had sold to the United States the vast territory that he had just acquired from Spain under the pretext of providing a French barrier to protect Spain's Mexican colony (including Texas!) from the ominous westward flow of American frontiersmen. Talleyrand replied diplomatically that "I can give you no direction; you have made a noble bargain for yourselves, and I suppose you will make the most of it." Napoleon's remark regarding the eastern extent of the Louisiana Purchase was even more cynical: If there had been no uncertainty about the borders "it would perhaps be good policy to put it there." If it led to conflict between Spain and the United States, with France as arbiter, so much the better![11]

When negotiations failed, Jefferson requested and received funds for the purchase of additional land and rivers from Spain but they never won acquiescence from either France or Spain. Madison even made several threats of

---

[10] It is ironic in this context that the "Rio Perdido" is Spanish for "Lost River."

[11] Robert R. Livingston to James Madison, May 20, 1803, cited in Brant, *James Madison: Secretary of State,* pp. 149-150.

war as perhaps the only solution but was frustrated by the failure of the Europeans to take them seriously. His insistence that West Florida was already American territory led to the break with the hot tempered Spanish diplomat, the Marquis de Casa Yrujo, who blatantly avoided meetings with Madison and thereafter spoke to the administration primarily through anonymous attacks in Federalist newspapers. Pichon commented frequently on Madison's intransigence regarding the Floridas, but he was only a chargé. General Louis Turreau, the blustering minister who finally arrived from France, was directed to improve Spanish-American relations. He soon reported that when he challenged Madison why he harped so exclusively about lands to the south (meaning Florida) rather than Canada or Nova Scotia, Madison responded that "the time has yet to come. When the pear is ripe, it will fall of itself." Madison did not add that the Spanish pear tree was a great deal less prickly than any British tree to the north. The pear metaphor would be a fine prophecy of how West Florida would fall to the hands of President Madison, part of it in peacetime 1810 and the remainder in wartime 1813. Turreau engaged in startlingly accurate prophecy when he advised his French superiors that the Americans would most likely not stop with Florida but would press across Texas and into Mexico.[12] Both Jefferson and Madison would have been offended to hear their territorial aspirations described as imperialism. Yet they were quite comfortable with references to an American "empire of liberty." To them, providing a larger laboratory for the great American experiment with republican government would serve world needs as well as American interests. If territorial expansion, and especially American access to the Gulf of Mexico and the Atlantic, also enhanced economic opportunities for Americans who had surged westward to fill the lands acquired by the peace treaty of 1783, again so much the better.

The Jefferson-Madison-Gallatin team was rewarded in 1804 for a spectacularly successful first administration by a huge electoral victory over the Federalist nominee, again Charles C. Pinckney. Jefferson was re-elected with 94 per cent of the electoral vote, prevailing even in diehard Massachusetts. Republicans would dominate the new Congress by nearly as large a percentage. Even before the election the Federalists were so weakened that their principal hope for survival as a political force was conspiracy with dissident Republicans, first with Aaron Burr and later with the Clintons, in hopes of achieving a new and more conservative nation based on New England and New York.[13] After this one-

[12] Ibid., pp. 276-278.

[13] Ironically Alexander Hamilton, the long-time leader of the Federalist Party, opposed Burr's campaign for governor of New York so vociferously and publicly that it led to his death in a

sided election, Jefferson's second term began with high expectations for domestic success. If only the super powers--France supreme on the European continent since the Battle of Austerlitz in December 1805 and England supreme on the seas since the Battle of Trafalgar in October 1805--would leave them in peace. They would justly be described as the tiger and the shark, each supreme in its sphere and each perhaps fatal to American interests.

ENGLAND AND FRANCE AT WAR AGAIN

The vast Louisiana Purchase and the resulting dreams of adding parts of Florida were among the most beneficial of the many impacts of the continual warfare, or preparation for war, between France and England that prevailed throughout most of Madison's long political career—from his arrival in the Virginia legislature in 1776 and through most of his presidency. For Americans and their leaders these wars brought economic success or diplomatic crisis, often a combination of the two. Madison was involved in all of them. Even more significant than the Louisiana Purchase was the warfare that made American independence possible in 1783. French royalists' valuable support for American independence from 1777 to 1783, followed by French revolutionists' assumed adoption of American republican ideals in and after 1789, led Madison long to assume the worst against Great Britain until France became too blatant in revealing its own ugly side. And however Jefferson and Madison responded to French depredations, Federalists would brand them as tools of the French dictator. In the series of European wars the United States would be the leading neutral nation, eager to dominate the carrying trade of both belligerents and insistent on neutral rights. American shipping and the American economy boomed while France and England each concentrated on trying to wipe its opponent's ships off the seas. But inevitably the belligerents would turn their attention to preventing neutral nations from feeding and supplying the enemy.

Madison and Jefferson generally sided as vigorously with the French as Hamilton and his political allies had with the English during the Federalist administrations. But the French squandered the opportunity to build upon the increased good will flowing from the Louisiana Purchase. France would have been wise to recognize the value of neutral shipping in maintaining a link to the Caribbean colonies, at least so long as the Royal Navy would permit it. Yet this

duel with Burr, while Burr was still Vice President in 1804. Thus Burr ended his term as a fugitive from justice in his own state.

was not a concern to French privateers (in effect legal pirates during wartime) who preyed so successfully on American merchant ships that Madison seriously considered arming them. Privateers heightened American antagonism for Spain as well as France when vessels seized by the French were taken before corrupt Spanish judges. Pichon admitted in diplomatic dispatches that the justice of Madison's complaints against French and Spanish conduct was undeniable. Madison and Jefferson had earlier achieved their greatest coup by reminding France of the slight value of a Louisiana colony if it was cut off by British control of the seas and the danger of pushing the United States into the arms of Great Britain. Madison again labored, although without similar success, to convince the French government that the United States might still be forced to ally with Great Britain against France for self protection.

British Assault on American Sailors

Because Great Britain controlled the seas it was in the best position to disrupt American commerce. For a while after war was resumed in May 1803, ship owners of Federalist New England made enough profit on those vessels that managed to reach ports that had been closed in peacetime to make them quite willing to absorb occasional depredations. It was the lowly seamen who suffered most by frequent seizures from American ships and forced service (the British called it impressment rather than "shanghaiing") in the British navy. Their plight became part of a diplomatic crusade first of Secretary Madison and later of President Madison. Conflict was inevitable in a situation where so many of these new Americans had previously been Englishmen. It was compounded because Great Britain did not recognize the right of Englishmen, *especially* able bodied seamen, to change citizenship. Even without war, seamen had every reason to prefer service on merchant ships rather than warships. During wartime neutral vessels were especially favored because they were less vulnerable to attack. Sailors and of course landlubbers who had been pressed unwillingly into the Royal Navy leaped at the opportunity to become "Americans" when their ships were in American ports. This provided all the justification that many British officers felt they needed to seize deserters in port or on American ships, especially when some of them were so foolish as to mock British captains from the presumed safety of American cities. Madison was embarrassed to learn that there were so many actual deserters on American merchant ships that American commerce would be severely crippled if he proceeded with a proposed guarantee not to prevent deserters from serving on American vessels. Seamen were seized from American vessels as early as the summer of 1803 and even in American ports in 1804. Sailors who could not prove American citizenship (and many who could have proved it if given the opportunity) were impressed into the Royal Navy. Naval commanders hurting for lack of sufficient manpower were often both judge and jury, clearly a severe conflict of interest.

Madison proposed the arming of American merchant ships and often threatened that French and English depredation of American commerce could lead to war, while hoping that the Europeans would change their conduct rather than call his bluff. His commitment to the wide gulf between executive and legislative authorities that he helped to institutionalize in the Constitution forced him to concede that the President could talk of war but only Congress could bring it into being. This was probably fortunate because of Republican economies, especially military and naval cutbacks since 1801. While Madison spoke loudly he carried a very small stick. British chargé d'affaires Edward Thornton protested the "bitterness of tone and of insinuation" in Madison's letter objecting to the seizure of native American seamen shortly after the resumption of war in 1803. He believed that President Jefferson "would not have acquiesced in either the language or the doctrine of Mr. Madison's" complaints.[14] When a British minister was finally sent to the United States, Anthony Merry was equally impressed by the Secretary of State's seeming antagonism toward Great Britain. Sadly Merry is best remembered for his aristocratic distaste for President Jefferson's democratic lapses in the courtly manners and consideration expected by European diplomats. He did not consider the Secretary of State any better. Madison chose Mrs. Gallatin as a dinner partner rather than Mrs. Merry, just as Jefferson had earlier chosen Mrs. Madison. Madison was embarrassed even to write to Monroe about this tempest in a teacup, but he proceeded to describe with interminable detail his own proposals for improving the administration's "informal" dinner parties. He assured Monroe that he and Jefferson were so committed to "a cordial society with them, and to manifest every proper respect for their characters and station that if any unfavorable impression has happened, it must be very transient."[15] Sadly Madison under-estimated the level of British dignity, as Federalist politicians and editors flocked to Merry's cause as he persistently chose their company in preference to the administrative leaders with whom he had been sent to negotiate.

---

[14] Brant, *James Madison: Secretary of State,* p. 161.

[15] December 26, 1803, and February 16, 1804, Hunt, *Writings of James Madison,* VII, pp. 76, 118-123.

Even before the British had cause to resume the impressment of American seamen, and only two months after his arrival in Washington, Madison wrote lengthy instructions to Rufus King, the competent minister to Great Britain whom he had inherited from President Adams, the first of several classic defenses of American rights against arbitrary seizure that he wrote. Blessed for the first time in his life with clerical assistance, this monumental author of legislation, resolutions, letters, and even constitutions flooded his representatives abroad with powerful exposition of international law and its guarantees of neutral rights. His instructions of July 24, 1801, persuasively document the illegality of the impressment of American seamen into the British Navy.[16] This practice never changed throughout Madison's remaining political career and it would remain a major issue, especially in his campaign for the presidency in 1808 and at the beginning of the War of 1812. James Monroe's chief assignment when he replaced King as minister to Great Britain in 1803 was to negotiate an end to impressment but he too found the British unbending.

OVERRULING THE RULE OF 1756

The other major bone of contention that Madison chose to pick with the British was the Rule of 1756, which was accepted by no country other than Great Britain because it was the only nation with the fleet that could impose and then enforce it. This rule is aptly, and fairly succinctly, described in the title of Madison's largest diplomatic document, "Examination of the British Doctrine which subjects to capture a Neutral Trade not Open in Time of Peace." The heart of his argument is that this rule had no legal standing and that admiralty decisions based on it were based on "a mere superiority of force" rather than on law or precedent. Unfortunately he continued for many pages "with increasing unreadability," according to his biographer Ralph Ketcham.[17] This rule was first imposed in the Seven Years War (1756-1783), known to Americans as the French and Indian War. It would later be modified or abandoned as suited future British governments. The Jay Treaty of 1794 had provided some relief by allowing neutral vessels carrying goods from the French West Indies to continue to Europe after a "broken voyage" in a United States port. The King had reinstated the Rule of 1756 in 1803, but Americans did not learn of this until their ships were seized in 1804-1805.

---

[16] Ibid., VII, pp. 428-432.

[17] Ketcham, *James Madison,* pp. 442-444.

Madison wrote *The Examination* while in Philadelphia tending his extremely ill wife. The title was the only succinct part of this massive pamphlet of nearly 70,000 words that was published anonymously and distributed to members of Congress in January 1806.[18] Two experienced American diplomats who would hardly be expected automatically to embrace Madison's views (John Quincy Adams, the son of the last Federalist President, and Federalist Rufus King) praised it, but another Federalist, Senator William Plumer of New Hampshire, doubtless spoke for more of his countrymen when he declared that he had "never read a book that fatigued me more." For all of its scholarly merits, the heavy book may have had its greatest impact when it was hurled loudly to the floor of the House by Representative John Randolph as the opening public salvo in the former Republican House leader's campaign to thwart Madison's presidential ambitions. This was a "highlight" of a tirade of more than two hours described as invective that was "the most severe that the English language can furnish." Randolph was so eager to demean the future President whom he had come to despise that he spouted a contrary defense of English policy, for which he was quoted with great glee in the British press. Whatever the strength of Madison's legal and historical arguments, the British controlled the seas and that was what really counted.[19]

CRISIS ON THE *CHESAPEAKE*

On May 20, 1807, Madison summed up the outrage he felt for impressment more effectively in a single sentence written to his agent and friend in England: "That an officer from a foreign ship should pronounce any person he pleased, on board an American ship on the high seas, not to be an American citizen, but a British subject, and carry his interested decision on the most important of all questions to a freeman into execution on the spot, is so anomalous in principle, so grievous in practice, and so abominable in abuse, that the pretension must finally yield to sober discussion and friendly expostulation."[20] Less than six weeks later he would be confronted with an act of impressment that was more an act of war. Impressment took its most nasty and warlike turn on June 22, 1807, when the U.S. frigate *Chesapeake* was stopped and boarded off the Virginia coast by *H.M.S.*

---

[18] Hunt, *Writings of James Madison,* VII, 204-375.

[19] Brant, *James Madison: Secretary of State,* pp. 312-316. As a Republican elector in 1820 Plumer would cast his vote for John Quincy Adams to prevent a unanimous election for Monroe as well as to advance Adams' political prospects.

[20] To George Joy, May 20 in William C. Rives and Philip R. Kendall, eds., *Letters and Other Writings of James Madison* (Philadelphia: J. B. Lippincott, 1865), II, p. 405.

Leopard. Captain Samuel Barron refused to allow the boarding of his ship in search of British deserters and for the surrender of three alleged deserters who were specifically named. Then for fifteen minutes cannon balls were fired into the unprepared *Chesapeake*, piercing its sides, breaking its masts, killing three and wounding nearly twenty more. Four sailors were seized and the principal target among them, because of his pugnacious anti-British conduct in American ports, was promptly hanged. The others were Americans who had previously been impressed into the Royal Navy and deserted.

Madison and Jefferson walked a difficult line after ordering the exclusion of British warships from American waters and demanding reparations. American shipping was summoned home and a declaration of war was considered but not implemented because the United States was so poorly prepared. The British diplomat assigned to seek a resolution demanded changes by the American government rather than volunteering any by the British.[21] The tone and teeth of Jefferson's presidential proclamation were sharpened by Madison. Ever since they had as young men rejoiced over occasional successes in the Revolutionary War, they had been firm believers that economic pressures by neutral trading partners must eventually compel belligerents to become reasonable. They had long experimented with limits on trans-Atlantic commerce. This should especially apply to Great Britain because Madison was convinced that Americans did not really need the many British goods that they imported, while the British and their West Indies colonies desperately needed the food exported from the United States. They kept alive the possibility of eventual warfare to get the attention of the belligerents, while doing all they could to halt the bullying by the European powers short of military response. War might indeed have come sooner if England and France had not seemed intent on competing as to who could be most offensive to the American neutrals—and if the United States had not been so woefully unprepared for military retaliation because of the Republican economies that had contributed so greatly to Jefferson's popularity. Under British Orders in Council the Royal Navy would sweep neutral shipping off the seas to prevent France from receiving supplies, while crassly allowing supplies to reach the European continent so long as they were in English bottoms or carried British licenses. Meanwhile various Napoleonic decrees were used to seize and often burn those few American ships and goods that somehow made their way into his "Continental System."

---

[21] Brant, *James Madison: Secretary of State,* pp. 404-405.

THE EMBARGO

The final "big gun" in the Jeffersonian arsenal was to prohibit *all* American exportations. The Embargo Act was rammed through Congress on December 22, 1807 with too limited discussion. English and the occasional French vessels that eluded the Royal Navy could still unload cargoes in the United States but they were required to sail away empty. The United States had been Great Britain's greatest trading partner since its independence, as well as a major contributor to the British dinner table, so it seemed inconceivable to Madison that the British would not eventually be starved into compliance. This might have been a good prediction, but unfortunately he vastly over-estimated American willingness to suffer for the good of the country, especially in the New England base of American shipping and Federalism. It rapidly became painfully obvious that New Englanders had not lost the smuggling skills that they had utilized so effectively when they were part of the British Empire. Turned on its tail as "Ograbme," a cartoon snapping turtle, the embargo was flouted so extensively that the administration had to follow up with highly un-Jeffersonian controls on American commerce and economy, extending even to internal waterways to prevent goods from being transported to Canada through Lake Champlain. Madison and Treasury Secretary Gallatin were prepared even to send the U.S. navy to patrol New England shores. Jefferson's unwillingness to admit defeat by cancelling the embargo was a political burden for Madison throughout his presidential candidacy. In his last annual message to Congress, Jefferson contended through wording supplied by Madison that this "experiment" should be allowed to run its course in order to learn if it was a "weapon" that could be relied on in some future crisis. He rationalized in addition that he should not interfere with possible options of his successor. Abandoning the embargo soon became one of the first legislative actions of the Madison presidency.

While the embargo was a burden for candidate Madison, it was very much one of his own making. He had written most of the legislation that was hustled through Congress in only four days, one in the Senate and three in the House. He was not entirely unrealistic about the likely success of trade restriction. One report that he wrote for a congressional committee speculated that the embargo might be followed by cessation of all trade and finally by war. How could it be otherwise when an undeclared maritime war was continually waged by England and France against the United States? Cabinet members recommended that the only option was to continue present policy or to declare war against *both* European giants Madison was outraged when his British counterpart, Foreign Secretary George Canning publicly ridiculed the embargo. Madison's was the most optimistic voice regarding its eventual success, while Treasury Secretary Gallatin was the perpetual pessimist, or even realist. Gallatin preferred actual warfare to a continual demonstration to the world that the United States was incapable of exercising the unpleasant domestic power that was required to enforce its own trade laws. In the short run, trade restrictions allowed the U.S. at least to delay a war for which it was entirely unprepared. Sadly it was not a great deal more prepared three years later when Madison would request a declaration of war. In 1809 he cautioned the new British Ambassador David M. Erskine that he would sacrifice a great deal to maintain peace, but not American honor or independence. Erskine warned his government that he believed Madison was hoping that the British would be first to declare war and thus unify Americans in their mobilization. Making the most of a difficult situation, Madison sounded almost Hamiltonian as he praised the growth of American manufacturing while trade restrictions kept European goods at a distance.[22]

Fortunately for Madison's reputation as Secretary of State the political attacks against him during the election year that would determine Jefferson's successor justified release by the President of extensive diplomatic correspondence that amply demonstrated Madison's tenacity, skill and sometimes eloquence in protecting American interests. Political enemies then learned, as had some supercilious European diplomats who at first tended to look down on Madison as a small man in talents as well as physical stature, what a tough and capable defender of American interests they were electing as President.[23]

[22] Ketcham, *James Madison,* pp. 457-463.
[23] Brant, *James Madison: Secretary of State,* p. 482.

Chapter 8

THE FOURTH PRESIDENT

Blatant campaigns *against* a Madison presidency began years before there was any evident campaign *for* it. As early as 1803 Robert R. Livingston of New York showed clear signs of a campaign for the vice presidency, which might then still be an avenue to higher office. Nomination and election of the aging George Clinton in 1804 as successor to the careening Aaron Burr headed off Livingston's possible ambitions by providing a political plum, though no longer a particularly juicy one, to Livingston's State of New York. Clinton would be 70 years old by the end of his first term as Vice President and unlikely to be a political factor by then. When Livingston was still stuck in France early in 1804, after his signature triumph with the acquisition of Louisiana, he urged Secretary of State Madison to consider coming to France to replace him as American ambassador.[1] More threatening to Madison's advancement was the bitter campaign of eccentric John Randolph of Roanoke that became public knowledge only in 1806, although hints of his enmity can be detected years earlier. When he was unable to prevent a successful Madison candidacy, the Virginia Congressman devoted his remaining years in Congress to continual warfare against the President from within his own political party.

Randolph's unceasing antagonism for Madison was justified in Randolph's view by his contention that the Secretary of State had declared Randolph unfit to serve as American ambassador to Great Britain. Madison had always been less eager than most leading Republicans to curry favor with the weirdly intimidating Randolph, but there is no evidence that Madison had publicly rebuffed him. Yet Randolph had let it be so widely known that he wanted such an appointment that

---

[1] Irving Brant's chapter "Candidate in Paris" makes a convincing case that Livingston was actively campaigning for higher office, *James Madison: Secretary of State*, pp. 213-229.

he considered it a personal slight when he did not receive it. He regarded the diplomatic appointment as a fitting reward for his leadership of Republicans in the House of Representatives during Jefferson's successful first term. There can be little question that the erratic Virginian would have been an embarrassment to the United States if he had become its official representative in any major European capital, so much so that the President surely would not have approved the appointment even if his Secretary of State had surprised him by such a recommendation. Jefferson would perhaps then have become Randolph's enemy rather than Madison, although Randolph preferred to attack the President indirectly through subordinates.

Running (Slowly) for the White House

Randolph's undermining of Madison began early in 1804 when President Jefferson finally announced publicly that he would not accept re-election in 1808. Randolph's opening salvo was in response to the proposed resolution of the notorious Yazoo land grab of 1795 that was submitted to Congress by an administrative commission that included Madison. Yazoo had been a national scandal since a corrupt Georgia legislature sold millions of acres of land along the Yazoo River in what is now the State of Mississippi for less than two cents an acre. The companies of speculators that made the initial purchase quickly unloaded their ill-gotten gains at a considerable profit to often innocent purchasers, many of whom were from New England, before a newly elected reform legislature rescinded the sale the following year. Shortly after his inauguration, President Jefferson appointed his Cabinet leaders (Madison, Treasury Secretary Gallatin, and Attorney General Lincoln) to a joint state and federal commission to propose a resolution to the dispute. In April 1802 they negotiated the purchase of Georgia's claims by the United States. Actual settlers, Georgia purchasers, and others with completed claims were first indemnified. Then the three Cabinet members were assigned a large parcel of land from which they were to provide equity for squatters and speculators. The least blatantly corrupt speculators would be allowed approximately what they had invested rather than what they wanted and demanded. Yet Randolph was so outraged that they receive anything that he succeeded in stalling these payments until 1810, by which time the United States Supreme Court took the issue out of Congress's hands by ruling in Chief Justice John Marshall's first great property rights decision, *Fletcher v. Peck.* Marshall ruled that the second Georgia legislature had acted unconstitutionally when it rescinded the completed action of its predecessor.

Only then did Congress rapidly enact the compromise that had been offered in 1804. During the delay Madison was persistently attacked by Randolph as a "Yazoo Man" even though Gallatin was the principal author of the report. Randolph next accused his new enemy of attempting to bribe France to pry West Florida from Spain without the approval of Congress, even though Randolph himself had made the motion and voted for the two million dollars that Congress had allocated for Florida negotiations.

Randolph's campaign went into high gear early in 1806 when William Pinkney, a moderate Maryland Federalist, was sent to augment Monroe's efforts to negotiate a treaty with Great Britain. Ironically, Monroe was offended in 1806, much as Livingston had been three years earlier when Monroe was sent to Paris to share in the glory that Livingston craved for the purchase of Louisiana. The irony was compounded by the fact that Livingston's 1803 treaty was a memorable triumph, while Monroe's and Pinkney's Treaty of 1806 was a political disappointment. Monroe's natural resentment was increased by correspondence in which Randolph persuaded him that Madison was attempting to undercut his only conceivable opposition for the Republican nomination for President, who was of course Monroe. Yet until then Monroe does not appear to have regarded himself as a presidential candidate. Virginians doing business in London reported that Monroe was heard to remark that he would "sooner be a constable" than to oppose Madison as President, although Monroe certainly was not this adamant in replies to Randolph's letters.[2]

Tale of a Rejected Treaty

It was Jefferson's handling of the treaty negotiated by Monroe and Pinkney that pushed Monroe into the presidential race. He did not learn of the President's refusal to submit the treaty to the Senate for ratification until his return to America in 1807. Although the Cabinet was unanimously opposed to the treaty because it did not solve the major issues between Great Britain and the United States, Monroe was persuaded by Randolph's innuendoes to assume that Madison alone had blocked the presidential aspirations that Monroe was by 1807 taking seriously. Even if Madison really was the only one persuading Jefferson to reject the treaty, Monroe should not have been surprised.

[2] George Joy to James Madison, January 28, 1808, cited in Brant, *James Madison: Secretary of State*, pp. 420-421; Donald O. Dewey, "John Randolph of Roanoke" and "Yazoo Land Grab" in Rutland, *James Madison Encyclopedia*, pp. 354-355 (Randolph) and pp. 457-458 (Yazoo).

The Secretary of State and President had ample reason to be dissatisfied. In the list of essential reforms in British policy that Madison provided for his diplomatic representatives, two loomed far above all others as *sine qua non.* Halting the impressment of American sailors on the high seas was the "point of honor" that dominated Madison's lengthy instructions to Monroe in 1804. The right of American neutrals to carry goods from a colony to its mother country also must not be impeded, so long as the ship landed in the United States before proceeding to Europe, was the second principle that was essential to Madison and Jefferson.[3] The Treaty of 1806 met neither of these key demands. The recently arrived British minister, David Erskine, even reported that Madison "expressed the greatest astonishment and disappointment" with what the treaty lacked and doubted that it could be accepted.[4] As a Senator who was an active participant in partisan attacks on the Jay Treaty of 1794, which had also failed to achieve anticipated English concessions, it is difficult to understand why Monroe felt that the 1806 treaty should be a political feather in his cocked hat. Monroe was in a position quite similar to that of John Jay a decade earlier. Neither could acquire what his President most wanted, so each gambled and negotiated for other concessions that the British were willing to concede—with political repercussions in each case. Nathaniel Macon of North Carolina, a personal friend of Monroe as well as Speaker of the House in 1807, remarked that published portions of the treaty did more damage to Monroe's reputation than its rejection by Jefferson.[5] Better friends than Randolph advised Monroe to bide his time and wait to succeed Madison, as of course he eventually did, rather than risk alienating the President and his numerous supporters.

FEDERALISTS FISH IN TROUBLED POLITICAL WATERS

Senator Timothy Pickering, who assumed leadership of the extremist wing of the Federalist Party following his dismissal as Secretary of State by President Adams in 1800, supported Monroe's candidacy as the lesser of evils. Monroe was Madison's "inferior in learning and discernment" to be sure, but this was offset because Monroe would at least represent a change from Jefferson. To Pickering

[3] James Madison to James Monroe, January 5, 1804, Hunt, *Writings of James Madison,* VII, pp. 79-114.

[4] March 6, 1897, cited in Brant, *James Madison: Secretary of State,* pp. 374-375.

[5] Nathaniel Macon to Joseph H. Nicholson, December 2, 1807, cited in ibid. p. 423; Donald O. Dewey, "James Monroe" in Rutland, *James Madison Encyclopedia,* pp. 305-308.

Madison was "as visionary in politics as Mr. Jefferson," who would from Monticello "direct all the movements of the little man at the Palace." While Monroe was "inferior in learning and discernment to Mr. Madison," he was at least "a more practical man" who was "more upright" than either Madison or George Clinton.[6] This comment is reminiscent of the desperation of the lame duck Federalists in the House of Representatives who attempted in 1801 to advance Aaron Burr to the presidency over Jefferson because, in the words of a Connecticut Congressman, "it is much safer to trust a knave than a fool."[7] The Federalists also toyed with support for Burr's Republican successor as Vice President, George Clinton, before finally throwing their support again to Charles C. Pinckney, who had been nominated by Federalists in 1800 with John Adams before the Twelfth Amendment mandated separate candidates for President and for Vice President, and then against Jefferson in 1804, and finally against Madison in 1808.

Madison received 83 of the 89 votes from the "official" Republican congressional caucus on January 23, 1808, with Monroe and Clinton each receiving three votes. Both of them denied the legitimacy of this caucus, claiming that it was not publicized sufficiently. Separate caucuses in Richmond, Virginia, nominated the two Virginians. Madison consistently had a greater number of supporters than Monroe and Clinton but the struggle among three Republican aspirants to succeed Jefferson continued throughout 1808. Even more peculiar than the conflict between the two long-time Virginia friends and near-neighbors was the candidacy of Jefferson's Vice President. Clinton managed to become Madison's official running mate while he was actively campaigning to defeat Madison for the presidency and bitterly savaging him in the process. Clinton complained of the "ill-timed and corruptly managed" Congressional caucus that had nominated him with Madison. Yet he never took the honorable step of rejecting the 79 votes that he had received from that caucus or withdrawing his name from the vice presidential ballot and devoting his full efforts to his personal campaign for President. Meanwhile he berated Jefferson for his efforts to manage the presidential succession. This gave the Federalists good reason to consider Clinton as a tool to head off Madison's candidacy. "It is in my opinion impossible," Clinton complained, "that the cause of republicanism can exist much longer under the present visionary, feeble and I might add corrupt management of our national affairs. It is calculated to disgust our best friends and it is fast doing

[6] Timothy Pickering to C. N. Ware, January 16, 1808, cited in Brant, *James Madison: Secretary of State,* p. 424.

[7] Roger Griswold, cited in ibid., p. 29.

so. The meditated successor will improve upon the example of his patron to whom he will owe his election and make our situation still worse if possible."[8] In this scenario Jefferson was of course the patron and Madison the meditated successor. Madison was in the unique position of being characterized in whispering campaigns as too physically fragile to do the job at the same time that he was portrayed as the power behind the scenes who pushed the President into any action, especially the Embargo on exportations to England and France, that might offend one group of voters or another.

The opposition erred spectacularly when they protested administrative secrecy regarding the Secretary of State's diplomatic instructions. Opening himself to counter-attack while presiding over an open session of the Senate, the Vice President had the secretary read diplomatic papers regarding the trade embargo that were clearly marked confidential. He then was unable to compel the secretary to deny evidence that it was marked confidential. The political implications of this assertion of secrecy inspired Pickering to demand the documentary evidence regarding American relations with France. As Secretary of State for both Presidents Washington and Adams, he should have known better! The President replied that he was "obliged," though he was really delighted, to complete the record by supplying reams of diplomatic correspondence with both France and England that demonstrated Madison's skill and persistence in defending American commerce from the incursions of both Great Britain and France. Clerks spent nearly a week reading these papers aloud while Clinton chafed in the Senate over what he called a waste of time and Randolph in the House frantically searched for flaws in the documentary record. Randolph personally read Monroe's lengthy defense of the treaty to present it in the best possible light but the public evidence of Madison's instructions and Monroe's justification for failing to implement them very likely doomed his presidential aspirations, at least for eight years. Public reading of the documents and publication in the newspapers brought the Secretary of State out from the shadow of the President. A New Jersey newspaper crowed that Madison "has dared to meet the most celebrated politicians of the British school in the diplomatic field, and has completely vanquished, disarmed and disgraced them." Even one of Jefferson's most bitter editorial critics had to admit that there was no justice to the continual assertions that Madison and Jefferson were trying to cause war with Great Britain at the behest of France.[9] Randolph and Pickering were not deterred. While clamoring to prove that Madison and Jefferson risked war to serve the

[8] March 10, 1808, cited in ibid., p. 431.

[9] Ibid., pp. 444-445.

interests of France, their widely publicized and unpatriotic justification of English policy against American commerce by Madison's political enemies confirmed British officials in their hard-line policies. Madison's view was vividly presented when he asked if neutral commerce should be "the victim and the sport of belligerents contesting with each other the priority of their destructive innovations."[10]

The belated decision of the beleaguered Federalists to nominate Pinckney rather than support one of the dissident Republicans saved Madison and the political party he had created from the greater factionalism of the so-called Era of Good Feelings. The lack of a viable Federalist opposition was not a problem in 1820 when Monroe was an incumbent running for a second term, but in 1824 the Republicans were nearly torn asunder when four Republicans battled for the succession. Dejected Virginia Federalists described by Chief Justice John Marshall as a "small and oppressed minority" that was "abused, insulted, & maltreated by all" threw their limited support to Monroe rather than Pinckney but were too weak to prevent a Madisonian sweep of all the state's electors. His seven years as Chief Justice had not made Marshall too "judicious" to participate in politics. He conceded that "the superior talents of Mr. Madison" would probably have compelled them to vote for him if they had not been so fearful of the presumed influence of France upon him.[11]

When the electoral votes were finally counted in February 1809, Madison overwhelmed his opposition, with 122 votes to 47 for Pinckney, six for Clinton, and none for Monroe. Madison swept the South and West and most of the middle states. With the exception of Vermont, which was culturally if not geographically part of Madison's western constituency, New England was equally solid for Pinckney. South Carolinian Pinckney's only votes outside of New England were three of fourteen North Carolina electors, two of eleven from Maryland and all three of tiny Delaware's votes. All of Clinton's votes, other than the many that he received for Vice President, were of course from New York.

---

[10] James Madison to John Armstrong (new American minister to France), May 2, 1808, Hunt, *Writings of James Madison,* VIII, pp. 27-31.

[11] October 19, 1808, Robert A. Rutland et al., eds., *The Papers of James Madison: Secretary of State Series* (Charlottesville: University of Virginia Press, 1986), I, pp. 184-185.

SURVIVING AN INAUGURATION

Madison's presidency would begin with distressing international issues that would provide a severe test case for the final year of his first term. New England's clamor for trade with Great Britain under any terms, which in effect meant old England's terms, led to the end of the hated Embargo just as Jefferson left office. Congress replaced it with continued non-intercourse with England and France; but authorizing the President to resume trade with either belligerent that would set a good example by rescinding its depredations against neutral commerce. Any diplomatic stumble in 1809 or 1812 and the young nation could be at war with one of the world's two most powerful nations—or perhaps both. In his final weeks as Secretary of State and first weeks as President, Madison sought to win peace while anticipating eventual war by offering American friendship and commerce to France *or* England. He reasoned that if one of the European powers saw the other one win American good will and support, then surely the other would be forced to follow suit. For his theory to be tested, one of the belligerents must take that first step. Because England ruled the seas it was the likeliest prospect; France could harm the Americans primarily when they sailed into the many European ports ruled by Napoleon. Madison hinted broadly to the newly arrived minister from Great Britain that American friendship was readily available. David Montague Erskine took Madison seriously but when he was unable to convince his own government he recklessly decided to take matters into his own hands. Madison's succession to the presidency in the first week of March 1809 was hectic and exhausting socially but was nothing compared to the roller coaster ride from euphoria to despair to which his administration was subjected the following month by the undiplomatic diplomacy of a neophyte minister who by then had represented Great Britain for two years but was still only thirty-one years old.

It was rare for James Madison to be clothed in anything but black, but at his inauguration on March 4, 1809, it was black with a difference. To demonstrate his patriotism he presented his inaugural address proudly clad in a suit made of wool that was sheared, spun and woven entirely in the United States; only the sheep were imported, and they were rapidly producing home-bred sheep as well. Shortly after noon he was sworn into office by Chief Justice John Marshall. No one was surprised that the small black-clad figure delivered an address of only ten minutes that was better in the reading than in the listening because too much time passed before he could even be heard.

The inaugural address was vintage Madison, interspersed with a few surprises. Of course the Constitution would for him remain "the cement of the

Union" with special attention to the religious freedom and free speech that he had sought to guarantee in the First Amendment. While the federal union was the basis of American peace and prosperity, the "rights and authorities reserved to the states and to the people" would be respected. He would strive as President as he had as Secretary of State to achieve friendly relations with all peaceful nations and strict neutrality with those at war. His administration would rely on diplomacy to protect American liberties in "the present state of the world" but significantly he broke from Republican tradition by justifying "a standing military force," so long as it was held within limits and augmented by an "armed and trained militia." He would honor the public debt but would liquidate it as rapidly as possible through the stringent economies that had been achieved by Treasury Secretary Gallatin's careful management of the budget for the previous eight years. He would encourage "improvements friendly to agriculture, to manufactures, and to external as well as internal commerce" but with the warning that they must be achieved through constitutionally "authorized means."[12] Praising the growth and competitiveness of American manufactures would be a perennial feature of his annual addresses to Congress—a feature that might not have been expected to be highlighted by a Jeffersonian President. There were frequent warnings directed at Great Britain that interference with neutral commerce would force the neutrals to supply their own needs, and thus curtail British exportations. Madison's first annual message to Congress, November 29, 1809, was also brief, only fourteen paragraphs. He reiterated that the "extension of useful manufactures" in the United States was "in no slight degree, a consequence of those impolitic & Arbitrary Edicts by which the contending nations, in endeavoring each of them to obstruct our trade with the other, have so far abridged our means of procuring the productions & manufactures, of which our own are now taking the place."[13] He would also be a frequent advocate for a national university, now that there was at last a national capital city to house it. A single national university has never materialized two centuries later, although Madison would play a major role in the establishment of Jefferson's beloved University of Virginia, near Charlottesville.

Social depression followed the political triumph of inauguration. Madison felt buffeted about when the house where he and Dolley resided while Jefferson remained in the presidential mansion was thrown open to an enthusiastic public that occupied nearly every inch of space. Later he was again overwhelmed by an

---

[12] Robert A. Rutland et al., eds. *The Papers of James Madison: Presidential Series* (Charlottesville: University of Virginia Press, 1984), I, pp. 15-18.

[13] Ibid., II, p. 94.

inauguration ball described as "the most brilliant and crowded ever known in Washington." In fairness it must be added that this was only the third inauguration in that frontier town and the first inauguration ball. Margaret Bayard Smith, the socialite wife of the editor of *The National Intelligencer,* which was for decades the public voice of the Republican Party, remained as close to Madison as she could and constantly contrasts him with both his triumphant wife and his relieved predecessor during her letter describing events of that day. The new President "seemed spiritless and exhausted." She said he had "the most woe begone face, and looking as if he could scarcely stand." When persuaded to remain for dinner he complained "I would much rather be in bed." Dolley Madison, who was seventeen years younger than her husband, sparkled as she became First Lady in her own right after years of playing that role during the presidency of the widower Jefferson. And to Margaret Smith Jefferson was almost a god.[14]

BUILDING A CABINET

But now to business. Candidate Madison had prevailed throughout the nation, except for quarrelsome New England. He had been the choice of seventy per cent of the electoral votes, very impressive compared with Jefferson's narrow victory in 1800 and Adams's even closer one in 1796. Madison was the first since Washington to begin the presidency with the advantage of a large margin of victory. Nevertheless he was confronted by a Congress where the limited Federalist votes were too often augmented by warring factions of nominal Republicans who even managed to disrupt his plans for his own Cabinet.

The quality of administrative cabinets alternated in distressing fashion for the earliest presidents, leaving President Madison on the down side. Washington was at first blessed with a great cabinet centered on Secretary of Treasury Hamilton and Secretary of State Jefferson, and augmented by at least adequacy in the other two positions. Partisan rancor in Washington's second administration, to which Madison contributed, discouraged strong leaders from accepting low-paying administrative appointments. Thus Adams inherited an inferior cabinet and evidently concluded that if that was the best that his great predecessor could manage, he might as well continue with the likes of Timothy Pickering and James McHenry. Sadly Adams's inherited cabinet was not just weak but disloyal; their allegiance was surreptitiously awarded to lawyer Alexander Hamilton in New

[14] Gaillard Hunt, ed., *The First Forty Years of Washington Society in the Family Letters of Margaret Bayard Smith* (New York: Frederick Ungar Publishing Co., 1906), pp. 59-63, 409-411.

York City, rather than to the President who kept them in office. Jefferson in turn was blessed with one of the great cabinets, led by James Madison. The key appointments were almost automatic, Madison as Secretary of State and Albert Gallatin as Secretary of the Treasury. Considering the scarcity of prominent Republicans in New England, which must somehow be represented in the cabinet, Levi Lincoln of Massachusetts was also an easy choice as Attorney General. Henry Dearborn and Robert Smith had been adequate as Secretary of War and Secretary of the Navy in an administration that was firmly committed to peace.

The political infighting that had disrupted the Republican Party as the Federalist Party declined denied Madison the ease with which Jefferson had staffed his cabinet. Because he was unwilling to confront a dissident Senate he began his presidency with one of the weakest cabinets in United States history. Madison had no doubt who should succeed him as Secretary of State. If the new President could have managed it, Gallatin might have brought the same genius and dedication to foreign affairs that he had contributed to the American economy since 1795, first in Congress and then in the Jefferson administrations. The Swiss background and manners that offended "America-firsters" in Congress gave great promise of diplomatic leadership. Sadly his personal enemies in Congress, several from his adopted state of Pennsylvania, had too much influence. Madison soon became painfully aware that Virginia Senator William Branch Giles lusted for the position and would lead the opposition against the "foreigner." Giles was out of the question for the position that he craved, so he would instead remain prominent among the so-called Senate "Invisibles," the obstructionist Republicans who had impeded Jefferson's policies in recent years and intended to do the same to Madison's. They were less blatant and corrosive than Representative John Randolph, who called his troublesome following "Old Republicans" because they professed that they were upholding the Republican faith of the 1790s, which they insisted had been betrayed by the "big government" policies of Jefferson and Madison. Their victims instead called them the *Tertium Quid* (third thing) or Quids. The weakened Federalists had for years grasped at alliances with ambitious dissident Republicans such as Aaron Burr and George Clinton; they now found new tools for their efforts to hinder Madison's goals and appointments, if not regain power.

Madison hoped to silence the most influential "Invisible," Senator William Smith of Maryland, by advancing his brother Robert Smith to Secretary of Treasury in exchange for Smith supporting Gallatin for Secretary of State. This would have been a remarkable advancement considering that Smith had only been Jefferson's *fifth* choice for the much less significant position of Secretary of Navy after it had first been offered to Samuel Smith in an unsuccessful attempt to win his political support. Gallatin balked at this arrangement because he had no confidence that Smith could deliver enough support for Gallatin's advancement and, much more important, he was certain that Gallatin would be forced to manage the economy as well as foreign affairs and the myriad of other responsibilities of the State Department because of Smith's inadequacy. The only way that Madison could be sure of maintaining his essential ally in the Cabinet was to leave him at the Treasury. Gallatin had gained Senate approval in 1801 when nominated by Jefferson so the Senate dissidents were deprived of a second shot at him. It was during discussion of the Gallatin-Smith appointments that Leonard D. White observed in one of his classic histories of American administrative history that "Madison's ineptitude for executive office has often been remarked. His figure was slight, his manner reserved, his speaking voice inadequate, his force of personality moderate."[15] Gallatin would continue as Secretary of the Treasury for thirteen years, a Cabinet tenure that would not be matched for well more than a century, when Harold Ickes served as Franklin D. Roosevelt's Secretary of the Interior a few months longer, from 1933 to 1946.

Madison surely would have been wiser to combat the dissidents at the outset, when he had just achieved a major electoral victory. Gallatin would long be used as a whipping-boy to attack the Madison administration without openly confronting the President, much as John Randolph had previously attacked the administration through Madison rather than openly confront President Jefferson. As a tradeoff for keeping Gallatin as Secretary of Treasury, the President consigned the nation to an ineffective figurehead as Secretary of State. Madison in effect continued as his own Secretary of State, unofficially assuming the many significant documentary responsibilities with which he dare not trust Smith. With the important positions decided, however unfortunately, the others went easily on a North-South-Middle basis. Dr. William Eustis of Massachusetts as Secretary of War and Paul Hamilton of South Carolina as Secretary of Navy were tolerable in peacetime but eventually very risky in time of war. Caesar Augustus Rodney of Delaware was another Jefferson holdover as Attorney General.

The new administration was barely settled when the new President was faced with his first need for internal diplomacy. Just three weeks after the inauguration Pennsylvania militia brandished bayonets under orders from the Governor, to prevent a United States marshal from implementing an order from the U.S. Supreme Court to seize the prize money from a British vessel that had been

[15] Leonard D. White, *The Jeffersonians: A Study in Administrative History, 1801-1829* (New York: Macmillan Company, 1951), p. 36. This was one of his few references to Madison. Ironically, a few years later White would become senior editor of the definitive multi-volume edition of Madison's writings, although he died before the first volume was published in 1964.

captured in the Revolutionary War and in turn seized from the captors by a Pennsylvania vessel. The state ignored decisions supporting the original captor, Gideon Olmstead, first in the Court of Appeals of the Confederation Congress and then in the United States District Court. It did not plan to give any more respect to Olmstead's latest triumph in the U.S. Supreme Court. Governor Simon Snyder used the President's own Virginia Resolutions of 1798 against him to justify state "interposition" against a court that was alleged to have exceeded its authority. Madison's support of the Supreme Court was firm but sufficiently gentle to gain Pennsylvania's retreat without a complete loss of face for its Republican Governor.[16]

A Brief, Thrilling Diplomatic Triumph

This minor triumph would be followed in April by a tremendous diplomatic success that would make Madison the hero of the day—although that day would be painfully brief. As his first full month as President began, he already feared that war could not be avoided, but he hoped at least to delay it until the country was better prepared. Of course he knew his Constitution well enough to remind his own diplomats as well as those of England and France that war was a legislative decision. The congressional repeal of the Embargo in the waning days of Jefferson's presidency opened new possibilities for the administration. He anticipated that the foe would be either England or France, whichever one continued to prey upon American commerce after the other would finally begin to treat the Americans with equity. He expected that the British would be the first to relent and therefore put greatest emphasis on wooing them. Meanwhile British Minister Erskine attempted to convince his government that Madison was serious in inviting an Anglo-American alliance, even though he suspected that Madison preferred war.

Early in April Erskine informed Madison that he was authorized to negotiate an end to the offensive Orders in Council that took advantage of war with France to force neutral American commerce monopolistically through British hands and cash registers, as well as reparations for the British assault on the *Chesapeake*. Madison eagerly grasped at this olive branch, never dreaming that Erskine had neglected to inform him of British thorns that limited his authority. American leaders were rightly perplexed by the offer to rescind the Orders in Council within

---

16 Irving Brant, *James Madison: The President 1809-1812* (Indianapolis: Bobbs-Merrill, 1956), pp. 28-30.

a mere week following the repeal of American restrictions on trade with Great Britain. How could the British act within a week when it took several weeks for news to cross the Atlantic? Their suspicions were painfully accurate because Erskine had neglected to inform Madison that official written notification of American action must be *received* by the British government before any such action by Erskine. The timely (or perhaps untimely) arrival of word from American Ambassador William Pinkney regarding rare conciliatory language from British Foreign Secretary George Canning emboldened Madison to gamble on Erskine's overtures. Otherwise months of salutary trade would be lost while each nation waited on its side of the Atlantic Ocean for the transmission of official papers. On April 19 Madison astonished and thrilled the nation by announcing that on June 10 the Orders in Council "will have been withdrawn" and therefore trade with Great Britain could resume on that same day. Federalist newspapers and politicians who had never expressed a kind word about Madison were joined even by Republican enemies such as John Randolph in treating Madison almost as a god, a spectacular change from the still Satanic Jefferson who now bore full blame for the Embargo and a decade of disputes with England. In its euphoric enthusiasm, Congress reduced military and naval funding (avidly desired by the penny-pinching Gallatin while Madison remained neutral) and rejected the request that the admission of British naval vessels be linked to a treaty of alliance, thus denying the President a bargaining chip that he very much desired.

THE REAL WORLD INTRUDES

Disturbing reports from England arrived just as Americans began celebrating their presumed safe return to the seas. An April 26 Order in Council seemed to end the grubby effort to siphon off profits from neutral trade while opening sections of eastern Europe to neutral trade, but it clearly maintained a paper blockade of most of Europe and denied neutral access to French and Dutch colonies. The astonished Erskine attempted to explain that it was a misunderstanding and Madison tried his best to believe him, until Erskine was summoned home in disgrace for exceeding his authority. Worse yet, the charming and affable Erskine was soon replaced by England's "hatchet man" of diplomacy. Francis James Jackson was widely known as "Copenhagen" Jackson because his most notable previous "diplomatic" achievement was calling on the British fleet to bombard the Danish capital while he was engaged in active negotiations with the Danes. The Attorney General recommended that the President refuse even to meet with so "personally obnoxious" a minister, suggesting that this rebuff should be justified because "we declined entering into a negotiation with [a] minister from whose personal character we could contemplate no favourable result."[17] Jackson soon lived up to his reputation by falsely accusing the administration of being fully aware of the limitations on Erskine's authority while deviously seducing him to exceed it. Writing letters that were signed by the Secretary of State, Madison denied the allegation and demanded its withdrawal. When instead it was repeated a second and then a third time, Madison, again through Smith, accused Jackson of "reiterating and even aggravating the same gross insinuation" which gave him no option other than "to inform you that no further communications will be received from you, and that the necessity of this determination will, without delay, be made known to your Government."[18]

Only five weeks after Jackson was first received by Madison, whom he described as a "plain and rather mean-looking little" President, the British bully was sent packing. The presumed weakling was by then described by Jackson as being as "stubborn as a mule."[19] Like too many other British diplomats both before and after 1809, Jackson's official reports of American attitudes would then for months reflect the views of ardent northern Federalist politicians who courted him to share tales about Jefferson and Madison. Jackson was especially endearing to Federalist editors who could conceive of no fault by the British government. For more than a year after Jackson's dismissal the British refused to recall him and he haunted the high society of Baltimore, New York and Philadelphia, using the Federalists for his own purposes and in turn being used by them even more for their own purposes.

Most Americans however were convinced that Madison and his Cabinet were victims of a high-handed British government. His first State of the Union address that same month sought to assure Congress that war was unlikely despite the continued injustices to American shipping from French and British alike. Most significant was his patriotic pride in American independence and manufactures that had resulted from those very injustices. Madison and his supporters would remain popular in 1810 and the Republican Party would make significant advances even in New England. Much of that year, though, would be devoted to determining whether Napoleon's promise of improved treatment of American shipping could or should be taken seriously.

---

[17] Caesar A. Rodney to James Madison, September 6, 1809, Rutland et al., eds., *The Papers of James Madison: Presidential Series,* I, p. 358.

[18] November 8, 1809, cited in Brant, *James Madison: President*, p. 101.

[19] Ibid., pp. 89, 94.

AMERICAN EXPANSION INTO FLORIDA

Although the administration remained frustrated in the goal of achieving security for American shipping, Madison in 1810 was at least able to take advantage of English and French preoccupation with war to achieve a significant goal that had tantalized him since 1803. Jefferson and Madison consistently asserted that West Florida, the small portions of Alabama and Mississippi that extend to the Gulf of Mexico, had been purchased then as part of the Louisiana Purchase. They bided their time so long as it, as well as East Florida, remained in the hands of the steadily weakening Spanish empire. That time arrived when Spain was torn asunder by French and English armies and by competing puppet monarchs.

Madison quietly encouraged western governors (both state and territorial) and generals to encourage the many American settlers in West Florida to throw off their colonial status. In September a convention in Baton Rouge, Louisiana, that was dominated by American speculators who had acquired considerable territorial claims from Spanish authorities actually broke their ties to Spain and declared themselves the independent state of West Florida, significantly not East Louisiana. Madison simply ignored their request for admission to the United States by treaty. Rather than allow the rebels to negotiate their status in the United States, and thereby guarantee their land holdings, Madison on October 27 proclaimed West Florida to be part of the United States, citing the Louisiana Purchase rather than the western uprising as justification. Remarkably Madison annexed West Florida by executive action without even consulting Congress. Indeed Congress was unaware that these western Americans had been "brought into the bosom of the American family" until it was announced December 3, 1810, in Madison's second annual message.[20] The President who was too often branded as a pawn of the legislature had maintained a level of secrecy that now seems beyond belief. When informed of the West Florida acquisition, surviving Federalists in Congress protested nearly as loudly as they had against the Louisiana Purchase. Louisiana would not become the eighteenth state in the union until April 1812 because its timely application for statehood was long overlooked during preparations for the War of 1812.

In March it even appeared that Spanish East Florida, the present state of Florida, might also fall into American hands as a wartime windfall. General George Mathews, former Governor of Georgia, was authorized to prevent "a foreign power," meaning Great Britain, from taking possession of East Florida.

[20] Rutland et al., eds., *The Papers of James Madison: Presidential Series,* II, pp. 305-320.

Based on the West Florida experience, but lacking the claim of possession by purchase and treaty rights, Mathews sent some two hundred adventurers across the St. Mary's River to declare independence and request annexation to the United States. Seizing Florida from weakened Spain was described by Monroe as "unlawful and unauthorized" and by Madison as a "strange comedy." Mathews, who had ambitions for Mexico and Peru as well as Florida, threatened to "blow them all up" but he died on his way to Washington.[21] If it had been the English whom he had confronted in East Florida, however, Mathews might well have been lionized. Madison's insistence that Britain must be excluded from Florida was a hint of the Monroe Doctrine, a decade in advance. For the present, however, annexation of East Florida was as unsuccessful, though fortunately not as costly, as that of Canada the following year.

Interpreting the Constitution

Secretary of State Madison had indirect and inadvertent impact on the American judiciary in 1801 when he refused to deliver to Federalist William Marbury appointment papers as a Justice of the Peace in Washington, D.C. that had been signed and sealed but left in the State Department offices by Madison's predecessor, John Marshall. Marbury's appeal provided that same John Marshall as Chief Justice the opportunity to deliver *Marbury v. Madison* (1803), the most historic decision in the development of judicial review of national legislation. Although Madison's name appeared on the docket, Marshall's scolding of the administration for failing to provide these documents to Marbury was felt more by Jefferson than by Madison, who fortunately never held the same personal animosity that Jefferson did for his distant cousin, John Marshall.[22] President Madison in 1811 had a much more direct impact on the further development of the Supreme Court when he appointed Joseph Story as Associate Justice, a position that he held until his death in 1845. Outstanding constitutional knowledge combined with judicial nationalism helped to make Story one of the greatest Associate Justices in American history. Story quickly became Chief Justice Marshall's principal ally, providing the scholarly judicial precedents to strengthen Marshall's sometimes more instinctive decisions. Like many other

---

[21] Brant, *James Madison: President,* pp. 45-46.

[22] Donald O. Dewey, *Marshall Versus Jefferson: The Political Background of Marbury v. Madison* (New York: A. A. Knopf, 1970), and "Supreme Court" in Rutland, *James Madison Encyclopedia,* pp. 392-393.

Presidents, Madison was surely unaware of what he had accomplished by this judicial (and highly judicious) appointment.

William Cushing of Massachusetts had been Washington's senior appointment as Associate Justice in 1789 but he was generally considered weak even in the 1790s and was senile well before his death in 1810, so any successor would surely be an improvement. But Cushing's successor would need to ride the New England circuit, and New England was the most difficult place to find an experienced and reliable Republican. Madison wishfully appointed former Attorney General Levi Lincoln, everyone's preferred candidate despite the rapid onset of blindness. Despite his quick confirmation by the Senate, Lincoln formally declined. Alexander Wolcott was next appointed as a reward for his political reorganization of Connecticut and his faithful implementation of the Embargo but he was quickly rejected by nearly a three to one Senate vote because of the lack of evidence that his judicial skills matched his political skills. John Quincy Adams was next unanimously confirmed. By the time his refusal arrived from St. Petersburg, Russia, where he was American ambassador, the position had been vacant for nearly a year and a second Associate Justice, Samuel Chase, had died.

After sounding out Lincoln one last time, Madison at last appointed 31-year old Joseph Story, despite Thomas Jefferson's intense disapproval because as a Republican member of Congress, Story had not been sufficiently supportive of the embargo in 1808-1809. Being well down the list of judicial preferences is not necessarily a sign of inadequacy. The only previous Supreme Court position that had been so frequently rejected was that of Chief Justice in 1800-1801. President Adams had received several rejections, including a failed attempt to reappoint Chief Justice John Jay to the position from which he had retired in 1795 to campaign for election as Governor of New York. As rejections continued he finally turned in despair to his Secretary of State John Marshall, who was already in Washington and from whom he could expect an immediate answer. Adams later justly described this appointment as one of his greatest achievements as President. Sadly prompt appointment was also no harbinger of judicial stardom. Attorney General Caesar A. Rodney was a popular choice to replace Justice Chase but Madison instead quickly appointed his close friend Gabriel Duvall, the Comptroller of the Treasury and a resident of Maryland as Chase had been. Duvall served without distinction until 1835.

Unfortunately at that same time Madison allowed his longing for constitutional consistency to stand in the way of the nation's well being. Alexander Hamilton's once-condemned Bank of the United States was scheduled to be given new life by Congress by March 4, 1811 or its charter would expire. Treasury Secretary Gallatin had no doubts that it must be renewed because it was essential to his persistent campaign through the Jefferson and Madison administrations to extinguish the national debt while doing away with internal taxes, just as it had been to Hamilton's economic programs of the 1790s. In his annual message of December 1810 Madison rejoiced in the budget surplus that allowed further reduction of the debt, yet provided no hint that the Bank of the United States had contributed significantly. Leaving Gallatin to carry the issue with Congress was a severe blunder Gallatin's enemies in Congress clubbed him with Madison's speeches and documents challenging its constitutionality when the bank was established in 1791. Fears and resentment of the Swiss-born Treasury Secretary, combined with Republican agrarianism, led to a 65-64 vote against renewal in the House. Next the seventeen Senate Republicans who voted against renewal equaled the ten Republicans and seven Federalists who supported it. Ironically the opposition was led by Senator Samuel Smith, the brother of Madison's Secretary of State, and the final blow was delivered by the vote of Madison's Vice President George Clinton for an 18-17 embarrassment.

Gallatin was probably correct years later in his assumption that these defeats were caused by the presidential ambitions of the Smiths and the Clintons. Yet he was too respectful of his friend Madison to add that the United States need not have waged war against the world's greatest power without an adequate financial structure if the Commander in Chief had lifted a finger to influence the razor-thin votes in Congress. A simple admission that twenty years of economic success seemed to have resolved the constitutional issue would have sufficed. Without that, Madison's powerful arguments of 1791 would be used unchallenged by his political foes. Even Madison's greatest biographical advocate admitted with regret that the First Bank could have been salvaged if the President could bring himself to admit that he was mistaken regarding a constitutional stance taken two decades earlier.[23] It is ironic that as the War of 1812 was bumbling to an end, Madison would himself be one of the "founding fathers" of the Second Bank of the United States (1816-1836), which President Jackson would declare unconstitutional in 1832.

Madison's few legislative vetoes of legislation in the first administration were more gratifying evidence of constitutional consistency. The first two supported his cherished "establishment of religion" clause of the First Amendment. He rejected Congress's attempt to grant Mississippi lands to the Baptists, although they had been his most consistent supporters throughout his political career. A second veto was for the proposed incorporation of an Episcopal Church in Alexandria, Virginia, which was then part of the District of Columbia. He also held then that

---

[23] Brant, *James Madison: President,* pp. 269-270.

federal authority for a church to support the poor and to educate their children was a dangerous "precedent for giving to religious societies as such a legal agency in carrying into effect a public and civic duty."[24] His third veto supported one of the first of the separation of powers arguments by the initial justices of the Supreme Court, in 1791, that they should not be assigned non-judicial functions. Congress did not attempt to override these vetoes. A major issue at that time that might have concerned Madison was the Erie Canal, the artificial waterway that enabled the produce of the Old Northwest to flow into New York City. It could be viewed as a political problem, being the brainchild of DeWitt Clinton, who would be Madison's principal opponent for President in 1812. Since it was a project of the State of New York, though, there was no constitutional question to be raised and Madison offered cautious support.

Locating a Real Secretary of State

The first faltering steps of a stately Virginia reel that would have dramatic impact on the presidency for the next decade were taken during Madison's first year as President. In addition they significantly increased the strength of Madison's administration. In November 1809 Jefferson initiated cautious efforts to reconcile his closest friends Madison and Monroe, who had so recently contested with spectacularly uneven results for the presidency. Old Republican John Taylor of Caroline had even earlier tried to persuade his ally Monroe to restrain his premature presidential ambitions and to accept appointment as Secretary of State if it was ever offered. In 1809 he advised Monroe that by then the office seemed to promise "presidential ermine." Philosophically sympathetic to John Randolph's insurgency against Jefferson and Madison, Taylor still advised Monroe to join the main stream. Meanwhile Randolph sent frantic warnings that Monroe's ambition for office had rendered him untrustworthy.

Only faltering steps had occurred until May 1810 when Monroe came to Washington to settle accounts from his diplomatic mission to Great Britain. The President's friendly reception of him encouraged further reconciliation. For the next several months there were increased rumors that Monroe might be offered the position of Secretary of State, especially after Jefferson arranged for the President to visit Monroe's Albemarle County home, where Madison received assurances of Monroe's friendship. Yet there was still no vacant office for

[24] Robert A. Rutland, *The Presidency of James Madison* (Lawrence: University of Kansas Press, 1990), p. 77.

Monroe to occupy. In January 1811, following Madison's appointment of Virginia Governor John Tyler to a federal judicial position, candidate Monroe publicly declared that if he was chosen to replace Tyler he would support President Madison and his administration. Madison's supporters in the legislature reciprocated by giving Monroe their votes. Although the raging Randolph had written "Judas" and "Monroe, Traitor" in his diary, he also asserted that he pitied the candidate whose presidential campaign that he had instigated only three years previously. He described Monroe as "more weak than wicked; that he is habitually and incurably ambitious; that he cannot live without office; the stimulus of public consideration having become necessary to his existence."[25]

GETTING RID OF THE SMITH BROTHERS

Now Madison needed to create a governmental vacancy for his old/new friend, and a timely blunder by Robert Smith paved the way. The President had made the best he could of his added burden of drafting much of the important diplomatic correspondence that would then be signed by his Secretary of State. But he could not disregard rumors in the winter of 1810-1811 of Smith's own political ambitions and lack of support for administration policies, especially when Smith incautiously showed him a proposed letter that would directly refute French claims that they were treating American trade fairly. Supposed French concessions to American trade had become essential to Madison's diplomatic policies—especially at a time when James Monroe was now waiting in the wings. Madison was not fooled by French overtures but was gambling that he could use the appearance of improved relations as a device that would bring Great Britain into line. Smith's proposed letter confirmed reports by the British chargé d'affaires that Smith had admitted orally that Madison's treatment of Britain was unjustified because French claims of reform were false. The President's outrage over betrayal of policy that was the Secretary of State's responsibility to implement was described by Smith as mere "peevishness." Smith could justly have argued during Cabinet deliberations that Madison had given too much credence to French assertions that American trade would be treated fairly. But after the President had decided to utilize French claims in the effort to coerce concessions from Great Britain, it was insubordinate and irresponsible to undercut the policy in private discussions with British officials. He should have resigned his office before publicly undercutting administrative policy.

---

[25] February 17, 1811, cited in Brant, *James Madison: President,* pp. 271-272.

Madison's political foes played into his hands while he awaited the adjournment of Congress that would enable him to offer Monroe a recess appointment that could not be impeded by a Senate influenced by Robert Smith's family and friends. The Invisibles, now augmented by Vice President George Clinton, New York City Mayor DeWitt Clinton, and William Duane's *Philadelphia Aurora,* increased their vituperative attacks on the Secretary of Treasury who had remained Madison's lone tower of strength in the Cabinet. Gallatin who was Madison's clear preference for Secretary of State in 1809 then helped make it possible for Madison to gain his 1811 preference for the position. Madison had retained Gallatin in the Treasury when it became clear that Smith's faction would ally with Federalists to prevent Senate approval of "the foreigner" from assuming this presumed threshold to the presidency. Gallatin had remained by default in the Treasury where no Senate action was required. As Madison became more and more dissatisfied by the Secretary of State that he never wanted, a Baltimore newspaper influenced by the Smiths joined the *Aurora* in open and violent attacks on Gallatin and, through him, on the President.[26]

Promptly after the adjournment of Congress Gallatin offered his resignation, declaring that the personal attacks on him threatened to make him a detriment to the administration and "a radical and speedy remedy has become absolutely necessary." Without the need to name Robert Smith, Gallatin referred to the need for, and lack of, "capacity and talents in the Administration" as well as "a perfect heartfelt cordiality amongst its members."[27] Madison immediately rejected Gallatin's resignation and delegated a Virginia Senator to gain a commitment from Monroe that he was willing to accept appointment as Secretary of State. Receiving an encouraging response, Madison on about March 20 demanded Secretary Smith's resignation and wrote personally on that day to offer the position to Monroe. About a month later Madison wrote in a "Memorandum as to Robert Smith" that he had told Smith that "the increase of the public business" prevented Madison from continuing to do Smith's job, as well as his own. Madison told Smith that his diplomatic letters were "almost always so crude and inadequate that I was in the more important cases generally obliged to write them anew myself, under the disadvantage sometimes of retaining, through delicacy, some mixture of his draft."[28]

---

[26] Ibid., pp. 275-281.

[27] Albert Gallatin to James Madison, ca. March 4, 1811, Henry Adams, ed., *The Papers of Albert Gallatin* (New York: Antiquarian Press Ltd. 1960), I, p. 495.

[28] Memorandum on Robert Smith, April 1811, Hunt, *Writings of James Madison,* VIII, pp. 137-149.

When Monroe was assured that peace with England, as well as with France, was administration policy he looked forward to restoration to national leadership. With the notable exception of Randolph, Monroe's political allies urged the reunion of the long-time friends. Old Republican legislator Littleton W. Tazewell even sounded the siren song that if relations with Britain improved, Monroe would not only gain the credit but would "then become in fact although not in name the President, and must hereafter inevitably succeed to the name also, provided the issues of your counsels are prosperous." Monroe expressed great interest on March 23 and formally accepted one week later.[29] On April 6, less than a week after Smith's resignation became effective, Monroe joined the Madison administration and the President need no longer manage American diplomacy from behind the scenes.

To sweeten the blow, and hopefully win a semblance of cooperation from Senator Smith, Madison offered to appoint Robert Smith as Minister to Russia.[30] On May 21 Smith proudly announced to the *National Intelligencer* that he was resigning to become Minister to Russia. Less than a week later, though, he decided that he should be offended and angrily rejected the appointment. When he asked instead to be appointed Minister to Great Britain, Madison responded with irritation that Smith lacked the talents for negotiating that would be required. Smith next suggested that he also would have liked to be on the Supreme Court or even President.[31] Rather than suffer the snows and rigors of Russia he resolved instead to remain in Maryland and publish a full account of his Cabinet career with the assumption that it would humble and humiliate "our panic-struck President." On the contrary, the forty-page pamphlet "Robert Smith's Address to

---

[29] Littleton W. Tazewell to James Monroe, March 17, 1811, Stanislaus M. Hamilton, ed., *The Writings of James Monroe* (New York: G P. Putnam's Sons, 1898-1903), V, pp. 172-173, 181-184.

[30] One cannot resist mentioning President Jackson's comment on sending another future President but then Secretary of State to St. Petersburg that he would send James Buchanan even farther away if possible.

[31] Ketcham, *James Madison,* pp. 485-489.

the People of the United States," that was also widely published in newspapers, so thoroughly demolished his career that Madison never felt any need to respond.[32]

Madison now had strong diplomatic leadership in the Cabinet, and this support had now become more important than ever. The two Virginians concentrated in the coming year on protecting American commercial rights, hopefully through diplomacy; if necessary through war.

[32] Brant, *James Madison: President,* pp. 302-303.

Chapter 9

MARCHING ALMOST TO WAR

From its birth the United States was either an economic and political beneficiary or victim of the persistent warfare between France and England. Wars were not then given momentous titles such as Hundred Years War or Thirty Years War, but the United States was born in the midst of more than a century of intermittent Anglo-French warfare. France's antagonism against Great Britain and its resultant military and financial support for American revolutionaries was essential to their achieving independence from Great Britain. Hardly had Americans achieved and solidified their independence with a new Constitution and viable government than the perpetual enemies were engaged again in a series of mini-wars from 1793 to 1818, the longest pause being from 1801 to 1803. As a member of the House of Representatives, Secretary of State and President, Madison was an important *civilian* participant in all of them.

As the western world's leading neutral with well established commercial shipping, the United States usually profited at the outbreak of war, becoming a valued trading partner to both belligerents until one or the other decided that American trade was too beneficial for the opponent. In April 1793 President Washington wisely proclaimed that the United States would remain neutral in spite of its 1778 Treaty of Alliance with France.[1] Congressman Madison and Secretary of State Jefferson favored neutrality that leaned decidedly toward the old ally France. As master of the seas it was almost inevitable that Great Britain would at first be the principal predator against American shipping. French resentments against the Treaty of 1794, which John Jay negotiated to win limited English concessions, in turn led to French attacks on American shipping and the

---

[1] Peterson, *George Washington,* pp. 219-220.

new nation's first (of what would become many) undeclared war. The so-called Quasi-War of 1798-1800 took place entirely on the seas. Madison had earlier led congressional opposition to funding the administrative aspects of the Jay Treaty and in 1803 he and Jefferson unfortunately allowed its beneficial commercial agreements to expire.

That same year Napoleon's preparation for the next phase of warfare led to the Louisiana Purchase, the enormous territorial windfall that solidified Jefferson's reputation as a great President and Madison's as at least a successful Secretary of State. But soon thereafter the two European rivals again began taking turns preying on American neutrals, to the point where eventually war seemed inevitable with one or the other, perhaps even both. The British ministry hampered neutral commerce with a series of Orders in Council that were countered by a series of French decrees that Napoleon, who in 1805 would proclaim himself Emperor, called the Continental System. Since Great Britain ruled the seas, his goal was to prohibit British commerce from the entire European continent other than Turkey and Sweden. The Order in Council of May 16, 1806, started the whip-sawing of neutral commerce with a paper blockade (meaning a blockade that was not enforced by naval vessels patrolling enemy shores) of northern Europe from France beyond most of Germany. France responded with the Berlin Decree of November 21 that declared an even more unrealistic and illegal blockade of the British Isles and threatened seizure of neutral vessels and goods that had entered British ports or had been boarded by the British navy.

The Order in Council of November 11, 1807, clearly demonstrated that the British blockades were not really designed to starve Europe into submission. On the contrary, their real intention was to seize what they regarded as Great Britain's "fair share" of profits by diverting neutral shipping to ports in England where fees could be collected. They were in effect warring against the neutral Americans who took advantage of war between the belligerents to dominate trade, as part of British warfare against France. Foreign Minister George Canning frankly admitted that the Orders in Council of November 1807 were "a measure of commercial rivalry" and Chancellor of the Exchequer Spencer Perceval asserted that they were designed to force European commerce into British ports: In effect they were challenging their French enemy that "If you will not take *our* trade, as far as we can help it you shall have none." The result was that neutrals must submit to British control if they intended to carry produce to Europe. Perceval admitted that American neutrals posed a greater threat to British commerce than Napoleon did. Some English editors were embarrassed by such blatant greed, but this offered little satisfaction to frustrated American shippers. Ironically, if Americans knew that Perceval who was so harsh in his policies toward the United States had been assassinated by a lunatic only five weeks before its declaration, the War of 1812 might never have been waged.[2]

Napoleon countered with still more decrees punishing neutral American shippers who were compelled to acquiesce in British restrictions. The Milan Decree authorized seizure of neutral vessels. Often the fact that they had managed to reach European ports controlled by France was all the evidence France needed to establish that they were tainted with British influence and therefore liable for seizure and sale. Competitive greed drove the two giants, each blaming the other, to seize some 900 American commercial vessels from 1807 to 1812, leaving many of them in ashes after removing their cargoes.

SEIZURE OF AMERICAN SEAMEN

The seizure of American sailors was one highly offensive area where only the British were in a position to antagonize their former colonists. The Royal Navy was regularly short of manpower in wartime, when British sailors would be much better paid as American merchant seamen and would be far more likely to survive than they would on a war vessel—at least until they were forced into the British navy. Captains who were short of manpower were easily convinced that some of those merchant seamen were really British deserters. The American position was weakened by the fact that a good proportion of them really were just that. It has been estimated that a fourth of American seamen were British, some deserters from the Royal Navy, and many more of them were British merchant seamen who had become or were trying to become American citizens. British captains with severe need to man their ships had every reason to convince themselves that able seamen were Englishmen whatever their papers, if any, might attest. It is likely that six thousand men were impressed by British naval vessels from 1804 to 1812, and a violent seizure led to the *Chesapeake* crisis of 1807. During Madison's first term as President, from 750 to a thousand men were impressed per year. It was an issue that might well have been negotiated if the Orders in Council could be cancelled at the same time. Yet it was a major psychological irritant as the former "mother country" refused to recognize the injustices for young men, some of whom had known no other nation than the United States, to be seized as runaway Englishmen and forced to serve a foreign nation. Resentful Americans considered impressment a threat to their young nationhood and therefore a symbolic return to colonial status.

---

[2] Brant, *James Madison: Secretary of State,* p. 397.

Regrettably at the very time that war loomed on the horizon, the popular economy measures of Treasury Secretary Gallatin (and of President Jefferson) had led to severe cutbacks in the army and navy and the rescinding of internal taxes. The government had come to rely primarily on tariffs on imported goods at a time when shipping became a pawn of powerful British navies and French armies. However unprepared, the American people were probably ready to declare war against Great Britain in the summer of 1807 after the U.S. frigate *Chesapeake* was shelled and severely damaged in American waters when its captain refused demands from the British warship *Leopard* that he turn over alleged British deserters. In response to the *Chesapeake* affair and British Orders in Council, Jefferson and Madison instead persisted in their series of attempts to use American commerce as a protective weapon short of war. The failure of their embargo of December 1807 and the creativity of American commercial men in finding surreptitious methods to continue shipping to Europe dominated the transition from President Jefferson to President Madison. Because Jefferson could not bring himself to admit defeat, the embargo remained in place until it was rescinded by Congress just as Madison assumed the presidency.

A Moment of Diplomatic Triumph

Madison's presidency was very soon enhanced by the euphoria of an agreement with David M. Erskine that momentarily seemed to resolve United States conflicts with Great Britain. Joyous Americans briefly compared their new President with their monumental first President. Jefferson wrote to congratulate Madison for bringing the nation "peace in your time." This ended abruptly when word crossed the Atlantic that the British Cabinet had summarily rejected the negotiations because Erskine had blatantly ignored his instructions. American vessels that had been lured to sea were promptly corralled by British vessels. Madison quickly halted trans-Atlantic commerce through executive action. This experiment with non-intercourse was more successful than most because economic depression at least induced English manufacturers to appeal for cancellation of the most offensive Orders in Council. It was supplanted in May 1810 by Macon's Bill No. 2, which was a replacement for a more realistic proposal written by Gallatin and sponsored by Nathaniel Macon, who had been Speaker of the House from 1801 to 1807. It sought to win a sort of peace by allowing American merchants to resume trade with Great Britain and France while promising a diplomatic reward to the first belligerent to offer "unconditional" revocation of its own incursions on American commerce.

Optimist that he was, Madison gambled that common sense, combined with the need for American produce, would force the laggard nation to fall quickly into line and end its own restrictions. Failing that, the United States was committed to resume non-intercourse against the nation that continued to violate American shipping rights. This was an open invitation to that famous French fisher in troubled waters, Napoleon, to hoodwink the Americans. On August 2, 1810, even before Napoleon had official knowledge of the American legislation, he dictated a letter that would be signed by Foreign Minister Jean Baptiste Champagny (the Duc de Cadore) declaring that the Berlin and Milan Decrees would be suspended on November 1, with the requirement that the United States would "cause their rights to be respected by the English." Because Napoleon was confident that the Americans would never be able to accomplish this goal, of course he never intended to suspend the decrees, nor did he ever actually suspend any part of them. From distant St. Petersburg in Russia, John Quincy Adams warned his brother that the United States was walking into "a trap to catch us into a war with England."[3]

The President seems not to have been deceived by the Cadore letter but he hoped that it could be used as a lever to force Great Britain to recognize its own self interest and promptly cease its attacks on American commerce in order to preserve its most valuable trading partner. Frustrated with the lack of corroboration from the United States minister to France, John Armstrong, Madison gambled that France would abide by its seeming commitment. He announced that, based on these French assurances the United States would resume its ban on trade with Great Britain if it failed to end its own interference with American shipping *and* the impressment of American seamen. Rather than winning improved relations with either belligerent, U.S. shipping would next be savaged by both.

The British were justified in demanding clear evidence that the French had changed their ways, while the French instead provided ample proof that the British suspicions were legitimate as they continued the seizure and burning of American ships on the seas when possible but usually in European ports. The French government ignored the gentle hints of its Minister to the U.S., Louis Serrurier, that it would be wise to cease depredations on American commerce. By the time that Armstrong finally forwarded the evidence that difficult strings were attached to the French offer, Madison had gone too far to retreat from his French

---

[3] Brant, *James Madison: President,* pp. 117-120, 139, 149-156; Rutland, et al., eds., *The Papers of James Madison: Presidential Series*, I, pp. 63-64, 89.

romance and he had little choice but to order cessation of trade with Great Britain effective February 1, 1811.

A Dangerous Gamble

When the Cadore agreement failed to bring England to terms, Madison concluded that war was inevitable. Since the United States could manage only "one contest on our hands at a time," he must choose the bully that was both most offensive and most accessible rather than attempt to quell both. The old enemy of three decades ago was certainly accessible, for the Royal Navy continued to patrol American waters, often clearly in sight of American ports. The huge disparity between American trade with England and that of France, almost from the time that American independence had been negotiated in 1783, should have impressed British officials, but too many British leaders took this relationship for granted. Furthermore they were not inclined to take Madison's attempts at peaceful coercion seriously, because they had seen so many starts and stops of American policy since 1803. Continued elements of economic colonialism made Americans sensitive to memories and fears of political colonialism. Too many in England, as well as New England, assumed the obligation of their quondam colonists to help Old England quell the despot across the English Channel who was threatening to control the world. For all these reasons, despite mounting news of American ships being destroyed in French-controlled ports, England continued to be regarded by most Americans, including their President, as the greater villain. As early as June 22, 1810 Madison had written that even though French depredations had temporarily diverted American attention, the public was finally recognizing mounting evidence that "the original sin agst. Neutrals lies with G.B. & that whilst she acknowledges it, she persists in it."[4] Psychological fears of a return to colonialism were still evident in Madison's first annual message to Congress as Commander in Chief. He proudly proclaimed that if Americans failed to resist British depredations they would betray "the magnificent legacy which we hold in trust for future generations." Standing up for national honor demonstrated that Americans were "an independent people" rather than mere "colonists and vassals."[5]

However offensive it had become to American interests, the French ally of the 1770s and 1780s was, on the other hand, at least an ocean away. The

[4] Hunt, *Writings of James Madison,* VIII, p. 103.
[5] November 4, 1812, ibid., VIII, p. 220.

possibility of war against France or even against both predator nations would be discussed through the first half of 1812, but the more immediate English threat and old enmities prevailed with the President as well as most of Congress, with the major exception of the waning Federalists of New England. Madison agreed with Congressman Nathaniel Macon that the two belligerents were "equally wicked" but wisely resisted war with both. His quandary was best expressed in letters to his favorite correspondent. He admitted to Jefferson that war against a French "conqueror roaming on the earth with havoc and destitution" could be as well justified as war against an English "pirate spreading misery and ruin over the face of the ocean." Only three weeks before war would be declared on June 17, 1812, Madison conceded to Jefferson that war against both belligerents "presents a thousand difficulties; above all, that of shutting all the ports of Europe against our Cruisers who can do little without the use of them." After admitting that even if he led the nation into war with France he could not win over the Federalists, he concluded that "The only consideration of weight in favor of this triangular war as it is called, is that it might hasten thro' a peace with G.B. or F. a termination, for a while at least, of the obstinate questions now depending with both."[6]

WAITING AND YEARNING FOR GOOD NEWS

Timely information was always a problem during an era when Europe and America were at best weeks and sometimes months apart. This crisis was compounded at this crucial time by diplomatic distance as well. John Armstrong reported too little and too late from France, influenced both by British seizure of the mails and Armstrong's innate laziness, leaving Madison too deeply committed to war by the time he finally learned of the extreme limits on French cooperation. He finally learned, but could not publicly admit, that the British were correct in their assumption that French repeal of the Berlin and Milan Decrees depended entirely on the Americans protection of their own rights against British incursions. Madison and Monroe spent the first half of 1812 waiting for vessels that were expected to bring good news from France or from England.

Meanwhile the United States had no official voice in Great Britain above the consular level as the two nations careened toward war. Minister William Pinkney was not replaced when he returned home. Rather than recognizing this as a diplomatic warning the British remained almost equally out of touch. They obstinately refused to replace "Copenhagen" Jackson, who had moved off to

[6] May 25, 1812, ibid., VIII, pp. 190-191.

Federalist salons after becoming unwelcome in Washington administrative circles in 1809. Thus his reports bore no understanding of the views of the American government to which he had been assigned. He could report only what his Federalist friends said about Madison and his government. Great Britain would not be represented diplomatically until the arrival of Sir Augustus John Foster at Annapolis, Maryland, on June 29, 1811, ironically the same day that Pinkney landed in America from a different vessel.

Foster had chafed at the informal treatment of British diplomats during his service as legation secretary during the first Jefferson administration, but he was pleased by his cordial reception by Madison in their new roles. He quickly recognized that the President seemed to prefer war to "their present embarrassments"[7] but he was unable to convince his government to take the threat seriously. Foster's options for serious negotiation were hampered by directives that he insist that the Americans force the French to admit British commerce to the Continent, which was close to a fool's errand that was impossible for the Americans to implement. Even though he found Madison unbending on the Orders in Council, Foster soon ceased to worry about warfare. Like most of his British predecessors he quickly fell under the sway of Federalists who convinced him that Madison's warnings were just political posturing. Whereas Jackson had described Madison as stubborn, Foster would generally view him as indecisive. Some Federalists were even convinced that Madison was in a no-win situation: that he would be defeated in 1812 if the Orders in Council remained in effect, yet a threat of war was an election gambit that could safely be ignored because war also would guarantee his electoral defeat. The *Baltimore Federal Republican,* edited by the chief clerk who Madison too humanely had kept in the State Department for six years despite his extreme Federalism, went so far as to predict Madison's impeachment. He was confident that Robert Smith's inside information about Madison's supposed "high crimes and misdemeanors" would exceed "the crimes of Charles II of England" who had been *beheaded* rather than merely impeached.[8] Too late, Foster would recognize that his first assessment of Madison's commitment to war with Great Britain was more accurate than the views fed to him by his Federalist sources. While he faithfully reported his discussions with Madison and Monroe to his government, they were too often tempered by intemperate remarks of Federalists who had no true insight regarding the policies and intentions of the administration.

---

[7] Brant, *James Madison: President,* pp. 366-367.

[8] July 25, 1811, ibid., pp. 343-344.

Madison called for the Twelfth Congress, which would soon be described as "the War Congress" because of significant changes in membership, to convene earlier than usual because of the international crisis. Recent elections had made war more likely due to the addition of young westerners and southerners to Congress to enhance the vigor and competence to a House of Representatives that had long been sorely lacking in leadership. Even disgruntled Federalists found it difficult to fault Henry Clay, who would be one of the most effective Speakers in the history of the United States before moving on to be numbered among the all-time greatest senators. He placed the so-called War Hawks in positions of power on important House committees, where they clamored loudly and forcefully—and competently—for American interests and recognition on the world scene. The Foreign Affairs Committee was packed with War Hawks, led by Peter B. Porter as chairman. Although he was from upstate New York, Porter would place more emphasis than even Madison on the continuing impressment of American seamen as a basis for war, increasing its status as a cause for war. Monroe met regularly with Clay and Porter, pressing for a declaration of war and a 60-day embargo prior to adjournment. Generations of historians have followed the leadership of Henry Adams' classic *History of the United States*[9] in branding Madison as a weakling who was dragged into the war by Clay and Company. On the contrary, Madison knew his own mind and other historians have applauded him for upholding America's national honor and rights as a neutral nation. Rather than bullying him, the War Hawks cooperated with him to achieve mutual goals. Not all of the Hawks would agree with that assessment, though. At the beginning of his monumental national career, South Carolina Representative John C. Calhoun wrote on April 4, 1812, that "our President tho a man of amiable manners and great talents, has not I fear those commanding talents, which are necessary to control those about him. He permits division in his cabinet."[10]

PREPARING FOR WAR

The first draft of Madison's third annual message to Congress, November 5, 1811, threatened "reprisals" against British policies, focusing primarily on the unfairness of the Orders in Council. When read to Congress, however, it was

---

[9] Henry Adams, *History of the United States During the Administrations of Jefferson and Madison* (New York: Charles Scribner's Sons, 1890-1891).

[10] R. L. Meriwether, et al., eds., *The Papers of John C. Calhoun* (Columbia: University of South Carolina Press, 1959), I, pp. 99-100.

toned down to an admonition for "an armor and an attitude demanded by the crisis and corresponding with the national spirit and expectations."[11] This resulted from Madison's recognition of an obvious lack of adequate military preparation, as well as his constitutional scruples that a declaration of war must be a legislative rather than executive function. Rather than recommending war then, he asked Congress to prepare for a war that seemed inevitable if the British persisted in their offensive Orders in Council. He urged Congress to increase the regular army to ten thousand men, call for volunteers, alert the militia, outfit and restore the remnants of the navy that had survived Jeffersonian economies, build new naval vessels, and stockpile munitions and supplies. While his emphasis on the Orders in Council made it obvious that Britain was the eventual target of all this preparation for war, he advocated careful monitoring of France as well. Historian Henry Adams' great grandfather, the patriarch John Adams, praised the President's address, which was read aloud by a clerk, as were all presidential messages to Congress between those of Adams himself and Woodrow Wilson in 1913. Adams declared that it did the President "great honor."[12] President Madison would devote every day of the next several months, and countless hours within them, to preparation for war. It was observed that he seemed never to leave the executive mansion. It was ironic that only eight days after Madison's "war message" he reported to Congress without fanfare that he had negotiated an end to the *Chesapeake* crisis that had threatened to take the U.S. to war with England in 1807.[13]

More Politics than Preparation

Regrettably Congress, even though dominated by War Hawks, could not for long maintain that level of commitment. Admittedly it had a very full agenda because the army had been decimated by Jeffersonian economies and the outstanding small navy developed in the Adams administration was cut even more drastically because of Republican fears of a military establishment. Before the end of November the Foreign Affairs Committee responded to Madison's requests, calling upon Americans' patriotism and resources. It recommended increasing the standing army of less than four thousand men to ten thousand and its

---

[11] Hunt, *Writings of James Madison,* VIII, pp. 158-165, especially p. 162; Brant, *James Madison: President,* pp. 356-359.

[12] Adams to Monroe, December 19, 1811, ibid., p. 361.

[13] Hunt, *Writings of James Madison,* VIII, pp. 166, 170-171.

augmentation by another ten thousand in new regiments, in addition to fifty thousand volunteers. The state militias were also to be alerted and the existing frigates outfitted for war duty. The committee added a proposal that merchant ships should be armed for their self protection. This led to extended debates with Madison in which British Minister Foster threatened that such action would surely lead to warfare. These recommendations were approved by the House by mid-December, after moderates were assured that they were only *preparations* for war and that negotiations could still continue. And continue they did as Representatives clung to the hope that all of these preparations might prove to be unnecessary. Politics then triumphed over patriotism when these proposals reached the Senate. The "Invisibles," the little group of Republican Senators who began the Madison administration as enemies of Albert Gallatin and then became enemies of Madison when he supported Gallatin rather than them, united with New England Federalists to stall military preparations. The Senate soon demonstrated that it was committed more to the oratory of warfare than to the military growth and expenses required for an international war. Senator William Branch Giles scoffed at the inadequacy of the new regiments and persuaded the Senate to insist on twenty five thousand men for five year terms rather than ten thousand for three years, thus assuring that those troops would never materialize. Three months after Madison called for military preparations, he grumbled about the Congress: "With a view to enable the Executive to step at once into Canada, they have provided after two months delay, for a regular force requiring 12 [months] to raise it and after 3 months for a volunteer force, on terms not likely to raise it at all for that object." Having been there, Jefferson certainly would have needed no explanation of Madison's cryptic comment that "The mixture of good & bad, avowed and disguised motives accounting for these things is curious eno' [enough] but not to be explained in the compass of a letter."[14]

Naval support was even more muddled in both houses of Congress. Most Jeffersonian Republicans, not just the dissidents, were even more fearful of a powerful navy than of a standing army. Despite Clay's strong support, Madison's proposal for twenty new frigates was rejected by 62 to 59 in the Senate; instead it funded only the outfitting of three of the sterling frigates that had survived the Quasi War of 1798-1800. Thus eight frigates, the twenty-gun *Adams,* and several small sloops and brigs that had been constructed for the so-called Tripolitan War[15] of 1801-1805, would in 1812 constitute the entire force that would sail against

---

[14] James Madison to Thomas Jefferson, February 7, 1812, ibid., VIII, p. 176; Brant, *James Madison: President,* pp. 394-395.

nearly one sixth of the world's greatest navy then sailing in North American waters. Great Britain had "more than a thousand ships of war, three *fighting ships* for every American *gun.*"[16] Unfortunately Gallatin's estimate of the cost of war preparations arrived during naval deliberations and only increased Congressional opposition to military expenditures.

Madison can certainly be criticized for speaking loudly and carrying *no* stick, in contrast with Theodore Roosevelt's famed admonition that the United States should speak softly and carry a big stick. He had realized for months that the country was ill prepared for war and that Congress had not made significant progress toward military preparedness. Indeed Madison shares some of the responsibility for the lack of American preparations because of his need to walk a narrow line between Gallatin's penchant for economy and balanced budgets while still striving to bring the nation to a war footing. Gallatin dragged his feet as long as possible because of the cost. His frugal management of the economy and budget had been a key element of Jefferson's success as President. Gallatin's worthy ambition to have the national debt entirely extinguished by the end of Madison's presidency had been realistic until the outbreak of the War of 1812 and related commercial interruptions. Internal taxes had been rescinded for political reasons so that the country relied almost exclusively on tariffs collected on foreign importations and on the sale of western lands. Of course income from tariffs was vastly diminished in time of war or even trade restrictions. The impact of limitation of commerce with Great Britain is demonstrated with its significance during peaceful interludes. Importations then from England were about twenty times greater in value than those from France—which in turn greatly exceeded importations from the rest of Europe. Naturally there was a comparably large disparity between American exportations to Great Britain and to continental Europe. Gallatin argued that war with England would force the doubling of duties on foreign trade, $3 million in direct taxes on the states, restoration of $2 million in taxes, as well as borrowing $10 million. These were modest estimates but they antagonized Congress, which eventually approved the taxes on March 2, but with the proviso that they would be collected only after war had been officially declared and they would lapse a year after the war's end.[17] Loans would be the economic backbone of this war. Yet while talking war in 1811 Congress (and

[15] This "war" would in later centuries probably be termed a "police action" since it consisted of naval action to quell the Barbary Pirates who preyed on Mediterranean commerce.

[16] Irving Brant, *James Madison: Commander in Chief, 1812-1836* (Indianapolis: Bobbs-Merrill Co., 1961), pp. 38-39.

[17] Albert Gallatin to Ezekiel Bacon, January 10, 1812, *Gallatin Papers*, I, pp. 501-517; Brant, *James Madison: President,* pp. 401-404.

Madison!) allowed the first national bank, the most likely source of these loans, to die.

Waiting and hoping for better news from England finally ended painfully on March 19, 1812 when dispatches from England demonstrated conclusively that there would be no British retreat. Madison wrote Jefferson that the continued power of "Perceval, &c." demonstrated conclusively that the British "prefer war with us, to a repeal of their Orders in Council." Therefore he felt that his only option was to "make ready for it." He proposed an embargo as a prelude to war, which was quickly adopted by Congress. While he favored the embargo as a step toward a declaration of war, Congress's revision of the embargo from sixty to ninety days demonstrated continued hesitance.[18] Meanwhile Monroe advocated a declaration of war before the adjournment of Congress. In an anonymous editorial in the *National Intelligencer,* he urged that war should "be forthwith proclaimed against England. With her there can be no motive for delay." Any further discussion, any new attempt at negotiation, would be "as fruitless as it would be dishonorable." As for France he reserved the option of similar action if it continued to violate American rights.[19] The hapless Foster, who believed that this editorial had been written without authority by Henry Clay, played his final cards on May 27. He showed dispatches written by Viscount Castlereagh, the new British Foreign Minister. The first message made it evident that Great Britain would not treat the United States differently from all other nations, even if France would be demonstrated to have excused the United States alone from the restrictions of the Continental System. Instead the French decrees must be "rescinded absolutely and unconditionally" for all nations, presumably including even Great Britain. When Madison responded with outrage, Foster countered with a more attractive offer to allow Americans a share in British trade with the French empire, and even offered to give up its own trade with the French as "a sacrifice of profit made for the sole purpose of conciliating the United States."[20] Madison delivered a war message to Congress four days after he and Monroe indignantly refused to bargain away neutral rights.

---

[18] April 3, 1812, Hunt, *Writings of James Madison,* VIII, pp. 185-186.
[19] April 14, 1811, cited in Brant, *James Madison: President,* pp. 434-436.
[20] Ibid., pp. 466-469.

DECISION FOR WAR

Madison's special message of June 1 succinctly spelled out the justification for war but characteristically left the decision to Congress. A considerable majority of the message focused on the Orders in Council, although only after a terse but vigorous protest against the more volatile issue of impressment of American seamen and British ships warring "on our shores." He complained that American commerce was the victim of the monopoly that Britain "covets for her own commerce and navigation." The final indictment was for the incitement of Indian attacks. He concluded that there existed "on the side of Great Britain a state of war against the United States, and on the side of the United States a state of peace toward Great Britain."[21]

Congress proceeded secretly, thereby preventing Federalists from airing their protests in public. The House voted 79 to 49 for war against Great Britain by June 3, but the Senate debates continued until June 17 when it approved a declaration of war by a vote of 19 to 13. Madison signed the legislation the next day. This most narrow war vote in American history was a victory of South and West, augmented by Pennsylvania, over largely opposed northern members of Congress. This demonstrated the strengths and weaknesses of Madison's (Democratic) Republican Party as it went to war, for 81 per cent of the Republican Senators and Representatives supported the war, while every Federalist voted in opposition.[22]

The President's eagerness to brand Federalist supporters of the British led to a financial blunder. He authorized Monroe to spend $50,000 for copies of letters by an English agent, John Henry, who professed to have evidence of covert negotiations in New England during the embargo crisis of 1807-1809. The documents caused great joy to Republicans and anxiety to New England Federalists when presented to Congress in March, 1812, but their impact declined rapidly when Henry's alleged contacts were not identified by name and especially when word of the payment was leaked. When it was further revealed that most of the money went to a notorious French swindler who was posing as Count Edward Crillon it was obvious that those precious dollars could have been more wisely expended on military preparations. Madison's war message nevertheless cited the actions of a "secret agent" as an additional justification for war.[23]

---

[21] June 1, 1812, Hunt, *Writings of James Madison,* VIII, 192-201.

[22] Donald F. Hickey, *The War of 1812: A Forgotten War* (Urbana: University of Illinois Press, 1989), p. 46.

[23] Brant, *James Madison: President,* pp. 413-420; Hunt, *Writings of James Madison,* VIII, p. 183.

Even after the vote Foster remained optimistic that war could still somehow be averted. He would have seemed prophetic if each nation had been aware of what was going on across the Atlantic. There was no way for Americans to know that their adversary Spencer Perceval, who had been Prime Minister since 1809 when Madison became President, had been assassinated by a lunatic on May 11 and that resignation of the British Cabinet had rapidly followed. Furthermore the British had begun retreating from the policies that most offended the United States, even offering Americans a legal share of the licensed trade to Europe. Paper blockades were quietly removed. Restraints were lessened in bits and pieces until, ironically, on the very day before the Senate voted for a declaration of war and two days before the President officially proclaimed it, the suspension of the offensive Orders was announced in Parliament. Madison would later admit that war could have been avoided if knowledge of these dramatic changes had reached America—but Madison made these concessions a decade after the War of 1812 had ended. Although he had been aiming toward war since July 1811, he was saddened that peaceful coercion had once again failed. By now American demands had increased. Rather than settle for repeal of the Orders in Council and later negotiations on impressment, he unsuccessfully demanded negotiations on impressment before war could be avoided. He still anticipated a quick and bloodless war.

Because of Republican-imposed secrecy in Congress, the American public was caught unawares. They knew that war was being discussed, but because this had been so often discussed since 1805, by those who welcomed it and especially those who detested it, they really could not believe it would ever happen.

Chapter 10

COMMANDER IN CHIEF

President Madison was true to his constitutional scruples when, after a year of preparations, he insisted that he was only recommending and that only Congress could actually declare a state of war. But once Congress had made that decision he moved rapidly and decisively. Except for some striking naval success, however, the results were dismal. British minister Augustus Foster argued for an armistice, hoping that recent English concessions might reconcile Mother Country and former colonies. Madison resisted a temporary truce, insisting that in addition to revocation of the offending Orders in Council, Britain must also renounce illegal blockades, end the impressment of American sailors, and return sailors who had already been impressed. After years of frustrating negotiations, he had reason to fear that, rather than negotiating in good faith, the British would deprive the Americans of presumed advantages gained from attacking while the enemy was still unprepared. This would have been wise strategy if the Americans themselves had been as well prepared as they thought they were. On the contrary, the army was in disarray. The military commanders were aged survivors from the Revolutionary War and the civilian leadership of the War Department would soon appear equally weak and inept. This more than offset the advantages gained by early naval triumphs.[1]

Madison's War Message to Congress of June 1, 1812 reviewed the causes of the conflict between the United States and Great Britain, in which the latter would be aided in this war by Canada, Bermuda, and segments of the Eastern Woodland Indians. The stage backdrop for the War of 1812, known as the "American War of 1812" in British history, had been the renewed conflict between Great Britain and

---

[1] Ketcham, *James Madison,* pp. 534-535.

France during the Napoleonic Wars. Therefore Madison stated in his June 1 message to Congress: "Without going back beyond the renewal in 1803 of the war in which Great Britain is engaged, and omitting un-repaired wrongs of inferior magnitude, the conduct of her Government presents a series of acts hostile to the United States as an independent and neutral nation."[2]

Madison systematically outlined the causes for his request for a declaration of war against Britain: "British cruisers have been in the continued practice of violating the American flag on the great highway of nations, and of seizing and carrying off persons sailing under it, not in the exercise of a belligerent right founded on the law of nations against an enemy, but of a municipal prerogative over British subjects. British jurisdiction is thus extended to neutral vessels in a situation where no laws can operate but the law of nations and the laws of the country to which the vessels belong, and a self-redress is assumed which, if British subjects were wrongfully detained and alone concerned, is that substitution of force for a resort to the responsible sovereign which falls under the definition of war." This violation of the rights of the U.S. as a neutral on the high seas and the illegal impressment of American citizens was a primary moral factor in Madison's request for a declaration of war by Congress. The President argued further that "thousands of American citizens, under the safeguard of public law and of their national flag, have been torn from their country and from everything dear to them; have been dragged on board ships of war for a foreign nation and exposed, under the severities of their discipline, to be exiled to the most distant and deadly climes, to risk their lives in the battles of their oppressors, and to be the melancholy instruments of taking away those of their own brethren."

Madison stated that his previous remonstrances sent to the British government had been in vain and had "passed without effect." He urged that the U.S. should seek its own redress as British cruisers continually violated "the rights and peace of our coasts. They hover over and harass our entering and departing commerce. To the most insulting pretensions they have added the most lawless proceedings in our very harbors, and have wantonly spilt American blood within the sanctuary of our territorial jurisdiction…." [3] As the British Orders in Council had sought to counter Napoleon's Continental System, both belligerents had sought to starve the other of neutral goods, especially food.

Madison's war message recognized this, saying that Britain had grossly interfered with neutral trade. "Under pretended blockades, without the presence of

[2] Madison's War Message to Congress, June 1, 1812, in Hunt, *Writings of James Madison,* VIII, pp. 192-201; see also *James Madison Writings,* edited by Jack N. Rakove (New York: The Library of America, 1999), pp. 685-692.

an adequate force and sometimes without the practicability of applying one, our commerce has been plundered in every sea, the great staples of our country have been cut off from their legitimate markets, and a destructive blow aimed at our agricultural and maritime interests." Madison conceded that because earlier efforts such as the Jefferson Embargo of 1807 had failed greater force was essential to avenge wrongs inflicted upon Americans.

Britain had been guilty of "laying waste our neutral trade," establishing "the sweeping system of blockades, under the name of Orders in Council, which has been molded and managed as might best suit its political views, its common jealousies, or the avidity of British cruisers." Madison would not allow U.S. commerce to be "sacrificed" to Britain's selfish European war aims and international ambitions to establish a "monopoly which she covets for her own commerce and navigation."[4]

Madison also held Britain accountable for stirring up trouble with the Indians on America's western frontier, stating that "In reviewing the conduct of Great Britain toward the United States our attention is necessarily drawn to the warfare just renewed by the savages on one of our extensive frontiers---warfare which is known to spare neither age nor sex and to be distinguished by features peculiarly shocking to humanity. It is difficult to account for the activity and combinations that have for some time been developing them selves among tribes in constant intercourse with British traders and garrisons without connecting their hostility with that influence and without recollecting the authenticated examples of such interpositions heretofore furnished by the officers and agents of that Government."[5]

Madison thus summarized the "spectacle of injuries and indignities" heaped upon the United States by Britain, stating that his previous "moderation and conciliation" had no effect and instead had been insultingly ignored. Smarting from these indignities, Madison continued to say that these injuries would continue unless redressed through war. "We behold our seafaring citizens still the daily victims of lawless violence, committed on the great common and highway of nations, even within sight of the country which owes them protection. We behold our vessels, freighted with the products of our soil and industry, or returning with the honest proceeds of them, wrested from their lawful destinations, confiscated by prize courts no longer the organs of public law but the

[3] Hunt, *Writings of James Madison,* pp. 193-194; Rakove, *James Madison Writings,* p. 686.
[4] Hunt, *Writings of James Madison,* p. 196; Rakove, *James Madison Writings,* p. 688.
[5] Hunt, *Writings of James Madison,* p. 198; Rakove, *James Madison Writings,* p. 690.

instruments of arbitrary edicts, and their unfortunate crews dispersed and lost, or forced or inveigled in British ports into British fleets…."[6]

Finally, because of these violations of American rights and national honor on the high seas, Madison declared that "we behold, in fine, on the side of Great Britain, a state of war against the United States, and on the side of the United States a state of peace toward Great Britain." It was time to redress this imbalance and answer blow for blow. "Whether the United States shall continue passive under these progressive usurpations and these accumulating wrongs, or, opposing force to force in defense of their national rights…" by declaring war was a choice for Congress which he recommended to their "early deliberations."[7] Congress did not disappoint President Madison, declaring war against Great Britain and her allies on June 18, 1812. America had contested British actions on the high seas as illegal and declared a war that would continue through 1815 and involve land and naval battles in the U.S., Canada, Nova Scotia and Bermuda.

The Twelfth Congress (1811-1813) that declared war by the close vote of 19 to 13 in the Senate and 79 to 49 in the House was also called the "War Hawks Congress" because a number of its members had loudly advocated reprisals against Britain for their atrocities on the high seas. The "War Hawks" were led by Speaker Henry Clay and future Vice President Richard Mentor Johnson of Kentucky, Peter B. Porter of western New York, future Vice President John C. Calhoun of South Carolina, and Felix Grundy of Tennessee.[8] These young enthusiasts for conflict blamed the British for troubles with the Indians on the western frontiers, especially exemplified by the agitations of Tecumseh and the bloody battle at Tippecanoe on November 7, 1811. They advocated the seizure of Canada from Britain and East and West Florida from Spain heralding the expansionist ideals of the frontiersmen. They expected that the West and the South would therefore join with the North to avenge America's national honor. Believing that Tecumseh had been aided by British agents in Canada with arms

---

[6] Hunt, *Writings of James Madison,* pp. 198-199; Rakove, *James Madison Writings,* p. 691.

[7] Hunt, *Writings of James Madison,* p. 199; Rakove, *James Madison Writings,* p. 691.

[8] Thomas A. Bailey, *A Diplomatic History of the American People* (New York: Appleton-Century-Crofts, 1964), pp. 131-146; W.H. Goodman, "The Origins of the War of 1812: A Survey of Changing Interpretations," *Mississippi Valley Historical Review,* XXVIII (1941): 171-186; G.R. Taylor, "Agrarian Discontent in the Mississippi Valley preceding the War of 1812," *Journal of Political Economy* XXXIX (1931): 471-505; Bradford Perkins, "George Canning, Great Britain, and the United States, 1807-1809," *American Historical Review* LXIII (1957): 1-22; Irving Brant, *James Madison: Commander in Chief, 1812-1836* (Indianapolis: Bobbs-Merrill, 1961); Reginald Horsman, *The Causes of the War of 1812* (New York: A.S. Barnes,1962); Bradford Perkins, *Prologue to War: England and the United States, 1805-1812* (Berkeley: University of California Press, 1961).

and ammunition they were determined to invade and conquer Canada to pacify the Great Lakes region and make safe the Old Northwest frontier. To win southern support, Florida should likewise be seized, as West Florida had been in 1810, justified by Madison's insistence that it had been part of the Louisiana Purchase. Seizure of East Florida (the present state of Florida) was declared necessary to stop runaway slaves, control the Seminole Indians, and punish Spain as an ally of Britain. Hence the "War Hawks" Congress was fueled by both maritime and frontier grievances that led to the War of 1812, which was declared in spite of the lack of military, naval, financial, or manufacturing preparedness for war. As Henry Clay had explained in a speech before Congress: "No man in the nation wants peace more than I, but I prefer the troubled ocean of war, demanded by the honor and independence of the country, with all its calamities and desolation, to the tranquil and putrescent pool of ignominious peace."[9] Emotions ran high as the United States entered "Mr. Madison's War."

The American strategy depended upon the calling up of the state militias to form a national fighting force. President Madison's original goal was to seize complete control of the Great Lakes region, capture Canada, and proceed to negotiations to eliminate America's maritime difficulties.

However the war on land started dismally for the U.S. troops seeking to invade Canada. The British Commander in Chief in North America was Lt. General Sir George Prevost who urged a defensive strategy to wear down the Americans until exhaustion would compel them to sue for peace on British terms. At war's beginning, the American regular army contained fewer than 12,000 men. Expansion to 35,000 was soon authorized but pay was low and the recruits were too few and too poorly trained. The British regular army forces in North America numbered only about 6,000 but they were more experienced and would be aided by the Canadian militia and some Indian warriors.

MORALE BOOSTING NAVAL SUCCESS

The British strategy began with a blockade of the U.S. coastline that devastated American agricultural exports but eventually had the effect of stimulating America's domestic factories and manufacturing. The British blockade was part of a larger defensive strategy because Britain's more important

---

9 *Annals of Congress,* 11 Congress, 1 session, I (February 22, 1810), p. 579. Clay's sentiments supporting war for national honor were echoed by Congressman John Adams Harper of New

theaters of war were in Europe, fighting against Napoleon. The American response to the British blockade was to send out hundreds of privateers (in effect pirates legalized in time of war) to attack British merchant ships especially in the West Indies. Further, President Madison sent two small squadrons under Commodore John Rodgers in the sloop *USS Hornet* to direct the U.S. naval opposition to the British blockade, and Captain Stephen Decatur in the brig *USS Argus* to patrol and protect American shipping off America's Atlantic coast. Decatur, who had fought so brilliantly in the War against Tripoli and the Barbary pirates, was later placed in command of the *USS United States.* By 1814 he was given command of a squadron composed of his flagship the *President,* the *Peacock,* the *Hornet,* and the *Tom Bowline.*

The British attempted to protect their merchant shipping to and from Canada and Nova Scotia to retain food and raw materials needed for their European war efforts, and to bottle up American ships through their blockade of American ports and thereby deprive Napoleon of U.S. food supplies and raw materials. The U.S. Navy was composed of far fewer ships than those of the British Royal Navy but a few American vessels were larger and heavier, 44-gun frigates compared with the British 38-gun frigates. The British had ninety-seven vessels off the U.S. coast in 1812, when the U.S. fleet totaled only twenty-two. Yet, early in the war the American Navy achieved several astonishing victories, the most famous of which was the engagement between the U.S. frigate *Constitution* with 55 guns and the British frigate *Guerrière* with 49 guns on August 19, 1812.

The *USS Constitution* commanded by Captain Isaac Hull was tracking the movement of British ships trading between Halifax and Bermuda, hoping to capture them as prizes and sell or seize their cargoes. Isaac Hull (1773-1843) was a distinguished naval officer and the nephew and adopted son of General William Hull, who ironically in that same month would become the greatest American military failure of 1812, when he surrendered Detroit to a vastly inferior British force. The confrontation between the *Constitution* and *Guerrière* took place 750 miles off the coast of Boston after the British had followed the American vessel from Chesapeake Bay. [10] Commander Hull brought up the *Constitution* to within

Hampshire who spoke of the need for war in order to achieve expansion of the U.S. in *Annals of Congress,* 12 Congress, 1 session I (January 4, 1812), p. 657.

[10] Henry Adams, "Naval Battles" in his book *The War of 1812* edited by Major H.A. DeWeerd (New York: Cooper Square Press, 1999 originally published Washington, D.C., 1944), pp. 39-43. This book consists of chapters taken from Henry Adams' nine-volume *History of the United States during the Administrations of Jefferson and Madison* published from 1889-1891; Theodore Roosevelt, *The Naval War of 1812* (New York: Modern Library, revised edition, 1999); Donald R. Hickey, *The War of 1812: A Forgotten Conflict* (Urbana: University of Illinois Press, 1990);

firing range of the *HMS Guerrière's* port side and his first broadside took down the enemy ship's main yard; another shot took out the mizzenmast and its fall ripped a hole in the ship's stern. Following additional broadsides, British Captain Dacres' ship suffered the loss of the foremast and mainmast and he was forced to surrender and ultimately he lost his life due to wounds. The Americans had lost seven men and the British 23. Hull was forced to burn the *Guerrière* because it was so badly damaged. His superior seamanship displayed in this most successful naval battle of the war earned him high regard. During this battle a seaman gave the victorious *Constitution* the name "Old Ironsides" as cannon shells seemed to bounce from her hull during the siege, causing the cry "Huzza, her sides are made of iron." Originally the *USS Constitution* had been authorized by Congress, designed by Joshua Humphreys, built in Boston by Edmund Hartt, and launched in 1797. The ship first saw service in the brief naval confrontations with the French during John Adams' presidency and then in the War with Tripoli against the Barbary pirates in 1804 during Thomas Jefferson's presidency. After its heroic action in the War of 1812, the *Constitution* was saved from demolition in 1830 because the poem "Old Ironsides" by Oliver Wendell Holmes immortalized the famed vessel, which is still preserved in Boston harbor.

In the next several months American morale was boosted by a series of naval victories over the world's greatest navy. Captain Decatur by then in the *USS United States* captured the *HMS Macedonian* in October 1812; Captain William Bainbridge commanding the *USS Constitution* captured the *HMS Java* in December off the coast of Brazil; Captain David Potter in the *USS Essex* in January 1813 successfully harassed British shipping in the Pacific before being captured in March 1814. Less successful was the effort by Captain James Lawrence, who cried out "Don't Give Up the Ship!" when he lay wounded and dying as his ship the *USS Chesapeake*, survivor of a peacetime British attack in 1807, was captured by the British off Boston in June 1813.

Despite these early victories and other heroic efforts, Britain slowly tightened its naval blockade of America's Atlantic coastline, strangling U.S. trade, and forcing American merchant and naval ships to remain in port. The blockade successfully allowed the British to ferry land troops to the North American war theaters and these forces became stronger especially after the first defeat of Napoleon in 1814. Halifax was the base for the Royal Navy in North America and Bermuda became increasingly expanded as a British base of naval and military operations as the Americans attempted to advance into Canada. British privateers

and J.C.A. Stagg, *Mr. Madison's War: Politics, Diplomacy, and Warfare in the Early Republic, 1783-1830* (Princeton: Princeton University Press, 1983).

sailed out of Halifax and Bermuda attempting to seize American ships as prizes. British Admiral Sir John Borlase Warren allowed licenses to be issued, however, to special New England vessels that were allowed to trade with London and the West Indies in violation of U.S. laws; this special treatment encouraged opposition against the American war effort to fester in New England, leading eventually to serious consideration of secession through the formation of the Essex Junto, a Federalist opposition group centered largely in Essex County, Massachusetts. Meanwhile, loyal and daring American privateers from other ports ran through the blockade and captured a total of 1,300 British vessels.

Gradually the British developed the strategy of engaging U.S. naval vessels only when they were assured of superior strength (usually in packs) as in January 1815 when four British vessels—*HMS Majestic, HMS Pomone*, *HMS Endymion*, and *HMS Tenedos* attacked and captured the single *USS President.*

DEMORALIZING BATTLES ON LAND

It was in the land battles especially in the region of the Great Lakes and Canadian theaters of war that the most dramatic battle action took place during the War of 1812. [11] Americans were sadly mistaken when they blithely assumed that the Americans would be seen as "liberators" when they marched into the British colony of Canada to achieve Canadian "independence" from Britain and to unite it with the United States. This conceit came to a rude awakening after American invasions of Upper and Lower Canada were repelled. To the Americans' surprise, the French Canadian populace too continued to seek British protection against the encroachments of Yankee land grabbers, just as their English elite Canadian counterparts did. The Great Lakes region was viewed as a potential military gateway into Canada due to its geography. Following the administration's strategy, the American forces attempted a three pronged attack into Canada using Lake Erie, the Niagara River between Lake Erie and Lake Ontario, and the Saint Lawrence River region, as well as Lake Champlain to the east between New York and Vermont. This entire region was viewed as a kind of 'soft underbelly' of

[11] Adams, *The War of 1812,* pp.1-37, 47-77, 169-188. For a discussion of the American militia see C. Edward Skeen, *Citizen Soldiers in the War of 1812* (Lexington: The University Press of Kentucky, 1999), pp. 4-184. For a Canadian perspective see Pierre Berton, *The Invasion of Canada, 1812-1813* (Boston: 1980 and Toronto: McClelland and Stewart, 1980 republished by Anchor Canada, 2001) and *Flames Across the Border: The Canadian-American Tragedy 1813-1814* (Boston and Toronto: McClelland and Stewart, 1981 republished by Anchor Canada, 2001).

Canada through which U.S. forces would scamper to seize Canada's major administrative cities—Montreal and Quebec.

During the first year of the war, however, the planned invasion and conquest of Canada would miss its mark and instead produce failures by American Generals William Hull at Detroit, Stephen Van Rensselaer and Alexander Smyth (at Black Rock near Buffalo, New York) on the Niagara River, and Henry Dearborn on Lake Champlain. In each of these theaters the American misjudgment of the tenacity of the Canadian defense was continually demonstrated by the determined Canadian resistance to the invaders.

Rather than fight in these western regions, the Americans would have been much wiser and probably more successful if they had focused all of their early efforts in the St. Lawrence Valley and thus broken British lines of communication and supply into Upper Canada. Canadians became bound more closely to their mother country and embraced anti-American attitudes that were later only partially dispelled by the conclusion of the Rush-Bagot Agreement of 1817 that offered a peaceful re-stabilization of the Great Lakes region. But this agreement was as yet far in the future and numerous battles ensued on the Great Lakes during the War of 1812, encouraged by naval rivalry and the desire for a water route to conquer Canada.

Even before the American settlers in Michigan were aware that the War of 1812 had been declared by Congress, the British had moved swiftly to secure a strategic advantage. The British forces at St. Joseph Island in Lake Huron learned that war had begun well before the American forces on Mackinac Island, (at the strait separating Lakes Michigan and Lake Huron) had received the word. On July 17, 1812 the British forced the surrender of Fort Mackinac, which persuaded the local Indians to side with Britain. This early demoralization of the Americans diminished their zeal and made them more cautious, even fearful, which had dramatic impact on the next military action.

The first major thrust aimed at Canada had begun July 12 when American Brigadier General William Hull (1753-1825) marched from Detroit with 2,500 militiamen onto Canadian soil, attacking at Sandwich (now Windsor, Ontario) and threatening that all Canadians and British should surrender immediately lest "the horrors and calamities of war will stalk before you." Hull made these pronouncements to protect non-combatants, and was over confident at least in part because of his faith in Thomas Jefferson's earlier boast that the capture of Canada was "a mere matter of marching." President Jefferson had appointed Hull governor of the Michigan Territory in 1805 and he was still in that position when he assumed military command in 1812. Hull was fifty-nine years old and had served capably in the Revolutionary War, but three decades had elapsed since then. Now he was charged by President Madison to defend Michigan and the surrounding areas and asked to take the point position in the invasion of Canada. Hull's troops threatened to kill all British soldiers who fought among Indian allies, and this bravado only strengthened his opponents' resolve.[12] Taken off guard by the news of the American loss of Fort Mackinac, Hull suffered reverses at Brownstown and Monguagon and decided to abandon the Canadian expedition and retreat to Fort Detroit. The officer who had directed the capture of Fort Mackinac and then forced the retreat of Hull's forces was British Major General Issac Brock.

Born on the Channel Island of Guernsey, and physically commanding at 6 feet 2 inches tall, Issac Brock was a veteran of the Battle of Copenhagen (1801) against Napoleon in Europe. He was assigned to Canada in 1802 as commander of an infantry regiment, promoted to Brigadier-General in 1807 by Canadian Governor-General Sir James Henry Craig, and given command of all British forces in Upper Canada by 1810. Brock had become acting Lieutenant Governor of the Province in 1811 when Craig returned to England to be replaced by Prevost. Brock had re-organized Canada's militia, supplies, fortifications around Quebec, and greatly improved defenses on the Great Lakes before the war with the U.S. had begun. Now he would direct the defense of Upper Canada, win early successes, and repel the first American invasion.[13]

Brock pursued Hull's troops to Fort Detroit where Hull surrendered without a fight on August 16, 1812. Although Brock's troops were seriously outnumbered, he fooled the Americans by dressing the Canadian militia in British regular uniforms to give the false impression that they were an experienced veteran force. He also employed large numbers of Indians as allies led by Tecumseh who had promised scalping and torture. Brock had even allowed a message asserting that he did not need reinforcements to fall into Hull's hands. He called on Hull to surrender, writing: "Sir: It is far from my inclination to join a war of extermination, but you must be aware that the numerous body of Indians who have attached themselves to my troops will be beyond my control the moment the

---

[12] Adams, *The War of 1812,* "The Invasion of Canada," p. 8; Department of War Papers are available on microfilm in the National Archives in Washington, D.C., Record Group 107 and include letters received and sent by the Secretary of War; also newspapers such as the *National Intelligencer* in Washington, D.C. and *Niles' Register* in Baltimore offer contemporary updates on the war's progress.

[13] Pierre Berton, *Capture of Detroit* (Toronto: McClelland and Stewart, 1991) and *Death of Issac Brock* (Toronto: McClelland and Stewart, 1991); W.K. Lamb, *The Hero of Upper Canada* (Toronto: Rous and Mann Press, 1962); Carl Benn, *The War of 1812,* (New York: Routledge, 2003); Walter R. Nursey, *The Story of Issac Brock: Hero, Defender and Savior of Upper Canada, 1812* (Toronto: William Briggs, 1909 republished 2006).

contest commences." Hull feared the possible Indian massacre of his troops, as well as the civilian population of Detroit, including his own family. After a brief bombardment of Fort Detroit by British cannon fire, accompanied by violent Indian war whoops, Hull agreed to Brock's demands on August 16, 1812. The capture of Detroit by Brock confirmed Tecumseh's alliance with the British, and Brock promised to secure an Indian homeland for the Shawnee in exchange for their further aid. Brock would be knighted for his success at Detroit. Following Hull's surrender President Madison appointed General William Henry Harrison supreme commander of the American Army of the Northwest. General William Hull's surrender of Detroit had taken place only three days before he would be somewhat avenged in another war theater by his nephew and adopted son Isaac Hull as commander of the *USS Constitution* over the British ship *Guerrière*. Young Hull may have helped to save the general from execution for treason, which was demanded by the politicians back east. In 1814, William Hull was sentenced by court martial to be shot for cowardice but this sentence was never carried out.

British forces and Indian allies led by General Brock, bolstered by his success in capturing Detroit, hurried eastward to confront American General Stephen Van Rensselaer who was planning to invade Canada from Lake Erie. Van Rensselaer was a Revolutionary War officer who had been Lieutenant Governor of New York from 1795 to 1801. Before the assault though, Governor-General Prevost negotiated a temporary armistice justified by the belated British repeal of the Orders in Council that had been a major cause of the American decision for war. When the armistice ended without peace, warfare resumed when Van Rensselaer crossed the Niagara River into Canada with advance forces and fixed a position on the steep slopes--the Queenston Heights--overlooking Queenston (later Queenstown) on October 13, 1812. Brock's British forces attacked the American position and, fortunately for American prospects for eventual victory, Brock was killed at age forty-three by American sharpshooters. Despite this loss, American disaster followed because the main body of New York militia had remained behind on the opposite side of the river and refused to leave their state. Brock died before he knew he had been knighted as "The British hero of Detroit."

With Brock fallen the British command was assumed by Major General Sir Roger Hale Sheaffe who enveloped the advance force of the Americans and captured them all—a force of 925 men including Lt. Colonel Winfield Scott. During this battle the rallying cry of British and Canadian forces was "Revenge for the General," their hero who had died so young. One of the sharpshooters who had killed Brock was his own brother who had become an American citizen. Mackenzie Brock was captured in the battle of Queenston Heights and was drawn and quartered for treason in revenge for his heroic brother's death. Thus the American "conquest of Canada" began with two disastrous defeats for the United States.

Brock's successor Sheaffe based his command of Upper Canada at the provincial capital at York (now Toronto).[14] He took both military and civilian control as administrator of the province. He endeavored to follow the cautious defensive tactics of Governor-General Prevost. Now Americans would seek revenge themselves for losses at Detroit and Queenston Heights.

The third and final prong of the American attempt to invade Canada was likewise a failure, though at least not a defeat. The senior general, Henry Dearborn, who had been Secretary of War throughout the Jefferson administrations, was ordered to lead an army through the Lake Champlain and Richelieu River route to threaten Montreal and Quebec. However he spent so much time trying to nationalize militia in rebellious New England states that by the time he neared the U.S. border his troops merely went into winter quarters and accomplished nothing militarily. On December 12, he wrote Madison with an appealing but entirely justified modesty that "it will be equally agreeable to me to employ such moderate talents as I possess in the service of my country, or to be permitted to retire to the shade of private life, and remain a mere but interested spectator of passing events."[15] Thus the opening year of the War of 1812 proved to be filled with major reverses on land and certainly the thrust into Canada had been foiled.

NOT CHANGING HORSES IN MID-STREAM

During the spring of 1812 President Madison maneuvered—although some would say that he was the one who was maneuvered—the United States into a declaration of war against an international military and naval giant that was infinitely better armed and financed and with an infinitely greater power than anything that the United States could mount, even considering Britain's added burden of simultaneous war against the other international giant, France. Then the months of August through October were devastated by the overwhelming and inexcusable defeats at Fort Detroit and Queenston Heights and the frustrating non-action at Lake Champlain.

---

[14] Frank H. Severance, ed., "Documents Relating to the War of 1812: The Letter-book of General Roger Hale Sheaffe," Buffalo Historical Society Publications (Buffalo, NY: 1913), 17: 271-381.

[15] Henry Adams, *History of the United States,* VI, pp. 360-361.

Meanwhile he was required to survive an electoral sideshow to retain the presidency. To no one's surprise the Republican Congressional caucus nominated Madison for re-election by 82-0. Several other states followed suit, but New York nominated its "favorite son" De Witt Clinton, mayor of New York City from 1803 to 1815 and nephew of that perennial presidential aspirant George Clinton. The aged Vice President died in April 1812, removing one possible impediment from De Witt's path.

Historian Henry Adams, grandson and great-grandson of American presidents, sagely remarked that "No canvass for the Presidency was ever less creditable than that of De Witt Clinton." Because the beleaguered Federalists were too weakened to mount a viable candidacy, they had to rest their hopes to overthrow the despised Madison on a rebel Republican. So they conspired with Clinton in 1812 just as they had with Aaron Burr in 1804. The Federalists kept their support as secret as possible because they were too well aware that their open support would be the kiss of death for their covert ally. So while Clinton was promising New England Federalists that he would quickly negotiate an end to the war with Great Britain, he was promising Republicans in the South and West that, unlike Madison, he would conduct the war efficiently and would soon seize Canada by warfare rather than diplomacy. As with his electoral victory in 1808 and with the declaration of war in June 1812, Madison's re-election was again a demonstration of the strength and popularity of his and Jefferson's Republican Party in the South and West. Madison won 128 electoral votes to Clinton's 89. Clinton prevailed in all of the seaboard states from New Hampshire to Delaware, including his home state, marking the first successful fissure in the Virginia-New York political coalition constructed by Madison, Jefferson and Burr in the 1790s. Madison carried Pennsylvania, Vermont, half of Maryland and all states to the south and west.[16]

ANNUAL MESSAGE OF THE COMMANDER IN CHIEF

The outcome of the election was expected but not known with certainty when Madison presented his fourth annual message on November 4. His goal was to rally his troops' and his nation's perseverance and resolve. He outlined the "pressures and vicissitudes" of the war at great length while summarizing

---

[16] Henry Adams, *History of the United States,* VI, p. 410; Irving Brant, *James Madison: Commander in Chief* (Indianapolis: Bobbs-Merrill, 1961), pp. 96-113; Ketcham, *James Madison,* pp. 544-545.

American war aims and the painful reversals they had encountered in the concluding month of 1812, as he wrote:

> "Fellow Citizens of the Senate and of the House of Representatives:
>
> On our present meeting it is my first duty to invite your attention to the providential favors which our country has experienced in the unusual degree of health dispensed to its inhabitants, and in the rich abundance with which the earth has rewarded the labors bestowed on it. In the successful cultivation of other branches of industry, and in the progress of general improvement favorable to the national prosperity, there is just occasion also for our mutual congratulations and thankfulness.
>
> With these blessings are necessarily mingled the pressures and vicissitudes incident to the state of war into which the United States have been forced by the perseverance of a foreign power in its system of injustice and aggression.
>
> Previous to its declaration it was deemed proper, as a measure of precaution and forecast, that a considerable force should be placed in the Michigan Territory with a general view to its security, and, in the event of war, to such operations in uppermost Canada as would intercept the hostile influence of Great Britain over the savages, obtain the command of the lake on which that part of Canada borders, and maintain cooperating relations with such forces as might be most conveniently employed against other parts.
>
> Brigadier-General Hull was charged with this provisional service, having under his command a body of troops composed of regulars and of volunteers from the State of Ohio. Having reached his destination after his knowledge of the war, and possessing discretionary authority to act offensively, he passed into the neighboring territory of the enemy with a prospect of easy and victorious progress. The expedition, nevertheless, terminated unfortunately, not only in a retreat to the town and fort of Detroit, but in the surrender of both and of the gallant corps commanded by that officer. The causes of this painful reverse will be investigated by a military tribunal.
>
> A distinguishing feature in the operations which preceded and followed this adverse event is the use made by the enemy of the merciless savages under their influence. Whilst the benevolent policy of the United States invariably recommended peace and promoted civilization among that wretched portion of the human race, and was making exertions to dissuade them from taking either side in the war, the enemy has not scrupled to call to his aid their ruthless ferocity, armed with the horrors of those instruments of carnage and torture which are known to spare neither age nor sex. In this outrage against the laws of honorable war and against the feelings sacred to humanity the British commanders can not resort to a plea of retaliation, for it is committed in the face of our example. They can not mitigate it by calling it a self-defense against men in arms, for it embraces the most shocking

butcheries of defenseless families. Nor can it be pretended that they are not answerable for the atrocities perpetrated, since the savages are employed with a knowledge, and even with menaces, that their fury could not be controlled. Such is the spectacle which the deputed authorities of a nation boasting its religion and morality have not been restrained from presenting to an enlightened age.

The misfortune at Detroit was not, however, without a consoling effect. It was followed by signal proofs that the national spirit rises according to the pressure on it. The loss of an important post and of the brave men surrendered with it inspired everywhere new ardor and determination. In the States and districts least remote it was no sooner known than every citizen was ready to fly with his arms at once to protect his brethren against the blood-thirsty savages let loose by the enemy on an extensive frontier, and to convert a partial calamity into a source of invigorated efforts.

This patriotic zeal, which it was necessary rather to limit than excite, has embodied an ample force from the States of Kentucky and Ohio and from parts of Pennsylvania and Virginia. It is placed, with the addition of a few regulars, under the command of Brigadier-General Harrison, who possesses the entire confidence of his fellow soldiers, among whom are citizens, some of them volunteers in the ranks, not less distinguished by their political stations than by their personal merits. The greater portion of this force is proceeding in relieving an important frontier post, and in several incidental operations against hostile tribes of savages, rendered indispensable by the subservience into which they had been seduced by the enemy - a seduction the more cruel as it could not fail to impose a necessity of precautionary severities against those who yielded to it.

At a recent date an attack was made on a post of the enemy near Niagara by a detachment of the regular and other forces under the command of Major-General Van Rensselaer, of the militia of the State of New York. The attack, it appears, was ordered in compliance with the ardor of the troops, who executed it with distinguished gallantry, and were for a time victorious; but not receiving the expected support, they were compelled to yield to re-enforcements of British regulars and savages. Our loss has been considerable, and is deeply to be lamented. That of the enemy, less ascertained, will be the more felt, as it includes among the killed the commanding general [Major General Issac Brock], who was also the governor of the Province, and was sustained by veteran troops from un-experienced soldiers, who must daily improve in the duties of the field.

Our expectation of gaining the command of the Lakes by the invasion of Canada from Detroit having been disappointed, measures were instantly taken to provide on them a naval force superior to that of the enemy. From the talents and activity of the officer charged with this object everything that can be done may be expected. Should the present season not admit of complete success, the progress made will insure for the next a naval ascendancy where it is essential to our permanent peace with and control over the savages.

Among the incidents to the measures of the war I am constrained to advert to the refusal of the governors of Maine and Connecticut to furnish the required detachments of militia toward the defense of the maritime frontier. The refusal was founded on a novel and unfortunate exposition of the provisions of the Constitution relating to the militia. The correspondences which will be laid before you contain the requisite information on the subject. It is obvious that if the authority of the United States to call into service and command the militia for the public defense can be thus frustrated, even in a state of declared war and of course under apprehensions of invasion preceding war, they are not one nation for the purpose most of all requiring it, and that the public safety may have no other resource than in those large and permanent military establishments which are forbidden by the principles of our free government, and against the necessity of which the militia were meant to be a constitutional bulwark.

On the coasts and on the ocean the war has been as successful as circumstances inseparable from its early stages could promise. Our public ships and private cruisers, by their activity, and, where there was occasion, by their intrepidity, have made the enemy sensible of the difference between a reciprocity of captures and the long confinement of them to their side.

Our trade, with little exception, has safely reached our ports, having been much favored in it by the course pursued by a squadron of our frigates under the command of Commodore Rodgers, and in the instance in which skill and bravery were more particularly tried with those of the enemy the American flag had an auspicious triumph.

The frigate *Constitution*, commanded by Captain [Isaac] Hull, after a close and short engagement completely disabled and captured a British frigate, gaining for that officer and all on board a praise which can not be too liberally bestowed, not merely for the victory actually achieved, but for that prompt and cool exertion of commanding talents which, giving to courage its highest character, and to the force applied its full effect, proved that more could have been done in a contest requiring more.

Anxious to abridge the evils from which a state of war can not be exempt, I lost no time after it was declared in conveying to the British Government the terms on which its progress might be arrested, without awaiting the delays of a formal and final pacification, and our chargé d'affaires at London was at the same time authorized to agree to an armistice founded upon them. These terms required that the Orders in Council should be repealed as they affected the United States, without a revival of blockades violating acknowledged rules, and that there should be an immediate discharge of American sea men from British ships, and a stop to impressment from American ships, with an understanding that an exclusion of the sea men of each nation from the ships of the other should be stipulated, and that the armistice should be improved into a definitive and comprehensive adjustment of depending controversies.

Although a repeal of the orders susceptible of explanations meeting the views of this Government had taken place before this pacific advance was communicated to that of Great Britain, the advance was declined from an avowed repugnance to a suspension of the practice of impressments during the armistice, and without any intimation that the arrangement proposed with regard to sea men would be accepted. Whether the subsequent communications from this Government, affording an occasion for reconsidering the subject on the part of Great Britain, will be viewed in a more favorable light or received in a more accommodating spirit remains to be known. It would be unwise to relax our measures in any respect on a presumption of such a result The documents from the Department of State which relate to this subject will give a view also of the propositions for an armistice which have been received here, one of them from the authorities at Halifax and in Canada, the other from the British Government itself through Admiral Warren, and of the grounds on which neither of them could be accepted.

Our affairs with France retain the posture which they held at my last communications to you. Notwithstanding the authorized expectations of an early as well as favorable issue to the discussions on foot, these have been procrastinated to the latest date. The only intervening occurrence meriting attention is the promulgation of a French decree purporting to be a definitive repeal of the Berlin and Milan decrees. This proceeding, although made the ground of the repeal of the British Orders in Council, is rendered by the time and manner of it liable to many objections.

The final communications from our special minister to Denmark afford further proofs of the good effects of his mission, and of the amicable disposition of the Danish government. From Russia we have the satisfaction to receive assurances of continued friendship, and that it will not be affected by the rupture between the United States and Great Britain. Sweden also professes sentiments favorable to the subsisting harmony.

With the Barbary Powers, excepting that of Algiers, our affairs remain on the ordinary footing. The consul-general residing with that Regency has suddenly and without cause been banished, together with all the American citizens found there. Whether this was the transitory effect of capricious despotism or the first act of predetermined hostility is not ascertained. Precautions were taken by the consul on the latter supposition.

The Indian tribes not under foreign instigations remain at peace, and receive the civilizing attentions which have proved so beneficial to them.

With a view to that vigorous prosecution of the war to which our national faculties are adequate, the attention of Congress will be particularly drawn to the insufficiency of existing provisions for filling up the military establishment. Such is the happy condition of our country, arising from the facility of subsistence and the high wages for every species of occupation, that notwithstanding the augmented inducements provided at the last session, a partial success only has attended the recruiting service. The deficiency has been necessarily supplied during the campaign by other than regular troops, with all the inconveniences and expense incident to them. The remedy lies in establishing more favorably for the private soldier the proportion between his recompense and the term of his enlistment, and it is a subject which can not too soon or too seriously be taken into consideration.

The same insufficiency has been experienced in the provisions for volunteers made by an act of the last session. The recompense for the service required in this case is still less attractive than in the other, and although patriotism alone has sent into the field some valuable corps of that description, those alone who can afford the sacrifice can be reasonably expected to yield to that impulse.

It will merit consideration also whether as auxiliary to the security of our frontiers corps may not be advantageously organized with a restriction of their services to particular districts convenient to them, and whether the local and occasional services of mariners and others in the sea port towns under a similar organization would not be a provident addition to the means of their defense.

I recommend a provision for an increase of the general officers of the Army, the deficiency of which has been illustrated by the number and distance of separate commands which the course of the war and the advantage of the service have required.

And I can not press too strongly on the earliest attention of the Legislature the importance of the reorganization of the staff establishment with a view to render more distinct and definite the relations and responsibilities of its several departments. That there is room for improvements which will materially promote both economy and success in what appertains to the Army and the war is equally inculcated by the examples of other countries and by the experience of our own.

A revision of the militia laws for the purpose of rendering them more systematic and better adapting them to emergencies of the war is at this time particularly desirable.

Of the additional ships authorized to be fitted for service, two will be shortly ready to sail, a third is under repair, and delay will be avoided in the repair of the residue. Of the appropriations for the purchase of materials for ship building, the greater part has been applied to that object and the purchase will be continued with the balance. The enterprising spirit which has characterized our naval force and its success, both in restraining insults and depredations on our coasts and in reprisals on the enemy, will not fail to recommend an enlargement of it.

There being reason to believe that the act prohibiting the acceptance of British licenses is not a sufficient guard against the use of them, for purposes favorable to the interests and views of the enemy, further provisions on that subject are highly important. Nor is it less so that penal enactments should be provided for cases of corrupt and perfidious intercourse with the enemy, not amounting to treason nor yet embraced by any statutory provisions.

A considerable number of American vessels which were in England when the revocation of the Orders in Council took place were laden with British manufactures under an erroneous impression that the non-importation act would immediately cease to operate, and have arrived in the United States. It did not appear proper to exercise on unforeseen cases of such magnitude the powers vested in the Treasury Department to mitigate forfeitures without previously affording to Congress an opportunity of making on the subject such provision as they may think proper. In their decision they will doubtless equally consult what is due to equitable considerations and to the public interest.

The receipts into the Treasury during the year ending on the 30th of September last have exceeded $16.5 million, which have been sufficient to defray all the demands on the Treasury to that day, including a necessary reimbursement of near $3 million of the principal of the public debt. In these receipts is included a sum of near $5.85 million, received on account of the loans authorized by the acts of the last session; the whole sum actually obtained on loan amounts to $11 million, the residue of which, being receivable subsequent to the 30th of September last, will, together with the current revenue, enable us to defray all the expenses of this year.

The duties on the late unexpected importations of British manufactures will render the revenue of the ensuing year more productive than could have been anticipated.

The situation of our country, fellow citizens, is not without its difficulties, though it abounds in animating considerations, of which the view here presented of our pecuniary resources is an example. With more than one nation we have serious and unsettled controversies, and with one, powerful in the means and habits of war, we are at war. The spirit and strength of the nation are nevertheless equal to the support of all its rights, and to carry it through all its trials. They can be met in that confidence.

Above all, we have the inestimable consolation of knowing that the war in which we are actually engaged is a war neither of ambition nor of vain glory; that it is waged not in violation of the rights of others, but in the maintenance of our own; that it was preceded by a patience without example under wrongs accumulating without end, and that it was finally not declared until every hope of averting it was extinguished by the transfer of the British scepter into new hands clinging to former councils, and until declarations were reiterated to the last hour, through the British envoy here, that the hostile edicts against our commercial rights and our maritime independence would not be revoked; nay, that they could not be revoked without violating the obligations of Great Britain to other powers, as well as to her own interests.

To have shrunk under such circumstances from manly resistance would have been a degradation blasting our best and proudest hopes; it would have struck us from the high rank where the virtuous struggles of our fathers had placed us, and have betrayed the magnificent legacy which we hold in trust for future generations. It would have acknowledged that on the element which forms three-fourth of the globe we inhabit, and where all independent nations have equal and common rights, the American people were not an independent people, but colonists and vassals.

It was at this moment and with such an alternative that war was chosen. The nation felt the necessity of it, and called for it. The appeal was accordingly made, in a just cause, to the Just and All-powerful Being who holds in His hand the chain of events and the destiny of nations.

It remains only that, faithful to ourselves, entangled in no connections with the views of other powers, and ever ready to accept peace from the hand of justice, we prosecute the war with united counsels and with the ample faculties of the nation until peace be so obtained and as the only means under the Divine blessing of speedily obtaining it." [17]

James Madison

As the first year of the War of 1812 came to a close, Madison and his generals re-directed their efforts to re-capture Detroit and outflank British strength throughout North America. President Madison promised that the United States would continue to offer "manly resistance" to British violations of American rights through the war and thus preserve for future generations "our best and proudest hopes."

---

[17] James Madison Annual Message to Congress November 4, 1812 in Hunt, *Writings of James Madison,* VIII, pp. 221-231.

Chapter 11

DEPTHS TO HEIGHTS: WASHINGTON, NEW ORLEANS, GHENT

Fortunately for the survival of President Madison and the United States, warfare was not then usually waged actively during winter. American forces under General William Henry Harrison, a future President, would attempt and fail in January 1813 to recoup the losses of General William Hull in the Northwest, but other than this successful defense, the British would bide their time until spring. This gave Madison time to introduce more competence into his Cabinet and to find more active and competent generals to lead American campaigns. His war ministers, Secretary of Defense Dr. William Eustis and Secretary of Navy Paul Hamilton, had been qualified for their positions only so long as the United States remained at peace. On December 3, 1812, the day on which the electoral college confirmed Madison's second term, Eustis succumbed to a long-term barrage by Congress and submitted his resignation. This was his second attempt for he offered to resign months earlier when war was declared. This time Madison accepted with regret because he was more supportive of Eustis than nearly anyone else in Washington. He respected Eustis for his contributions in the Revolution and blamed Congress for not authorizing the assistants that might have allowed Eustis to succeed.

At the end of December Madison asked Hamilton to resign. Even though the only American military successes in 1812 had occurred on the high seas, and Hamilton's naval strategy had some positive effect, his widely known public intoxication over-shadowed his achievements, usually rendering him effective for only half-days. Madison became convinced that Congress would authorize the ships that were so desperately needed only if he could replace Hamilton with an official who could be guaranteed to use them effectively.

Replacing Hamilton with William Jones was a coup for Madison. A sea captain and merchant, Jones had also been a Congressman from Philadelphia. He served with distinction until late in 1814, even acting in place of the presumably irreplaceable Albert Gallatin as Secretary of the Treasury so that Gallatin could participate in the successful Treaty of Ghent that would bring an unbelievably successful end to this painful war. He resigned in 1814 only because his commercial interests had failed while he worked long days in Washington.

Replacing the Secretary of War was a very different story. Monroe acted competently while Madison searched, but he refused to accept the position permanently, in part because the position seemed to lessen rather than strengthen his presidential ambitions.[1] After the position was rejected also by General Henry Dearborn and Congressman William H. Crawford, Madison finally turned with anguish to General John Armstrong of New York, who ironically had the goal of supplanting Monroe in the presidential succession. Armstrong was also suspect because of his involvement in an abortive mutiny against General Washington in the Revolutionary War, as well as his indolent and sometimes insubordinate performance as U.S. Minister to France while Madison was Secretary of State. Armstrong had convinced many that he could not be trusted, and his irascible temper too often antagonized those around him, yet he was at least aggressive and well organized, sadly a step up from Eustis. The Senate seemed to share Madison's reservations, when it voted only 18 to 15 to approve the appointment. Ironically Armstrong's administrative career would end with his presidential ambitions in August 1814 when he was held in large part responsible for the disastrous sacking and burning of Washington D.C. Monroe would at the same time enhance his reputation by replacing Armstrong while continuing to serve as Secretary of State.

More Frustration in the Old Northwest

The American surrender of Detroit and the Michigan Territory in August 1812 gave the British control of much of the region tributary to the Upper Great Lakes in the American heartland, causing great alarm. Thus the strategy of President Madison shifted in 1813 to the American Northwest with attention focused on Brigadier General Harrison's plans to re-take Fort Detroit as a base for another attempted Canadian invasion. Detroit was defended by General Henry Procter.

---

[1] Brant, *James Madison: Commander in Chief,* pp. 125-126.

American planning went horribly awry on January 22, 1813 when Harrison was defeated at the River Raisin near Frenchtown in which nearly 400 Americans were killed. It soon become remembered as a "Massacre" after Procter failed to restrain his Indian allies from scalping thirty wounded and unarmed American prisoners in a drunken night raid when they were not properly guarded. This provided some rationalization, though months after the fact, for the terror of Indian warfare that had led to the abject surrender of Detroit by General Hull without even being attacked.[2] "Remember the River Raisin" would long remain a rallying battle cry for Harrison's rebuilt forces, comparable to Texans' call to "Remember the Alamo" prior to the Mexican-American War. Inspired by this success, Procter's regulars and Tecumseh's Indian forces unsuccessfully attacked Fort Meigs, near Toledo, Ohio, in April-May and again in July. The American troops bitterly defended their homes in the Ohio Valley and deeply resented foreign intrusions on their soil, especially the harsh tactics of using the local Indians as their fearsome allies. The war in the Northwest had reached a fevered pitch but after a failed attempt by Tecumseh and Procter to capture the American Fort Stephenson on the Sandusky River in Ohio, the British abandoned their entire Ohio campaign.

CONTROLLING THE LAKES

A timely and fortunate naval victory on Lake Erie enhanced American opportunities to re-capture Detroit. Youthful American Master-Commandant Oliver Hazard Perry had built a fleet on Lake Erie that won a decisive naval victory on September 10, 1813 finally giving Americans control of this vital waterway.[3] Perry had seen action in the naval Quasi-War with France and in the War against Tripoli. Commodore Isaac Chauncey, who had commissioned a comparable fleet on Lake Ontario, assigned Perry the command of Lake Erie. At Erie, Pennsylvania, Perry constructed a ten-ship fleet that he based at Put-in-Bay north of Sandusky. He was challenged there by British fleet commander Captain Robert Heriot Barclay, whose six vessels drastically outgunned Perry's nine ships. Perry's only hope against the British long-range cannonading was to move to

---

[2] Henry Adams, *The War of 1812,* pp. 47-57; Helen Koutras Bozonelis, *Primary Source Accounts of the War of 1812* (Berkeley Heights, NJ: Enslow Publishers, 2006), p. 37; A. J. Langguth, *Union 1812: The Americans Who Fought the Second War of Independence* (New York: Simon & Schuster, 2006).

[3] C.S. Forester, *The Age of Fighting Sail,* (Sandwich, MA: Chapman Billies, 1956), pp. 153, 173-174, 178-86, 188.

close quarters. His heroic victory off the Ohio coast proved to be the decisive naval engagement of the War of 1812 and made him a Commodore at the tender age of twenty-eight.

Perry's flagship in this crucial fresh water battle was the *USS Lawrence* which flew a flag with the inscription "Don't Give Up the Ship." This was the dying command of Captain James Lawrence as he fell during the capture of the *Chesapeake* near Boston, only three months earlier on June 1. At the Battle of Lake Erie, Perry transferred from his badly damaged flagship to the *Niagara* to direct the final broadside bombardment into the British ships *Detroit* and *Queen Charlotte* that were commanded by British fleet commander Barclay. Perry then returned to his ship the *Lawrence* to receive the formal British surrender. Barclay, who had lost an arm fighting with Nelson at the Battle of Trafalgar in 1805, lost his other arm in this action. The victorious American Perry sent a message to General Harrison that would resound through American history: "We have met the enemy and they are ours, two ships, two brigs, one schooner, and one sloop." The exultant John Adams declared that "Perry's triumph is enough to revive Mr. Madison if he was in the last stage of a consumption." He added that the President, whom he had often opposed politically, should "long continue to live and be well, and to see the good work of the war prospering in his hands, for a more necessary war was never undertaken." So much for historians who have described this as the "unnecessary war!"[4]

British General Henry Procter's position in Detroit had become untenable because the Lakes were essential for supply of his troops. He attempted to retreat to Lake Ontario with General Harrison in hot pursuit. Ferried by Perry's victorious fleet, Harrison pursued Procter along Lake St. Clair and the Thames River. Procter was overtaken on October 5 near Thamesville where Harrison won the famed Battle of the Thames where Tecumseh was killed.[5] British regulars fought on the British left side while the Shawnee allies fought on the right side. A mounted charge directed by Harrison was led by Colonel Richard Mentor Johnson whose cavalry broke through the British ranks and forced their surrender. The Indians led by Tecumseh attempted to fight on, listening to his bellows for inspiration, but when he fell they disappeared into the forests. This proved to be a turning of the tide, for the Americans recaptured the Detroit region and remained there throughout the remainder of the war. Harrison would be heralded as the

[4] Brant, *James Madison: Commander in Chief,* pp. 214-215; William S. Dudley, ed., *The Naval War of 1812: A Documentary History* (Washington, D.C.: Naval History Center, Department of the Navy, 1985).

[5] Forester, *The Age of Fighting Sail,* pp. 186-188.

'hero of the Battle of the Thames'. American troops had answered the British forces, in Madison's words exchanging "blow for blow," to avenge American national honor. The battles of Lake Erie and the Thames had recaptured the American Old Northwest and catapulted both General Harrison and Colonel Johnson to future political prominence—Harrison briefly as President in 1841 and Johnson as Vice President in 1837-1841 with President Martin Van Buren. Shawnee defeats were memorialized in their careers, the former for 'Tippecanoe and Tyler Too' and the latter for the phrase 'Rumpsey Dumpsey, He Killed Tecumseh'. In addition to successful election in 1840 and one month in office, Harrison was territorial governor of Indiana from 1801 to 1813, briefly held seats in the U.S. House of Representatives and Senate, and was the Whig candidate for President in 1836 as well as 1840. Johnson served ten years in the House and ten years in the Senate.

Niagara Campaigns of 1813

American strategy called for seizing and maintaining control of the Great Lakes and the Saint Lawrence River pathway from the Atlantic to the interior to safeguard communications. The Americans were as successful in stopping British incursions into the Niagara River area as they were in impeding the British offensives in the Great Lakes.

On April 27, 1813 American troops had seized and eventually burned the British city of York (now Toronto) which was the administrative capital of Upper Canada.[6] Its defender General Roger Hale Sheaffe was ordered by Governor Prevost to strengthen the Canadian militia but he was able to raise only one battalion rather than the three that were needed, due to inadequate funding. Thus despite his efforts, York was inadequately prepared for the American attack. When an American fleet landed 1,700 men, on April 26, Sheaffe could counter with only 700 British regulars and militia, augmented by fewer than 100 Indians.

---

[6] Forester, *The Age of Fighting Sail*, pp. 155-159; D.B. Read, *The Lieutenant-Governors of Upper Canada and Ontario, 1792-1899* (Toronto: William Briggs, 1900); C.P. Stacey, *The Battle of Little York* (Toronto: Toronto Historical Board, rev. ed. 1977); J. Mackay Hitsman, *The Incredible War of 1812: A Military History* (Toronto: University of Toronto Press, 1965); See an article on the letter-book kept by Sir Roger Hale Sheaffe through the War of 1812 edited by Frank H. Severance, "Documents Relating to the War of 1812: the letter-book of General Roger Hale Sheaffe," Buffalo Historical Society (Buffalo, New York, 1913), 17: 271-381; Henry J. Morgan, *Sketches of Celebrated Canadians and Persons Connected with Canada* (London: Hunter, Rose, 1934); Walter R. Borneman, *1812: The War that Forged a Nation* (New York: HarperCollins, 2004).

He attempted a cautious delaying action in order to preserve his troops, before deciding to move his administration to Kingston. Thus Sheaffe abandoned the provincial capital of Upper Canada. He attempted to take necessary official papers with him and to blowup stores of powder to prevent their capture and use by the Americans. His goal was to "carry off the kernel, leaving only the shell." He was nevertheless later removed by Governor General Prevost for inadequate defensive preparations and was recalled to London.

The British would never forgive the Americans for burning government buildings in York and would later capture and burn Washington, D.C. in retribution. In the siege of York, the British Parliament buildings and the main library were destroyed. The British regarded this as a depraved act, while the Americans justified it as essential to break the enemy's morale and force concessions at the peace table. Kingston remained in British hands however, and continued to supply British troops fighting in Upper Canada from points in Lower Canada. On May 27, 1813 American forces aided by Isaac Chauncey's fleet, captured Fort George near where the Niagara River falls spectacularly into Lake Ontario. Despite a brief counter-offensive at Stoney Creek on June 5, the British abandoned the entire Niagara frontier to the Americans. The British Fort George was destroyed as the Americans took up defensive positions at Fort Niagara.

When American General George McClure attacked and burned Newark (now called Niagara-on-the-Lake) on December 10 the wanton destruction of Canadian citizens and their homes it further inflamed British sensibilities, and would later be used to justify wanton retribution against American cities, eventually including even Washington D.C. The British attacked Fort Niagara on December 19, 1813 and burned three New York towns, Youngstown, Manchester, and Lewiston, in retaliation for the destruction of Fort George. Now holding the upper hand, the British crossed the Niagara River and even burned much of Buffalo.

Madison's Account of Military Events of 1813

Shortly before these inflammatory attacks against civilians, the Commander in Chief summed up military strategy and events through 1813 in his fifth State of the Union Address to Congress, on December 7. President Madison demonstrated an informed knowledge of the battle action and troop operations throughout this war that would prove to be the principal focus of his entire second administration. Madison declared:

"Fellow-Citizens of the Senate and House of Representatives:

In meeting you at the present interesting conjuncture it would have been highly satisfactory if I could have communicated a favorable result to the mission charged with negotiations for restoring peace. It was a just expectation, from the respect due to the distinguished Sovereign who had invited them by his offer of mediation, from the readiness with which the invitation was accepted on the part of the United States, and from the pledge to be found in an act of their Legislature for the liberality which their plenipotentiaries would carry into the negotiations, that no time would be lost by the British Government in embracing the experiment for hastening a stop to the effusion of blood. A prompt and cordial acceptance of the mediation on that side was the less to be doubted, as it was of a nature not to submit rights or pretensions on either side to the decision of an umpire, but to afford merely an opportunity, honorable and desirable to both, for discussing and, if possible, adjusting them for the interest of both.

The British cabinet, either mistaking our desire of peace for a dread of British power or misled by other fallacious calculations, has disappointed this reasonable anticipation. No communications from our envoys having reached us, no information on the subject has been received from that source; but it is known that the mediation was declined in the first instance, and there is no evidence, notwithstanding the lapse of time, that a change of disposition in the British councils has taken place or is to be expected. Under such circumstances a nation proud of its rights and conscious of its strength has no choice but an exertion of the one in support of the other.

To this determination the best encouragement is derived from the success with which it has pleased the Almighty to bless our arms both on the land and on the water. Whilst proofs have been continued of the enterprise and skill of our cruisers, public and private, on the ocean, and a trophy gained in the capture of a British by an American vessel of war, after an action giving celebrity to the name of the victorious commander, the great inland waters on which the enemy were also to be encountered have presented achievements of our naval arms as brilliant in their character as they have been important in their consequences.

On Lake Erie, the squadron under command of Captain Perry having met the British squadron of superior force, a sanguinary conflict ended in the capture of the whole. The conduct of that officer, adroit as it was daring, and which was so well seconded by his comrades, justly entitles them to the admiration and gratitude of their country, and will fill an early page in its naval annals with a victory never surpassed in luster, however much it may have been in magnitude.

On Lake Ontario the caution of the British commander, favored by contingencies, frustrated the efforts of the American commander to bring on a decisive action. Captain Chauncey was able, however, to establish ascendancy in that important theater, and to prove by the manner in which he effected everything possible that opportunities only were wanted for a more shining display of his own talents and the gallantry of those under his command.

The success on Lake Erie having opened a passage to the territory of the enemy, the officer commanding the Northwestern army transferred the war thither, and rapidly pursuing the hostile troops, fleeing with their savage associates, forced a general action, which quickly terminated in the capture of the British and dispersion of the savage force.

This result is signally honorable to Major-General Harrison, by whose military talents it was prepared; to Colonel Johnson and his mounted volunteers, whose impetuous onset gave a decisive blow to the ranks of the enemy, and to the spirit of the volunteer militia, equally brave and patriotic, who bore an interesting part in the scene; more especially to the chief magistrate of Kentucky, at the head of them, whose heroism signalized in the war which established the independence of his country, sought at an advanced age a share in hardships and battles for maintaining its rights and its safety.

The effect of these successes has been to rescue the inhabitants of Michigan from their oppressions, aggravated by gross infractions of the capitulation which subjected them to a foreign power; to alienate the savages of numerous tribes from the enemy, by whom they were disappointed and abandoned, and to relieve an extensive region of country from a merciless warfare which desolated its frontiers and imposed on its citizens the most harassing services.

In consequences of our naval superiority on Lake Ontario and the opportunity afforded by it for concentrating our forces by water, operations which had been provisionally planned were set on foot against the possessions of the enemy on the St. Lawrence. Such, however, was the delay produced in the first instance by adverse weather of unusual violence and continuance and such the circumstances attending the final movements of the army, that the prospect, at one time so favorable, was not realized.

The cruelty of the enemy in enlisting the savages into a war with a nation desirous of mutual emulation in mitigating its calamities has not been confined to any one quarter. Wherever they could be turned against us no exertions to effect it have been spared. On our southwestern border the Creek tribes, who, yielding to our persevering endeavors, were gradually acquiring more civilized habits, became the unfortunate victims of seduction. A war in that quarter has been the consequence, infuriated by a bloody fanaticism recently propagated among them. It was necessary to crush such a war before it could spread among the contiguous tribes and before it could favor enterprises of the enemy into that vicinity. With this view a force was called into the service of the United States from the States of Georgia and Tennessee, which, with the nearest regular troops and other corps from the Massachusetts Territory, might not only chastise the savages into present peace but make a lasting impression on their fears.

The progress of the expedition, as far as is yet known, corresponds with the martial zeal with which it was espoused, and the best hopes of a satisfactory issue are authorized by the complete success with which a well-planned enterprise was executed against a body of hostile savages by a detachment of the volunteer militia of Tennessee, under the gallant command of General Coffee, and by a still more important victory over a larger body of them, gained under the immediate command of Major-General Jackson, an officer equally distinguished for his patriotism and his military talents.

The systematic perseverance of the enemy in courting the aid of the savages in all quarters had the natural effect of kindling their ordinary propensity to war into a passion, which, even among those best disposed toward the United States, was ready, if not employed on our side, to be turned against us. A departure from our protracted forbearance to accept the services tendered by them has thus been forced upon us. But in yielding to it the retaliation has been mitigated as much as possible, both in its extent and in its character, stopping far short of the example of the enemy, who owe the advantages they have occasionally gained in battle chiefly to the number of their savage associates, and who have not controlled them either from their usual practice of indiscriminate massacre on defenseless inhabitants or from scenes of carnage without a parallel on prisoners to the British arms, guarded by all the laws of humanity and of honorable war. For these enormities the enemy are equally responsible, whether with the power to prevent them they want the will or with the knowledge of a want of power they still avail themselves of such instruments.

In other respects the enemy are pursuing a course which threatens consequences most afflicting to humanity. A standing law of Great Britain naturalizes, as is well known, all aliens complying with conditions limited to a shorter period than those required by the United States, and naturalized subjects are in war employed by her Government in common with native subjects. In a contiguous British Province regulations promulgated since the commencement of the war compel citizens of the United States being there under certain circumstances to bear arms, whilst of the native emigrants from the United States, who compose much of the population of the Province, a number have actually borne arms against the United States within their limits, some of whom, after having done so, have become prisoners of war, and are now in our possession. The British commander in that Province, nevertheless, with the sanction, as appears, of his Government, thought proper to select from American prisoners of war and send to Great Britain for trial as criminals a number of individuals who had emigrated from the British dominions long prior to the state of war between the two nations, who had incorporated themselves into our political society in the modes recognized by the law and the practice of Great Britain, and who were made prisoners of war under the banners of their adopted country, fighting for its rights and its safety. The protection due to these citizens requiring an effectual interposition in their behalf, a like number of British prisoners of war were put into confinement, with a notification that they would experience whatever violence might be committed on the American prisoners of war sent to Great Britain. It was hoped that this necessary consequence of the step unadvisedly taken on the part of Great Britain would have led her Government to reflect on the inconsistencies of its conduct, and that a sympathy with the British, if not with the American, sufferers would have arrested the cruel career opened by its example.

This was unhappily not the case. In violation both of consistency and of humanity, American officers and non-commissioned officers in double the number of the British soldiers confined here were ordered into close confinement, with formal notice that in the event of a retaliation for the death which might be inflicted on the prisoners of war sent to Great Britain for trial the officers so confined would be put to death also. It was notified at the same time that the commanders of the British fleets and armies on our coasts are instructed in the same event to proceed with a destructive severity against our towns and their inhabitants.

That no doubt might be left with the enemy of our adherence to the retaliatory resort imposed on us, a correspondent number of British officers, prisoners of war in our hands, were immediately put into close confinement to abide the fate of those confined by the enemy, and the British Government was apprised of the determination of this Government to retaliate any other proceedings against us contrary to the legitimate modes of warfare.

It is fortunate for the United States that they have it in their power to meet the enemy in this deplorable contest as it is honorable to them that they do not join in it but under the most imperious obligations, and with the humane purpose of effectuating a return to the established usages of war. The views of the French Government on the subjects which have been so long committed to negotiation have received no elucidation since the close of your late session. The minister plenipotentiary of the United States at Paris had not been enabled by proper opportunities to press the objects of his mission as prescribed by his instructions.

The militia being always to be regarded as the great bulwark of defense and security for free states, and the Constitution having wisely committed to the national authority a use of that force as the best provision against an unsafe military establishment, as well as a resource peculiarly adapted to a country having the extent and the exposure of the United States, I recommend to Congress a revision of the militia laws for the purpose of securing more effectually the services of all detachments called into the employment and placed under the Government of the United States. It will deserve the consideration of Congress also whether among other improvements in the militia laws justice does not require a regulation, under due precautions, for defraying the expense incident to the first assembling as well as the subsequent movements of detachments called into the national service.

To give to our vessels of war, public and private, the requisite advantage in their cruises, it is of much importance that they should have, both for themselves and their prizes, the use of the ports and markets of friendly powers. With this view, I recommend to Congress the expediency of such legal provisions as may supply the defects or remove the doubts of the Executive authority, to allow to the cruisers of other powers at war with enemies of the United States such use of the American ports as may correspond with the privileges allowed by such powers to American cruisers.

During the year ending on the 30th of September last the receipts into the Treasury have exceeded $37.5 million, of which near $24 million were the produce of loans. After meeting all demands for the public service there remained in the Treasury on that day near $7 million. Under the authority contained in the act of the 2nd of August last for borrowing $7.5 million, that sum has been obtained on terms more favorable to the United States than those of the preceding loans made during the present year. Further sums to a considerable amount will be necessary to be obtained in the same way during the ensuing year, and from the increased capital of the country, from the fidelity with which the public engagements have been kept and the public credit maintained, it may be expected on good grounds that the necessary pecuniary supplies will not be wanting.

The expenses of the current year, from the multiplied operations falling within it, have necessarily been extensive; but on a just estimate of the campaign in which the mass of them has been incurred the cost will not be found disproportionate to the advantages which have been gained. The campaign has, indeed, in its latter stages in one quarter been less favorable than was expected, but in addition to the importance of our naval success the progress of the campaign has been filled with incidents highly honorable to the American arms.

The attacks of the enemy on Craney Island, on Fort Meigs, on Sacketts Harbor, and on Sandusky have been vigorously and successfully repulsed; nor have they in any case succeeded on either frontier excepting when directed against the peaceable dwellings of individuals or villages unprepared or undefended.

On the other hand, the movements of the American Army have been followed by the reduction of York, and of Forts George, Erie, and Malden; by the recovery of Detroit and the extinction of the Indian war in the West, and by the occupancy or command of a large portion of Upper Canada. Battles have also been fought on the borders of the St. Lawrence, which, though not accomplishing their entire objects, reflect honor on the discipline and prowess of our soldiery, the best auguries of eventual victory. In the same scale are to be placed the late successes in the South over one of the most powerful, which had become one of the most hostile also, of the Indian tribes.

It would be improper to close this communication without expressing a thankfulness in which all ought to unite for the abundance; for the preservation of our internal tranquility, and the stability of our free institutions, and, above all, for the light of divine truth and the protection of every man's conscience in the enjoyment of it. And although among our blessings we can not number an exemption from the evils of war, yet these will never be regarded as the greatest of evils by the friends of liberty and of the rights of nations. Our country has before preferred them to the degraded condition which was the alternative when the sword was drawn in the cause which gave birth to our national independence, and none who contemplate the magnitude and feel the value of that glorious event will shrink from a struggle to maintain the high and happy ground on which it placed the American people.

With all good citizens the justice and necessity of resisting wrongs and usurpations no longer to be borne will sufficiently outweigh the privations and sacrifices inseparable from a state of war. But it is a reflection, moreover, peculiarly consoling, that, whilst wars are generally aggravated by their baneful effects on the internal improvements and permanent prosperity of the nations engaged in them, such is the favored situation of the United States that the calamities of the contest into which they have been compelled to enter are mitigated by improvements and advantages of which the contest itself is the source.

If the war has increased the interruptions of our commerce, it has at the same time cherished and multiplied our manufactures so as to make us independent of all other countries for the more essential branches for which we ought to be dependent on none, and is even rapidly giving them an extent which will create additional staples in our future intercourse with foreign markets. If much treasure has been expended, no inconsiderable portion of it has been applied to objects durable in their value and necessary to our permanent safety. If the war has exposed us to increased spoliations on the ocean and to predatory incursions on the land, it has developed the national means of retaliating the former and of providing protection against the latter, demonstrating to all that every blow aimed at our maritime independence is an impulse accelerating the growth of our maritime power.

By diffusing through the mass of the nation the elements of military discipline and instruction; by augmenting and distributing warlike preparations applicable to future use; by evincing the zeal and valor with which they will be employed and the cheerfulness with which every necessary burden will be borne, a greater respect for our rights and a longer duration of our future peace are promised than could be expected without these proofs of the national character and resources. The war has proved moreover that our free Government, like other free governments, though slow in its early movements, acquires in its progress a force proportioned to its freedom, and that the union of these States, the guardian of the freedom and safety of all and of each, is strengthened by every occasion that puts it to the test.

In fine, the war, with all its vicissitudes, is illustrating the capacity and the destiny of the United States to be a great, a flourishing, and a powerful nation, worthy of the friendship which it is disposed to cultivate with all others, and authorized by its own example to require from all an observance of the laws of justice and reciprocity. Beyond these their claims have never extended, and in contending for these we behold a subject for our congratulations in the daily testimonies of increasing harmony throughout the nation, and may humbly repose our trust in the smiles of Heaven on so righteous a cause."7

James Madison

BACK AND FORTH IN 1814

When war resumed in the summer of July 1814, some of the bright young officers recently appointed by the Madison administration would be tested and they rose to the occasion. Major General Winfield Scott quickly became a much-needed hero following his exchange from the captivity that began at Queenston. On July 3 he and Brigadier General Jacob Brown captured Fort Erie, giving Americans a welcome birthday present for Independence Day. Scott pressed ahead to defeat the British at the Chippewa River on July 5. Next Scott's troops engaged the British in a brutal battle at Lundy's Lane near Niagara Falls on July 25.[8] They then fell back to defend Fort Erie. Wounds received at the battle of Lundy's Lane prevented Scott from being sent later to join another rising military star, Andrew Jackson, at New Orleans.

Meanwhile the British were able to gain mastery of Lake Ontario by constructing what was then the largest ship of its kind, the 112-gun *HMS St. Lawrence* commanded by Sir James Lucas Yeo. This see-saw struggle in the Great Lakes region would continue throughout the duration of the war.

The British had kept the supply lines and communications open with Montreal in July by capturing Ogdensburg, an American site that controlled shipping on the St. Lawrence River. This foiled an American attempt by Major General Wade Hampton and General James Wilkinson to capture Montreal. Shortly after this failure, Wilkinson resigned his command and the American army was finally free of an officer who had long been insubordinate and incompetent, a spy for other nations while commanding American troops and

---

7 Hunt, *Writings of James Madison,* VIII, pp. 265-276.

8 Adams, *The War of 1812,* pp. 169-187, 188-200.

drawing American pay. President Madison is justly criticized for allowing Wilkinson to command men for so long. He had held the highest military command as early as 1796, and even became territorial governor of Louisiana, despite involvement in the Burr conspiracy, courts of inquiry and even court martial following the unnecessary deaths of his troops resulting from his incompetent decisions regarding encampment in Louisiana. Although he was acquitted by court martial Madison had ample cause to remove him. Preceding presidents had also been at fault, but the stakes were seldom so high.[9]

In 1814 the strategy of the war was slowly changing with both sides seeking military advantages for the sake of winning better terms in peace negotiations. In Europe, Napoleon abdicated in April following his first defeat at the Battle of Nations, thereby freeing seasoned and freshly trained British troops for action in North America. With Napoleon set aside, Great Britain was able to turn full attention to the American conflict. But they too were war weary, after years of bitter warfare in Europe. They wanted a swift end to military problems everywhere. Peace negotiations had begun in earnest in June 1814 at Ghent, Belgium, but both sides were eager to inflict severe military damages to press for peace on their terms. With the goal of an early end to warfare, but with the greatest possible gains, Great Britain rushed an additional 15,000 British troops commanded by four of the Duke of Wellington's veteran commanders to fight against the Americans and force them quickly to terms.

Limited fighting continued in the western regions of the Great Lakes through that year with activity on Lake Huron. Canadian Lt. Colonel Robert McDougall recaptured Fort Mackinac and from there sent forces that on July 20 captured Fort Prairie Du Chien in far off Wisconsin. The British held this relatively isolated region in the far west and countered the attempts of Major Zachary Taylor, another future President, to re-capture this area.

The naval battles on the high seas that had provided inspiring boosts of morale to Americans during the early months of the war were few and far between throughout 1813 and 1814. Blockades by the superior British navy bottled up American naval vessels in port, limiting American naval successes largely to privateers preying on British commerce and the fresh-water fleets of the Great Lakes.

9 C. Edward Skeen, "James Wilkinson," in Rutland, *James Madison Encyclopedia,* pp. 449-451; Rutland, *The Presidency of James Madison,* pp. 57-59, 136-138.

WASHINGTON, D.C. IN FLAMES

In August 1814 the British hit the United States with what they were sure would be the one-punch knockout that would immediately force the Americans to terms. For centuries the culminating blow in wartime was the seizure and often razing of the opponent's capital. Governor-General Prevost prompted this major campaign by suggesting that Washington be burned in retaliation for the burning of York. Rear Admiral George Cockburn initiated the campaign when he carried troops under General Robert Ross in seventeen ships that had just become available because of British successes in the Peninsular War. After blockading Chesapeake Bay and raiding Virginia's coastal towns, the British focused on their main objective, Washington, D.C., which had been the American capital city for only fourteen years.

British commanders were well aware of the importance of Chesapeake Bay and its proximity and easy naval access to Washington, D.C. American naval defenses proved inadequate when the British neutralized the squadron led by American commander Joshua Barney on August 19-20. This opened the way to Washington for the British. The Battle of Bladensburg was the final defensive stand for the Americans composed of 6,000 Maryland and District militia, Barney's seamen who had re-grouped, and too few regular U.S. forces.[10] The Americans were led by Major General William Winder but could not turn back the tide of Ross's experienced tide of British regulars who marched rapidly into Georgetown and central Washington, D.C.

President Madison and his administrative staff including Secretary of War Armstrong, Secretary of State James Monroe, and Attorney General Richard Rush were briefly involved militarily in the field of battle in Washington before fleeing to Virginia. Dolley Madison carefully stored White House valuables in her possessions and made her own escape as her husband was at the front. She removed from the White House the most widely recognized portrait of George Washington, that by Gilbert Stuart, as well as important presidential papers.[11]

---

[10] Adams, *The War of 1812,* pp. 215-227; Red Reeder, *The Story of 1812* (New York: Duell, Sloan and Pearce, 1960); Anne Todd, *The War of 1812* (Mankato, Minnesota: Capstone Books, 2001); David Stephen Heidler, *The War of 1812* (Westport, CT: Greenwood Press, 2002); John R. Elting, *Amateurs, to Arms! The Military History of the War of 1812* (New York: Da Capo, 1995); John K. Mahon, *The War of 1812* (Gainesville: The University of Florida, 1972); Donald R. Hickey, *The War of 1812: A Forgotten Conflict* (Urbana: University of Illinois Press, 1990).

[11] Zall, *Dolley Madison,* pp. 56-64; "Dolley Payne Todd Madison" by Irving Brant, in Edward T. James, ed., *Notable American Women* (Cambridge, MA: Belknap Press of Harvard University, 1971), II, pp. 483-485.

General Ross's forces stormed into Washington, D.C., in the evening of August 24, occupied the White House, and sat down to devour a dinner that had been prepared for President Madison, before setting fire to the presidential home.[12] The White House, the Capitol, and the Treasury building were burned by British troops. Fortunately a hurricane drenched the destructive flames before the entire city could go up in flames. But the U.S. Treasury and the buildings holding the records of the Department of State and Department of War, as well as the office of the *National Intelligencer,* the journalistic voice of the Jefferson and Madison administrations, were all in ruins. Secretary of War Armstrong was later compelled to resign for failing to make adequate preparations for the defense of Washington.

Ross's forces marched next toward Baltimore where the general was killed.[13] Naval reinforcements sent by sea to occupy Baltimore failed when Americans successfully defended Fort Henry, which guarded the entrance to the harbor. The bombardment of Fort Henry with shells exploding in the darkness overhead and the sight of the inspiring American flag still flying gave rise to the words of the famed "Star-Spangled Banner" by Francis Scott Key.

James and Dolley Madison hovered in Virginia near Washington, not knowing that they were separated by only a few miles. The President angrily rejected a proposal for capitulation and spent several days largely on horseback attempting with Monroe to organize the defense. The Madisons were reunited in Virginia. The President returned to Washington on August 27. The Madisons were given the use of Octagon House by the French minister. In place of the Capitol, the President directed that the Post Office and Patent Office, which had survived the fire though not the hurricane, be repaired to serve as meeting rooms for the Senate and House of Representatives. When Secretary of War Armstrong finally returned with explanations for his failings, Madison ordered him to leave Washington and appointed James Monroe in his place.[14]

After the destruction inflicted on Washington in August 1814, British North American commander Sir George Prevost was ordered to strike further into the U.S. with an attack on upper New York and Vermont. Prevost moved south along Lake Champlain to invade New York with 14,000 troops, all seasoned veterans of

---

[12] Anthony S. Pitch, *The Burning of Washington, The British Invasion of 1814* (Annapolis: Naval Institute Press, 1998), pp. 86-153; Randy Schultz, *Washington Ablaze: The War of 1812* (Vero Beach, FL: Rourke Publishers, 2007); Don Nardo, *The War of 1812* (San Diego, CA: Lucent Books, 2000).

[13] Ibid., pp. 180-218; Irvin Molotsky, *The Flag, The Poet, & The Song, The Story of the Star-Spangled Banner* (New York: Dutton, 2001), pp. 44-149.

[14] Ketcham, *James Madison,* pp. 582-583.

Wellington's successful campaigns in Spain in the Peninsular War. They were opposed by American General Alexander Macomb who commanded only 2,500 militia and 1,500 regular U.S. troops. The Americans had taken up a defensive position on the Saranac River near Plattsburg, New York, where they were supported by a small flotilla commanded by Thomas Macdonough. In the famous Battle of Plattsburg Bay on September 11, Prevost's main naval support led by the British naval commander Captain George Downie was soundly defeated by Macdonough, with Downie being killed, in large part because Prevost failed to cross the Saranac River to support Downie.[15] Lacking his naval support, Prevost turned back to Canada where criticism of his failure forced his recall to London. There he died before a scheduled court martial inquiry. The British lost through these circumstances their most knowledgeable former wartime leader in North America. Prevost's defeat at Plattsburg contributed to British willingness to negotiate for peace and even weakened their demands at the peace table. Most important for Madison's reputation, it gave the first slim rationalization for calling Mr. Madison's War a victory. In combination with Andrew Jackson's stunning victory at New Orleans five months later, it would convince Americans that their victories had forced the greatest world power to acquiesce to the Treaty of Ghent.

Nearly a month after Washington was burned and shortly after the Battle of Plattsburg, President Madison presented his unusually brief Sixth State of the Union Address to Congress on September 20, 1814, a most unusual date for this address because of the extraordinary circumstances. He described the operations of the war, the need for money to prosecute it successfully, and the overtures made for peace. He demonstrated that he was still firmly in command and could press on to a successful conclusion of the War of 1812.

> "Fellow-Citizens of the Senate and House of Representatives:
>
> Notwithstanding the early day which had been fixed for your session of the present year, I was induced to call you together still sooner, as well that any inadequacy in the existing provisions for the wants of the Treasury might be supplied as that no delay might happen in providing for the result of the negotiations on foot with Great Britain, whether it should require arrangements adapted to a return of peace or further and more effective provisions for prosecuting the war.
>
> That result is not yet known. If, on the one hand, the repeal of the Orders in Council and the general pacification in Europe, which withdrew the

---

15 Adams, *The War of 1812,* pp. 201-214; David G. Fitz-Enz, *The Final Invasion, Plattsburg, the War of 1812's Most Decisive Battle* (New York: Cooper Square Press, 2001), pp. 1-197. Richard Morris, *The War of 1812* (Minneapolis: Lerner Publications, 1985).

occasion on which impressments from American vessels were practiced, suggest expectations that peace and amity may be re-established, we are compelled, on the other hand, by the refusal of the British Government to accept the offered mediation of the Emperor of Russia, by the delays in giving effect to its own proposal of a direct negotiation, and, above all, by the principles and manner in which the war is now avowedly carried on to infer that a spirit of hostility is indulged more violent than ever against the rights and prosperity of this country.

This increased violence is best explained by the two important circumstances that the great contest in Europe for an equilibrium guaranteeing all its States against the ambition of any has been closed without any check on the over-bearing power of Great Britain on the ocean, and it has left in her hands disposable armaments, with which, forgetting the difficulties of a remote war with a free people, and yielding to the intoxication of success, with the example of a great victim to it before her eyes, she cherishes hopes of still further aggrandizing a power already formidable in its abuses to the tranquility of the civilized and commercial world.

But whatever may have inspired the enemy with these more violent purposes, the public councils of a nation more able to maintain than it was to require its independence, and with a devotion to it rendered more ardently by the experience of its blessings, can never deliberate but on the means most effectual for defeating the extravagant views or unwarrantable passions with which alone the war can now be pursued against us.

In the events of the present campaign the enemy, with all his augmented means and wanton use of them, has little ground for exultation, unless he can feel it in the success of his recent enterprises against this metropolis and the neighboring town of Alexandria, from both of which his retreats were as precipitate as his attempts were bold and fortunate. In his other incursions on our Atlantic frontier his progress, often checked and chastised by the martial spirit of the neighboring citizens, has had more effect in distressing individuals and in dishonoring his arms than in promoting any object of legitimate warfare; and in the two instances mentioned, however deeply to be regretted on our part, he will find in his transient success, which interrupted for a moment only the ordinary business at the seat of Government, no compensation for the loss of character with the world by his violations of private property and by his destruction of public edifices protected as monuments of the arts by the laws of civilized warfare.

On our side we can appeal to a series of achievements which have given new luster to the American arms. Besides the brilliant incidents in the minor operations of the campaign, the splendid victories gained on the Canadian side of the Niagara by the American forces under Major-General Brown and Brigadiers Scott and Gaines have gained for these heroes and their emulating companions the most unfading laurels, and, having triumphantly tested the progressive discipline of the American soldiery, have taught the enemy that the longer he protracts his hostile efforts the more certain and decisive will be his final discomfiture.

On our southern border victory has continued also to follow the American standard. The bold and skillful operations of Major-General Jackson, conducting troops drawn from the militia of the States least distant, particularly Tennessee, have subdued the principal tribes of hostile savages, and, by establishing a peace with them, preceded by recent and exemplary chastisement, has best guarded against the mischief of their co-operations with the British enterprises which may be planned against that quarter of our country. Important tribes of Indians on our northwestern frontier have also acceded to stipulations which bind them to the interests of the United States and to consider our enemy as theirs also.

In the recent attempt of the enemy on the city of Baltimore, defended by militia and volunteers, aided by a small body of regulars and sea men, he was received with a spirit which produced a rapid retreat to his ships, whilst concurrent attack by a large fleet was successfully resisted by the steady and well-directed fire of the fort and batteries opposed to it.

In another recent attack by a powerful force on our troops at Plattsburg, of which regulars made a part only, the enemy, after a perseverance for many hours, was finally compelled to seek safety in a hasty retreat, with our gallant bands pressing upon them.

On the Lakes, so much contested throughout the war, the great exertions for the command made on our part have been well repaid. On Lake Ontario our squadron is now and has been for some time in a condition to confine that of the enemy to his own port, and to favor the operations of our land forces on that frontier. A part of the squadron on Lake Erie has been extended into Lake Huron, and has produced the advantage of displaying our command on that lake also. One object of the expedition was the reduction of Mackinaw, which followed with the loss of a few brave men, among whom was an officer justly distinguished for his gallant exploits. The expedition, ably conducted by both the land and the naval commanders, was otherwise highly valuable in its effects. On Lake Champlain, where our superiority had for some time been undisputed, the British squadron lately came into action with the American, commanded by Captain Macdonough. It issued in the capture of the whole of the enemy's ships. The best praise for this officer and his intrepid comrades is in the likeness of his triumph to the illustrious victory which immortalized another officer and established at a critical moment our command of another lake.

On the ocean the pride of our naval arms had been amply supported. A second frigate has indeed fallen into the hands of the enemy, but the loss is hidden in the blaze of heroism with which she was defended. Captain Porter, who commanded her, and whose previous career had been distinguished by daring enterprise and by fertility of genius, maintained a sanguinary contest against two ships, one of them superior to his own, and under other severe disadvantages, until humanity tore down the colors which valor had nailed to the mast. This officer and his brave comrades have added much to the rising glory of the American flag, and have merited all the effusions of gratitude which their country is ever ready to bestow on the champions of its rights and of its safety. Two smaller vessels of war have also become prizes to the enemy, but by a superiority of force which sufficiently vindicates the reputation of their commanders, whilst two others, one commanded by Captain Warrington, the other by Captain Blakely, have captured British ships of the same class with a gallantry and good conduct which entitle them and their companions to a just share in the praise of their country. In spite of the naval force of the enemy accumulated on our coasts, our private cruisers also have not ceased to annoy his commerce and to bring their rich prizes into our ports, contributing thus, with other proofs, to demonstrate the incompetency and illegality of a blockade the proclamation of which is made the pretext for vexing and discouraging the commerce of neutral powers with the United States.

To meet the extended and diversified warfare adopted by the enemy, great bodies of militia have been taken into service for the public defense, and great expenses incurred. That the defense everywhere may be both more convenient and more economical, Congress will see the necessity of immediate measures for filling the ranks of the Regular Army and of enlarging the provision for special corps, mounted and un-mounted, to be engaged for longer periods of service than are due from the militia. I earnestly renew, at the same time, a recommendation of such changes in the system of the militia as, by classing and disciplining for the most prompt and active service the portions most capable of it, will give to that great resource for the public safety all the requisite energy and efficiency.

The monies received into the Treasury during the nine months ending on the 30th day of June last amounted to $32 millions, of which near $11 millions were the proceeds of the public revenue and the remainder derived from loans. The disbursements for public expenditures during the same period exceeded $34 millions, and left in the Treasury on the first day of July near $5 millions. The demands during the remainder of the present year already authorized by Congress and the expenses incident to an extension of the operations of the war will render it necessary that large sums should be provided to meet them.

From this view of the national affairs Congress will be urged to take up without delay as well the subject of pecuniary supplies as that of military force, and on a scale commensurate with the extent and the character which the war has assumed. It is not to be disguised that the situation of our country calls for its greatest efforts. Our enemy is powerful in men and in money, on the land and on the water. Availing himself of fortuitous advantages, he is aiming with his undivided force a deadly blow at our growing prosperity, perhaps at our national existence. He has avowed his purpose of trampling on the usages of civilized warfare, and given earnests of it in the plunder and wanton destruction of private property. In his pride of maritime dominion and in his thirst of commercial monopoly he strikes with peculiar animosity at the progress of our navigation and of our manufactures. His barbarous policy has not even spared those monuments of the arts and models of taste with which our country had enriched and embellished its infant metropolis. From such an adversary hostility in its greatest force and in its worst forms may be looked for.

The American people will face it with the undaunted spirit which in their revolutionary struggle defeated his unrighteous projects. His threats and his barbarities, instead of dismay, will kindle in every bosom an indignation not to be extinguished but in the disaster and expulsion of such cruel invaders. In providing the means necessary the National Legislature will not distrust the heroic and enlightened patriotism of its constituents. They will cheerfully and proudly bear every burden of every kind which the safety and honor of the nation demand. We have seen them everywhere paying their taxes, direct and indirect, with the greatest promptness and alacrity. We see them rushing with enthusiasm to the scenes where danger and duty call. In offering their blood they give the surest pledge that no other tribute will be withheld.

Having forborne to declare war until to other aggressions had been added the capture of near one thousand American vessels and the impressment of thousands of American sea faring citizens, and until a final declaration had been made by the Government of Great Britain that her hostile orders against our commerce would not be revoked but on conditions as impossible as unjust, whilst it was known that these orders would not otherwise cease but with a war which had lasted nearly twenty years, and which, according to appearances at that time, might last as many more; having manifested on every occasion and in every proper mode a sincere desire to arrest the effusion of blood and meet our enemy on the ground of justice and reconciliation, our beloved country, in still opposing to his persevering hostility all its energies, with an undiminished disposition toward peace and friendship on honorable terms, must carry with it the good wishes of the impartial world and the best hopes of support from an omnipotent and kind Providence."[16]

James Madison

The President wished to continue to press the enemy in the war's battle action to win military advantages that would bring Britain to America's terms at the peace table. Like Jefferson's, Madison's writing style was elegant and impassioned as he praised Americans for their wartime sacrifices—bearing "every burden of every kind" by paying their taxes and offering their blood in the fight

[16] Hunt, *Writings of James Madison,* VIII, pp. 306-312.

for national honor and the protection of American rights and freedoms. His was a refined plea to persevere to win the war.

SHAKING UP THE ADMINISTRATION

During 1814 Madison had to shake up his cabinet even more severely than in the previous year when ineffective Secretaries of War and Navy were replaced by the extremely controversial John Armstrong and the extremely effective William Jones. Armstrong had been appointed despite strong objections from Madison's principal advisors, Monroe and Gallatin. There had been frequent criticism of Armstrong for months that could no longer be ignored after the virtual non-defense of Washington. Monroe, whose own presidential ambitions might be threatened by those of Armstrong, succeeded Armstrong as Secretary of War in August 1814 while continuing to serve also as Secretary of State. He had trouble deciding which office was the best pathway to the presidency during time of war so now he had both. Colonel James Monroe had long fancied himself a military leader despite limited experience. Neither he nor Madison had achieved laurels during the escape from Washington, but at least Monroe did not have military responsibilities at the time of the disaster. Thomas Jefferson regretted that his young neighbor assumed so thankless a position. He wrote that he "much regretted" Monroe's acceptance of the war department. "Not that I know a person who I think would better conduct it. But, conduct it ever so wisely, it will be a sacrifice of yourself. Were an angel from Heaven to undertake that office, all our miscarriages would be ascribed to him. Raw troops, no troops, insubordinate militia, want of arms, want of money, want of provisions, all will be charged to want of management in you."[17] He did not add that Armstrong's fall provided living proof of the hazards of this position.

Navy Secretary Jones had also taken on double duty for an even longer period, from June 1813 to February 1814, because Treasury Secretary Albert Gallatin was on leave when he sailed for St. Petersburg in response to a proposed mediation of the war by Russian Tsar Alexander. Madison, Gallatin and most of all Jones could not have imagined that Gallatin would be bouncing around through Europe for a year and a half in search of the site of negotiations until they were finally consummated at Ghent in December 1814 by Great Britain.

[17] Thomas Jefferson to Colonel James Monroe, January 1, 1815, Andrew A. Lipscomb, ed., *The Writings of Thomas Jefferson* (Washington, D.C.: Thomas Jefferson Memorial Association, 1905), XIV, p. 229; Ketcham, *James Madison,* p. 583.

Gallatin's long absence and Armstrong's abrasive personality contributed to the initial change of office holders in February 1814. Confronted by a pending Senate resolution that recognized that the Treasury position was vacant because it was unlikely that Gallatin would resume his duties, Madison was forced hurriedly to fill that position and several others. The ideal candidate, Alexander J. Dallas, a Philadelphia attorney and admirer of Madison, Jones, and Gallatin, privately expressed his willingness to serve with *them* but never with Armstrong. Pressed to appoint someone immediately, Madison had named George W. Campbell, a Tennessee senator who had not demonstrated particular interest or qualifications for the position. Fortunately the dismissal of Armstrong, and the prompt resignation by Campbell when he realized how far he was in over his head, enabled Dallas to accept a second offer. Dallas contributed significantly to the peacetime success of the Madison administration, lessening the severe financial burdens that he inherited and developing plans for a second national bank. Henry Dearborn was appointed again as Secretary of War on March 1 to replace the exhausted Monroe in the War department, but he was rejected the very next day by the Senate. The former president pro tempore of the Senate, William H. Crawford of Georgia, was immediately appointed and confirmed, but he was currently sailing from France where he had been U.S. minister since 1813, after he refused to replace William Eustis as Secretary of War. Fortunately Crawford accepted when he landed in America. On October 21, he succeeded Dallas as Treasury Secretary. Crawford would therefore be both Madison's fourth and final Secretary of War as well as his fourth and final Secretary of Treasury.[18]

Another Cabinet change in February was the appointment of Madison's close friend and admirer Comptroller Richard Rush as Attorney General in place of William Pinckney, who resigned due to increasing pressures for the Attorney General to reside in Washington. A powerful advocate in court as well as in diplomacy, Pinkney had replaced Caesar Augustus Rodney as Attorney General in 1811 when that worthy refused to reduce his legal practice in Delaware. Pinkney had served since then while continuing his lucrative practice in Baltimore, which at least was much closer than Wilmington, Delaware. Finally in December, William Jones was forced by physical exhaustion and fiscal ruin to resign as Secretary of the Navy. Madison appointed Boston merchant Benjamin W. Crowninshield, who at first declined but then relented when he received the commission.[19]

---

[18] Brant, *James Madison: Commander in Chief*, pp. 329-330, 382.

[19] Ibid., pp. 241, 346.

The Postmaster General did not become a member of the Cabinet until 1820 but this office had long been one of the most important controllers of political patronage. Madison had retained Jefferson's Postmaster General Gideon Granger in the position even though he was a part of the Senate "Invisibles" who undercut so many of Madison's policies from within his own party. Granger tested his strength when he ignored Madison's wishes and appointed Senator Michael Lieb, who was one of the three senators at the heart of this malcontent group, as Philadelphia postmaster. Lieb resigned from the Senate because he was unlikely to be re-elected. Madison dismissed Granger the next day and replaced him with Return J. Meigs, Jr., who quickly dismissed Lieb.[20] Meigs had been an Ohio chief justice, governor and senator. Granger's threat to Jefferson that he would spread lurid rumors about Dolley Madison did not persuade the former President to intervene.

Madison's inability to attract top-level appointees to key positions, then to keep on the job those who were appointed and performed with success, and finally to unload those who deserved dismissal, led to his severe censure by the most renowned historian of American public administration, Leonard D. White Especially as Commander in Chief White described Madison as "irresolute [and] weak in his judgment of men."[21] Political leaders had ample reason to avoid public duty in perilous times and Madison had to cope with dissidents within his own party who too often augmented the open political opposition, but he shares blame for the quality of his appointments and his unwillingness to confront Congress to achieve better ones. Though there was not a Gallatin among them, by the end of 1814 Madison had an administrative team that would successfully lead the United States into a peaceful future. Four of Madison's late appointments would serve in succeeding administrations. William H. Crawford would continue as Secretary of the Treasury until succeeded by Richard Rush in the John Quincy Adams administration. Meigs would in 1820 become the first Postmaster General in the Cabinet. Crowninshield remained Secretary of Navy during the first two years of the Monroe administration. Crawford was the "official" (Democratic) Republican presidential candidate in 1824 by virtue of the Congressional caucus. Indeed, he was narrowly defeated in the 1816 caucus even though he publicly announced that he would not oppose Monroe. By the time of the 1824 caucus Crawford had already been victimized by a stroke that left him severely

[20] Ibid., pp. 243-245.

[21] Leonard D. White, *The Jeffersonians* (New York: Macmillan Co., 1951), p. 221. Although White would be the senior editor of *The Papers of James Madison* from its inception in 1956, he was no admirer of Madison as an administrator. Madison citations in the index of *The Jeffersonians* include "ineptitude for executive office" and "incompetence in selecting generals."

incapacitated and nearly blind. He survived for another decade but never really recovered, nor did the Congressional caucus as a political institution. Ironically supporters of Monroe in 1816 argued that Monroe should be honored as the last of the "revolutionary heroes" while Crawford was young and should bide his time.

JACKSON'S CRUCIAL VICTORY AT NEW ORLEANS

Meanwhile, amid Madison's domestic administrative changes with new appointments, a hero had emerged in a very different theater of the ongoing war—Andrew Jackson in the Southwest. On March 26, 1814 Jackson had led a successful force composed of Tennessee militiamen, U.S. regular army troops and allied Cherokees to halt the ravages of the Creek Indians on American settlers of the frontier. At the Battle of Horseshoe Bend on March 26 Jackson and General John Coffee defeated Creek warriors led by Chief Menawa who had taken numerous lives in massacres such as that at Fort Mims on August 30, 1813 near Mobile, Alabama.[22] Jackson's military successes in Indian warfare earned him appointment as Major General in the U.S. army and orders to defend New Orleans; until then he had held the same rank in the militia.

In the fall of 1814 Sir Edward Pakenham, the brother-in-law of the Duke of Wellington, the British military hero of the Napoleonic Wars, led a British fleet of fifty vessels towards the Gulf of Mexico carrying 7,500 troops experienced in European wars.[23] Their goal was to capture New Orleans and by controlling the mouth of the Mississippi River block America's western territories from the sea; thus the bellicose western War Hawks would be punished. Louisiana Governor William C.C. Claiborne called for U.S. reinforcements to defend the city and Jackson marched his troops south, arriving in New Orleans on December 1, shortly before Pakenham.

Although the large British fleet defeated the small American fleet on Lake Borgne near New Orleans fairly easily, the American resistance gave time for Jackson to organize the defenses of the city. Next on December 14 American gunboats led by Lieutenant Thomas ap Catesby Jones resisted the British attack at the Malhereux Island Passage, defending part of the city's eastern fortifications long enough to win still more time for Jackson's defense of New Orleans. The

---

22 Adams, *The War of 1812,* pp. 106-116.

23 "Sir Edward Pakenham," by Barbara Bennett Peterson in *The Encyclopedia of the French Revolutionary and Napoleonic Wars, A Political, Social and Military History* edited by Gregory Fremont-Barnes (Santa Barbara, CA and Oxford, UK: ABC-CLIO, 2006) Vol. Two, pp. 733-734.

British sustained unsuspected losses and the river defenders contributed to Jackson's eventual victory. British troops had crossed the swamps and positioned themselves below New Orleans after the battle of Lake Borgne. By the time of their arrival, Jackson had used his 6,000 to 7,000 troops mustered from Louisiana, Kentucky, and Tennessee militias plus army regulars to prepare and man breastworks for defending the city.

General Jackson's victory at New Orleans on January 8, 1815 was a strategic victory for the Americans and an enormous morale boost for a nation that had long had little to cheer. Significantly it was against a British general who had seen battle action in Martinique and in the Peninsular War in Spain, and who would not live to see his British professionals decimated in the Louisiana lowlands. Pakenham had stationed his troops seven miles south of New Orleans at the Villere Plantation by Christmas Day 1814. His strategy was to capture the American positions on both sides of the Mississippi River. He attacked Jackson's fortified lines before the American guns on the west bank had been seized. On the east bank his forces were decimated by Jackson's searing line of fire. In a valiant attempt to rally his forces to advance, Pakenham remounted his horse after he had been dismounted by a cannonball but rode too close to the action and was hit by a volley of bullets. He died after issuing an order for British reserves to advance but it was too late. In action lasting about half an hour, more than two thousand British troops were lost, with 289 of them killed; a number of officers were lost in addition to Pakenham. Jackson lost fewer than one hundred men with only thirteen killed.[24]

Jackson was justly honored as the 'Hero of New Orleans' and his political star shone brightly and helped to advance him to the American presidency, just as a lesser victory would elevate General William Henry Harrison, the 'hero of the Battle of the Thames'. The Battle of New Orleans was thought to save the Mississippi Valley from invasion, but ironically it had no impact other than American pride on the outcome of the war. The Treaty of Ghent had already been signed unbeknown to the combatants on Christmas Eve 1814, two weeks before Jackson's victory. The peace treaty was ratified by the U.S. on February 17, 1815 officially ending the War of 1812. News of New Orleans arrived in Washington before news of Ghent, so Americans were left with the buoyant feeling they had won the war rather than merely survived it. The British forces departed as soon as they were informed of peace. General Pakenham who had fought so gallantly without the knowledge that peace had already been achieved was later honored by

[24] Winston Groom, *Patriotic Fire, Andrew Jackson and Jean Laffite at the Battle of New Orleans* (New York: Alfred A. Knopf, 2006), pp. 135-219; Adams, *The War of 1812,* pp. 302-323.

a statue commissioned with publicly raised funds for display in St. Paul's Cathedral in London.

THE TREATY OF GHENT

President Madison had actually attempted to produce a peace settlement long before when on June 26, 1812 his government had made preliminary overtures for talks to the British government. However his demands for terms exceeded British willingness to agree. Only three months later the Russian government proposed to mediate an end to the war. After all, Russia was also involved in its own War of 1812 with Napoleon storming its gates, so they had every reason to seek peace between its ally Great Britain and the United States. (Piotr Ilyitch Tchaikovsky composed his famed Russian "1812 Overture" in honor of the 70th anniversary (1882) of the Russian defeat of Napoleon in 1812. It was originally written in 1880 and premiered in 1882.) This offer of mediation was only made public in the week after Madison's second inauguration of March 4, 1813, when it was accepted by Washington, only to be rejected by Great Britain. Meanwhile the war had seesawed back and forth exchanging 'blow for blow' until Lord Castlereagh's ministry offered eight months later, on November 4, to establish direct negotiations. This olive branch was quickly grasped by Madison and accepted on January 15, 1814. He then assembled a diplomatic team of which any nation would be proud. It was headed by the transplanted Swiss Albert Gallatin, who had been Secretary of the Treasury since 1801. Others included John Quincy Adams, who had been minister to St. Petersburg from 1809 to 1811; James A. Bayard, who had been a Federalist senator from Delaware since 1805 and had been a key House figure in negotiating Jefferson's rise to the presidency following the tie electoral vote between Jefferson and Aaron Burr; Henry Clay, who had been Speaker of the House of Representatives since 1811 and would continue in that office for eight years after the war; and Jonathan Russell, who was longtime U.S. chargé d'affaires in London and later minister to Sweden. Unfortunately for Madison, he also sent as a secretary the step-son whom he inherited when he married Dolley Payne Todd for the overseas experience. Payne Todd's experience was largely in gambling debts and expensive purchases that the president later had to cover.

This band of worthies traveled to various European cities before negotiations were finally established in Ghent, Belgium, where they were met by British representatives Baron James Gambier, a successful naval commander who would later be Admiral of the Fleet, Henry Goulburn, Under Secretary of State to Lord

Bathurst, a young man who would later hold a major government position, and Dr. William Adams, a Doctor of Civil Law.[25] Recent American battle victories had made several British demands untenable, most importantly their original demand for military control over the Great Lakes and the establishment of an Indian buffer zone in the American Northwest. The Americans agreed to respect the rights of the Indians but without a territorial allotment and the Great Lakes were neutralized with an un-militarized common border. After the capture of Washington, D.C., the British argued for the principle of *uti possidetis*, a diplomatic principle that combatants maintain control over property seized in the conflict. However following American victories on Lake Champlain, U.S. negotiators insisted upon the contrasting diplomatic principle of mutual restitution of all properties captured during the war, or the restoration of the *status quo ante bellum* which fortunately prevailed. Thanks to the arguments of the heroic Duke of Wellington the British receded from their hard-line arguments for *uti possidetis* and agreed upon the *status quo ante bellum.*[26] Americans in return abandoned their specific demands for clauses outlawing impressment and gave up their demands for financial reparations for wartime commercial damages inflicted. Fortunately impressment would be one of those crises that would go away during the decades of Pax Britannica, when there was no longer need for Britain to adopt bullying tactics to maintain control of the seas. Impressment basically ceased when Napoleon was defeated. "Striking confirmation of this was found when Napoleon's return forced England once more to man her Navy by impressment" but she never considered involving Americans. United States consul James Maury at Liverpool "had the singular satisfaction to observe that the utmost courtesy was used towards the crews of our ships and every disposition manifested by the officers of the impress service at this port to avoid all occasion of vexation." If the Treaty of Ghent had "contained the full draft of the American article on

[25] Adams, *The War of 1812,* pp. 328-329.

[26] Adams, *The War of 1812,* p. 341; The Duke of Wellington was quoted in Henry Adams' *History* and in his shorter volume *The War of 1812* stating "In regard to your present negotiations [at Ghent], I confess that I think you have no right, from the state of the war, to demand any concession of territory from America....You have not been able to carry it into the enemy's territory, notwithstanding your military success and now undoubted military superiority, and have not even cleared your own territory on the point of attack. You cannot on the principle of equality in negotiation claim a cession of territory excepting in exchange for other advantages which you have in your power....Then if this reasoning be true, why stipulate for the *uti possidetis?* You can get no territory; indeed, the state of your military operations, however creditable, does not entitle you to demand any." This quote was expressed by Wellington in a letter he wrote to Lord Liverpool of November 9, 1814. In this same letter Wellington declined to take command of the British and Canadian forces in Canada offered by the British government.

impressment, it could have achieved no more than was brought about by the spontaneous effect of the war that ended without a decision."[27]

The Christmas Eve Treaty of Ghent, ratified by the U.S. Senate on February 17, 1815, also assured American fishing rights in the Newfoundland fisheries, the same goal that had first been achieved by John Quincy Adams's father, John Adams, in the Treaty of 1783 that ended the Revolutionary War.[28] All war incurred debts were to be paid and seized property was to be returned, except for freed slaves who had fought with the British. The British honored their service by granting them their freedom, purchased by British cash payments. Both sides agreed to end the Atlantic slave trade. Boundary commissions were established that would be highly successful in resolving and avoiding potential conflicts between the two countries. With old controversies such as impressment of American seamen no longer an issue, diplomacy became the pattern for the two nations gradually to resume friendly relations that would eventually blossom into close and powerful alliances.

The former Indian threat in the West was internally solved by the American army and local militia, allowing pioneers to push further west along the Oregon Trail to colonize the Pacific coastline in the Oregon Country. President Polk would later negotiate the Oregon Treaty in 1846 with the British allowing the annexation of the Oregon Territory. Problems or disputes would be settled peacefully among friends in the post War of 1812 era. Canada saw itself as "rescued" from American invasion and believed that Canadian militia had "saved the day" and been the most important weapon in resisting the American invasions through the Great Lakes, thus fostering a new sense of pride and independent nationalism. In the postwar period the Great Lakes would remain unfortified as well as the common border, but Canadians did erect La Citadelle in Quebec City to protect against a future American invasion attempt. This remained an important bulwark operating with Canadian forces along with the British port of Halifax in Nova Scotia. In the 1830s these bulwarks would be augmented by the construction of the Rideau Canal that connected Montreal to Lake Ontario and the construction of Fort Henry at Kingston to defend this canal.

British held Bermuda was catapulted into additional prominence by the War of 1812 when it became the British Royal Navy's base of operations for North American waters. Britain built a shipyard there for ship construction and a series of docks marking this as the British 'Gibraltar of the West'. Great Britain endeavored to use Bermuda to build up its Royal Navy to defend its far-flung

---

[27] Brant, *James Madison: Commander in Chief,* VI, p. 392.

[28] Adams, *The War of 1812,* pp. 334-345.

empire and to remain mistress of the seas. They emulated American ship construction, building larger, heavier vessels with numerous additional guns with greater accuracy. British diplomacy strengthened a trading partnership with America and resumed trade with France and the continent following Napoleon's defeat.

As President Madison was packing to return permanently to Virginia, he received the greatest commendation of "Mr. Madison's War" that he could have imagined. After years of disdain and contempt heaped on him by New England Federalists, the only one of them ever to become President, John Adams, praised Madison's achievement as Commander in Chief. After writing to Jefferson on February 2, 1817, to express his pity that Madison had neither children nor grandchildren, he concluded: "I therefore pity Brother Madison, and especially his Lady." After describing the worth of such offspring, however trying, he concluded that "I pity him the more, because Notwithstand[ing] a thousand Faults and blunders, his Administration has acquired more glory, and established more Union, than all three Predecessors, Washington, Adams and Jefferson." If Jefferson was delighted to be told that his disciple had transcended both him and Washington, he did not put it in writing. When he finally replied more than three months later, Jefferson's only reference to Adams's comments on Madison was that Adams need not worry about the lack of children because if Madison succeeded in his efforts with Jefferson and Monroe to establish the University of Virginia it "will raise up children for Mr. Madison to employ his attentions thro' life."[29] It was probably a kindness that he did not go on to refer to the countless expenses and worries that Madison had received from his step-son Payne Todd.

---

[29] Lester J. Cappon, *The Adams-Jefferson Letters* (Chapel Hill, University of North Carolina Press, 1959), pp. 507-508, 513. Adams felt that however muddled the waging of the war, the important thing was its success and the terms of the peace. Alfred J. Zarcher parts from many other historians when he uses the same logic to argue that, despite the capture and burning of Washington, D.C., and the series of American defeats, James Madison was one of those rare presidents whose second term could be described as successful. He advanced this view in *Trial and Triumph: Presidential Power in the Second Term* (Fort Wayne, Indiana: Presidential Press, 1996), pp. 60-66, 331.

Chapter 12

WAGING PEACE, 1815-1817

For President Madison the year in which ratification of the Treaty of Ghent *officially* ended the War of 1812 was divided in two quite distinct parts. Worries whether diplomacy could be trusted and lasting peace could be assured consumed the first six months. American and British negotiators signed the peace treaty on Christmas Eve 1814 in the Belgian city of Ghent six months before Great Britain achieved its own security at the Belgian city of Waterloo from June 18 to 21 of 1815. Napoleon's bold attempt to regain power was thwarted by the Duke of Wellington and allies in the bloody Battle of Waterloo that claimed heavy losses from both armies. Yet fears remained that the seeming final removal of Britain's perennial enemy might embolden the victors to resume the punishment of their quondam colonies, as they had quite consciously attempted by shifting troops to North America when Napoleon was captured and exiled in 1814. Madison had gambled and lost much when he led the nation to war in 1812, greatly influenced by his assumption that surely France or England (and hopefully both) would come to their senses and halt their depredations on American commerce short of warfare. In 1815 he gambled that if Napoleon was again defeated by the powerful European coalition of Great Britain, Prussia, Austria, and Russia the British would go home content and allow Americans to resume their trading relations; or in the unlikely event that Napoleon prevailed he would not resume his quest for North American empire. Madison won this gamble and the United States would through most of the nineteenth century remain at peace with Great Britain and the rest of Europe. Madison avoided recognition of any new French government and even took strenuous measures to prevent a possibly embarrassing visit at Montpelier by Napoleon's brother Joseph Bonaparte, the deposed King of Spain.[1]

This victory would give Madison leeway to wage and win a great political struggle: the decimation of the opposition Federalist Party and the executive dominance of what would long be described as the Virginia Dynasty. Madison's Secretary of State (and recently Secretary of War) James Monroe would be the principal beneficiary but the Era of Good Feelings really had its birth in Madison's last two years at Washington D.C. There were many pains and embarrassments associated with the achievement of a lasting peace with Great Britain, but once achieved the war-weary President was by the end of 1815 able to propose and support legislation that usurped enough of the Federalist programs to blend with his traditional (Democratic) Republican philosophy, that the already weakened New England Federalists could do little but complain. Even Old Republicans such as John Randolph of Roanoke and John Taylor of Caroline, who had long considered Jefferson and Madison betrayers of their own Virginia and Kentucky Resolutions, were largely silenced during those years.

THE JOYS OF PEACE, AT LEAST WITH EUROPE

Two days after the Senate had rapidly and unanimously approved the Treaty of Ghent on February 16, President Madison sent a special message praising Congress and the American people for this "event which is highly honorable to the nation, and terminates with peculiar felicity a campaign signalized by the most brilliant successes." He insisted that the war had been necessary to maintain American "rights and independence." Congressmen were praised for their wisdom, their constituents for their patriotism, and the military for their public spirit and valor. He sought to stem the inevitable, already characteristically American, political goal to demobilize as rapidly as possible. He lectured Congress that because "neither the pacific dispositions of the American people nor the pacific character of their political institutions" would protect the nation from external forces, Congress must "provide for an adequate regular force; for

[1] Brant, *James Madison: Commander in Chief,* p. 394; Barbara Bennett Peterson, "Joseph Bonaparte," in *Encyclopedia of the French Revolution and Napoleonic Wars,* edited by Gregory Fremont-Barnes (Santa Barbara, CA and Oxford, UK: ABC-CLIO, 2006), I, pp. 159-161. After leaving Napoleonic France and after the Congress of Vienna confirmed the throne of Spain upon Ferdinand VII, Joseph Bonaparte came to the United States and lived in Bordentown, New Jersey for seventeen years, becoming an American citizen. He later moved to

the enhancement of the naval establishment; for improving all the means of harbor defense; for adding discipline to the distinguished bravery of the militia; and for cultivating the military art in its essential branches." His optimism was not entirely misplaced, although Congress provided considerably less force than he recommended.

Later in this message he gave a broad hint of changes that would surface in his ground-breaking annual message in December. Despite his successful opposition to Alexander Hamilton's creative proposal to support the development of American manufactures early in the history of the United States, Madison had throughout his presidency, and especially during the recent war, become an enthusiastic supporter of this segment of the American economy. Like Jefferson he had long been a spokesman for agrarian America, but he happily predicted for postwar America a balanced economy based on commerce and manufactures as well. He felt that "there is no subject that can enter with greater force and merit into the deliberations of Congress than a consideration of the means to preserve and promote the manufactures which have sprung into existence and attained an unparalleled majority throughout the United States during the period of the European wars. This source of national independence and wealth I anxiously recommend, therefore, to the prompt and constant guardianship of Congress. He concluded with his hope that the treaty would "be the foundation of the most friendly intercourse between the United States and Great Britain" as well as "productive of happiness and harmony in every section of our beloved country." [2]

A week later he sent another special message to Congress, urging legislation that would require that the navigation of American vessels be "exclusively by American seamen, either natives, or such as are already naturalized." This would not only improve relations with other nations but would also "increase the number of our seamen" and thereby "render our commerce and navigation independent of the service of foreigners."[3] Because an end to impressment of American seaman for which he had campaigned since 1801 was not achieved in the treaty, he moved finally to make it unnecessary.

Robert A. Rutland, editor of *The Papers of James Madison* as well as several other valuable volumes on James Madison, argues persuasively that the heady month of February 1815 marked a "sudden turn of fortune [that] had no precedent in American history."[4] Not only had the August disaster of the seizure and

Britain, then Italy where he died in 1844. His body was later re-buried in Les Invalides in Paris near his brother Napoleon.

[2] February 18, 1815, Hunt, *Writings of James Madison,* VIII, pp. 324-326.

[3] February 25, 1815, *ibid.,* pp. 126-127.

[4] Rutland, *The Presidency of James Madison,* p. 187.

burning of the nation's capital been followed by surprising success on Lake Champlain, and then by the astonishing victory of Jackson at New Orleans and even by naval victories that were known, and sometimes even waged, after the successful negotiations at Ghent.

Frosting on the cake was the timely arrival of a delegation of New England Federalist party bosses sent to lay down the terms that would keep New England within the Union. The Hartford Convention met in Connecticut from December 15 to January 4 to discuss possible disunion and, failing that, New England's role in the United States. High Federalists who had rejoiced in Madison's military embarrassments and had hampered war efforts sometimes to the point of treason, beginning in the summer of 1812, were there to force upon Madison the peace that was already being celebrated as they arrived in Washington. Their demands for peace with Great Britain were accompanied by demands for political amendments that would further limit the President, the Republican Party, and his beloved South. The three visitors from Hartford were largely ignored in the midst of delirious celebrations of American "victory," and never had the opportunity to present their demands. If given a platform they would have demanded that any future war, as well as commercial restrictions and admission of new states, must be approved in Congress by a super majority of two thirds. New western states that always seemed to vote for Jefferson and Madison had always been resented by the Federalists. Future presidents would be limited to a single term and must be from a different state than that of his predecessor. They would halt the Virginia Dynasty with Madison rather than Monroe. Foreign-born citizens, too many of whom became Jeffersonians, would be precluded not just from the presidency as provided by the Constitution but from holding *any* federal office. Finally to weaken the South, slaves would no longer be counted as three-fifths toward electoral representation. Until 1849 every President, other than the single terms of Adams father and son and Martin Van Buren, was from Virginia or Tennessee.[5] The three-fifths of the black population who counted for representation but were denied the vote contributed significantly to that series of southern Presidents. The spirit of the New Englanders' celebration of American victory was best expressed by their leader Harrison Gray Otis, who protested "the tinsel and vulgarity" of the reception by the President. He did not attend the President's reception because "we have received no invitation from Mr. Madison. What a mean and contemptible little blackguard." Otis consoled himself with the satisfaction that

[5] Washington, Jefferson, Madison, Monroe, Harrison and Tyler were all born in Virginia. Jackson and Polk were born in the Carolinas but were raised in Tennessee.

"the little pigmy shook in his shoes at our approach."[6] Jefferson wrote that the administration was wise to let the Hartford survivors "live as the laughing stocks of the world, and punish them by the torment of eternal contempt." Even before news of New Orleans and Ghent, Madison himself had laughed aloud while reading the published demands from Hartford.[7]

Madison rewarded the American diplomats who negotiated the Treaty of Ghent with prime European assignments. Albert Gallatin served as minister to France from 1816 to 1823 and then as minister to Great Britain in 1826-1827. John Quincy Adams, who had previously been minister to Prussia and Russia followed in his father's steps as minister to Great Britain; each President Adams was sent to London after successful negotiations to end a war against Great Britain. Their descendant Charles Francis Adams would also be American minister to Great Britain throughout the Civil War. John Quincy Adams' service was brief because he was soon summoned home as Monroe's Secretary of State. In that brief time he cooperated with Gallatin in successful commercial negotiations with Great Britain. As Secretary of State he would be engaged in ground-breaking diplomacy including the development of the Monroe Doctrine that attempted to exclude European interference with the western hemisphere. James A. Bayard was appointed American minister to St. Petersburg, though he died before his departure, and Jonathan Russell resumed his position as minister to Sweden. Only Henry Clay returned directly home, by choice, to reclaim his long-term position as Speaker of the House of Representatives. William H. Crawford, who would have been added to the negotiations at Ghent if he were not considered indispensable as American minister to France, became Secretary of War upon his return and then Secretary of the Treasury during the last four months of Madison's presidency and all of Monroe's two terms. Less triumphal was the return of Madison's step-son John Payne Todd, who had been Gallatin's secretary during the negotiations. He arrived with expensive purchases and much larger debts than Madison had authorized or could have imagined. Payne Todd would long remain a burden on his step-father, with his magnificent gaming debts tolerated by his indulgent mother and ignored by Madison in deference to his wife.

---

[6] Brant, *James Madison: Commander in Chief,* p. 370.

[7] Ketcham, *James Madison,* p. 597; Brant, *James Madison: Commander in Chief,* p. 361.

SMALL WAR WITH SOMEONE CLOSER TO OUR OWN SIZE

Only a week after the War of 1812 was officially ended by the unanimous ratification of the Treaty of Ghent, Madison asked Congress to declare another much less dangerous war. He had sent to Congress as early as November 17, 1814, reports of the hostile proceedings of the Dey of Algiers, who had cut down the American flag because of delays in the payment of tribute required to protect commerce from Mediterranean pirates. These were followed by "acts of more overt and direct warfare against the citizens of the United States trading in the Mediterranean, some of whom are still detained in captivity, notwithstanding the attempts which have been made to ransom them." It was "unnecessary and unimportant to commence hostile operations on the part of the United States against acts of piracy and demands for tribute in the Mediterranean from the Barbary states of North Africa" until achievement of the "peace with Great Britain, which opens the prospect of an active and valuable trade [for American] citizens within the range of the Algerian cruisers." He recommended that Congress declare "the existence of a state of war between the United States and the Dey and Regency of Algiers, and of such provisions as may be requisite for a vigorous prosecution of it to a successful issue."[8]

Once war was declared, Madison quickly dispatched ships and commanders who had won distinction in the recent war. Stephen Decatur had won his initial reputation and promotion to captain in the Tripolitan War of 1801-1805, in which Jefferson and Madison first attempted to force an end to Barbary invasions on American commerce in the Mediterranean. These triumphs were followed against more formidable opposition with his victory by the *United States* over the British ship *Macedonian* in October 1812 and by the *President* over the *Endymion* on January 15, 1815, one of the naval victories that occurred after peace had been negotiated. He led his squadron to the Mediterranean Sea, followed by a second group under Captain William Bainbridge, who arrived primarily for mop-up duties and negotiations. By the time Decatur was prepared to sail, word arrived late in April that Napoleon had escaped from his exile on the Mediterranean island of Elba, had been welcomed back in France and was again on the march. Madison was forced to decide whether to hold back Decatur's squadron for possible use against one of the recent foes if Napoleon's resurgence wrecked the peace of Ghent. Fortunately for the status of the United States in world commerce and politics, Madison gambled and won. Napoleon's "Hundred Days" ended at

---

[8] Message to Congress, February 23, 1815, James D. Richardson, ed., *A Compilation of the Messages and Papers of the Presidents* (New York: Bureau of National Literature, 1897), II, p. 539.

Waterloo on June 18. He abdicated his rule for a second time on June 22, surrendered on July 15, and was a captive on the barren island of St. Helena from October 1815 until his death in 1821.

The Algerian venture finally gave Madison the opportunity to boast of a successful war on a timely basis in a State of the Union message. His seventh annual message on December 5, 1815 began on a triumphal note, lacking only Decatur's famous toast at a dinner in his honor when he returned to Norfolk, Virginia, in November 1815: "Our country! In her intercourse with foreign nations may she always be right; but our country right or wrong!"[9]

The opening paragraph of Madison's triumphal message focused entirely on the victory over Algiers. "I have the satisfaction on our present meeting of being able to communicate to you the successful termination of the war which had been commenced against the United States by the Regency of Algiers. The squadron in advance on that service, under Commodore Decatur, lost not a moment after its arrival in the Mediterranean in seeking the naval force of the enemy then cruising in that sea, and succeeded in capturing two of his ships, one of them the principal ship, commanded by the Algerian admiral. The high character of the American commander was brilliantly sustained on the occasion which brought his own ship into close action with that of his adversary, as was the accustomed gallantry of all the officers and men actually engaged. Having prepared the way by this demonstration of American skill and prowess, he hastened to the port of Algiers, where peace was promptly yielded to his victorious force. In the terms stipulated the rights and honor of the United States were particularly consulted by a perpetual relinquishment on the part of the Dey of all pretensions to tribute from them. The impressions which have thus been made, strengthened as they will have been by subsequent transactions with the Regencies of Tunis and Tripoli by the appearance of the larger force which followed under Commodore Bainbridge, the chief in command of the expedition, and by the judicious precautionary arrangements left by him in that quarter, afford a reasonable prospect of future security for the valuable portion of our commerce which passes within reach of the Barbary cruisers."[10]

---

[9] Alan Westcott, "Stephen Decatur," in Allen Johnson and Dumas Malone, eds., *Dictionary of American Biography* (New York: Charles Scribner's Sons, 1946), V, p. 189.

[10] Hunt, *Writings of James Madison,* VIII, p. 335.

PEACE AND A LONG DELAYED VACATION

Before leaving for his long-deferred vacation in Virginia, Madison took precautions to assure that neither army nor navy be weakened to the level that had prevailed prior to the war. A Board of Naval Commissioners was formed to provide professional guidance to the Secretary of the Navy. Because the law establishing the Board did not provide any link to the President, Madison insisted that they report to him through Secretary Crowninshield. Commodore John Rodgers and Captain David Porter agreed to these terms but Captain Isaac Hull refused and transferred to another position. This opened a position for Decatur when he returned, although his service was cut tragically short when he was killed in a duel with Captain James Barron, only five years later at the young age of forty one. Indeed the position contributed directly to his death because the duel was caused by Decatur's opposition to the reinstatement of Barron after suspension.[11] Much as successful naval commanders were kept in service and involved in administration, the best of the young generals who had risen from 1813 to 1815 kept their commands and united to form an advisory group to restructure the peacetime army and recommend officers of lower ranks. This group lacked the official status of the Naval Commissioners but their role was crucial because immediate decisions had to be made as to who would continue in service, who released, and who pensioned. Acting Secretary of War Dallas told Madison that "your first selection of general officers is as good as can be made." Yet before it could even begin Madison and Dallas must walk a fragile tightrope before contenting the most obvious choice for high command. William C.C. Claiborne who had been territorial governor of Mississippi and Louisiana before becoming the first state governor of Louisiana in 1812 wrote angrily and extensively about the harsh martial law imposed on New Orleans by General Andrew Jackson, which was still in effect in February. Jackson had expelled the French consul and scores of French citizens from the city, and even deported the federal judge who dared to issue a writ of habeas corpus for a state legislator whom he had arrested. Before Dallas's gentle admonition providing reminders of pertinent sections of the United States Bill of Rights arrived, Jackson had ended martial law and left for Nashville; he was fined $1000 for contempt of court by the judge who had returned, but that was paid by grateful citizens. Constitutionalist Madison hated to see martial law develop from the will of a commander rather than from conditions facing the army. Yet he insisted that

---

[11] Brant, *James Madison: Commander in Chief,* p. 388; Westcott, "Stephen Decatur" in Johnson and Malone, eds., *Dictionary of American Biography,* p. 189.

Jackson be judged "with a liberality proportioned to the greatness of his services, the purity of his intentions, and the peculiarity of the circumstances." Jackson certainly did not ease the situation by countering with a demand for the names of those who reported him, but Dallas assured Jackson on July 1 that he was regarded by the President with "confidence and esteem. Indeed, you have found in his late acts, relative to the military peace establishment, the best proofs of respect for your character, and of his recognition of your services."[12] Dallas was referring to the appointment of Jackson as one of two continuing lieutenant generals. Jackson was given command of the entire southern department, while Lieutenant General Jacob Brown was northern commander. Generals Alexander Macomb, Edmund P. Gaines, Winfield Scott, and E. W. Ripley were appointed brigadier generals. These six generals appointed by Madison would establish the army as it would remain until the Civil War.[13] Fortunately Madison and Dallas did not encounter an unending conflict as would William H. Crawford, appointed by Madison but serving under Monroe, when he was required to censure the hot-headed Jackson for his military incursion into Spanish Florida in 1818. The restored King Ferdinand VII who returned with a full measure of despotism and religious intolerance implied war in response to American incursions in Florida, but fortunately this remained a war only of words.[14]

A reward for peace was that James and Dolley Madison were finally able to vacation again in the Virginia uplands. Whether to Virginia or to Massachusetts, Presidents both before and after Madison would flee the capital city during the sickly season. Presidents were seldom in Washington, D.C., or in Philadelphia before that, in July and August. The realities of war kept Madison on the job far more than any of his predecessors. He had escaped to Virginia in August 1814, but it was an escape from British attackers and he and his government hovered as close to Washington as they dared. As soon as British troops withdrew, Madison and his fellow administrators returned to pick up the pieces, living in rented rooms while official buildings were repaired. Late in March of 1815 the Madisons finally departed with the usual entourage of Dolley's relatives providing the youthful companions that Madison cherished. Madison spent much of April at Monticello working through Jefferson's magnificent library and helping to select the 10,000 volumes that Jefferson would donate to replace the Library of Congress that had been burned by the British. This was in part a working vacation

---

[12] Brant, *James Madison: Commander in Chief,* pp. 383-385.

[13] Ibid., p. 385.

[14] Ibid., p. 393.

to be sure, but Madison was doing what he loved most, poring over old books—and best of all doing it with his best friend Thomas Jefferson.

Madison returned to Washington for six weeks in June and July, during which news was received of a commercial treaty negotiated in Great Britain by Gallatin and Clay while on their way home from Ghent. It provided hope for the future, but also disappointing evidence that Britain would not welcome the return of American shipping to some areas, most important the West Indies trade that was so crucial to American commerce. The President kept the disappointment to himself until his annual message to Congress in December. He also recommended that Congress provide funds to maintain a naval presence in the Mediterranean as well as the Great Lakes.

The Madisons left again for Montpelier on July 19 and did not return until October 12. The difference in Madison's life between 1814 and 1815 (between war and peace) is highlighted by the fact that the only "writings" in the eighth volume of *The Writings of James Madison* between February proclamations ending the war with Great Britain and his seventh State of the Union Message in December 5 are *two letters*. One was written March 4 to apologize to Henry Dearborn for Madison's appointment of Dearborn as Secretary of War without first clearing it with the Senate, and the other on March 12 to forward a printed copy of the "Exposition on the Causes and Character of the War" to Jefferson. Madison initiated this project that was largely written by Dallas and eventually published by Congress.[15] A week after the Jefferson letter, Madison left for the first portion of his vacation. As was always the case, historians suffered when Jefferson and Madison were in close enough proximity to visit by horseback that there was no reason for them to write letters. A number of Cabinet members also visited at Montpelier, as well as foreign diplomats who also relished the opportunity to abandon Washington in favor of the Virginia highlands in the summer. During these months dramatic improvement of the nation's economy and fiscal stability were achieved by Dallas—and of course by the return of peace--and several Indian treaties were negotiated, all of which would be reported in the buoyant State of the Union message.

Extensive Legislative Agenda

During this long vacation Madison was able to reflect at length while preparing his penultimate, and triumphant, annual message. It began with

---

[15] Hunt, *Writings of James Madison,* VIII, pp. 327-335.

Decatur's and Bainbridge's naval and diplomatic success in the Mediterranean but turned rapidly to the greater peace assured by the end of the European wars. Decatur had returned to a hero's welcome in mid-November and provided full details of American success. Then without expressing his concern that Great Britain had not been more receptive of American trade, Madison emphasized that the "convention on the subject of commerce" that followed the peace treaty demonstrated a mood in both countries "which it may be hoped will be improved into liberal arrangements on other subjects on which the parties have mutual interests, or which might endanger their future harmony." Fortunately this was an accurate prediction. Since the issue of impressment of American sailors by the Royal Navy had been ignored in the peace treaty, he reiterated his prior admonition that American shipping should be confined to American seamen. Peace treaties with a large number of Indian tribes were described and praised, with the caution that the country must be prepared to repress "restlessness" among some tribes along the southern frontier. After a lengthy description of administration efforts to assure "an efficient military peace establishment" he urged Congress to provide equitably for those who would continue to serve as well as for the many more returning to civilian life. Congress was "best calculated to give support and solace to the veteran and the invalid, to display the beneficence as well as the justice of the Government, and to inspire a martial zeal for the public service upon every future emergency."

Jefferson and Madison had won their narrow victory in the "Revolution of 1800" in large part because of fears of militarism in the closing years of the Adams administration. One of Madison's many lessons from the recent war was that armies and navies were not to be reviled in peacetime, as they had been when he was Secretary of State. He lectured Congress that "the character of the times particularly inculcates the lesson that, whether to prevent or repel danger, we ought not to be unprepared for it." In addition to "immediate extension and gradual improvement of the works of defense" the military academy at West Point must be enlarged and others established. A direct response to the dismal performance of New England and New York militia in the recent war was his call for reorganization of the state militias that would enable "the political authority of the Union to employ promptly and efficiently the physical power of the Union in the cases designated by the Constitution." He did not express it directly, but in future national crises state militias must not again be prevented by their governors from crossing national or even state borders. As for the navy the "soundest policy" was for Congress to "preserve the ships now in sound state, to complete those already contemplated, to provide amply the imperishable materials for prompt augmentations, and to improve the existing arrangements into more advantageous establishments for the construction, the repairs, and the security of vessels of war."

CONSTITUTIONAL ISSUES OF THE ERA

When Madison turned to domestic affairs he confronted the three issues that would for decades remain the core of Henry Clay's "American System": a national bank, protective tariffs to encourage American industry and commerce, and internal improvements of roads, canals, and harbors to ease the transportation of that commerce and manufactured goods. Madison's stance on this issue was not partisan, although he had since 1810 been closely allied with Clay. Support for or opposition to these issues was key to American political debate once neutral trade and impressment of seamen could be set aside.

Suspicion of a national debt had been a Madisonian article of faith since 1791 when he led the opposition to Hamilton's economic program that sought to make debt a virtue by linking the fiscal interests of capitalists to the new government; Hamilton's Bank of the United States was central to this strategy. Extinguishing the debt was never as crucial to Madison as it had been to his Treasury Secretary Albert Gallatin, but he was invariably a peacetime ally of Gallatin. The war had demolished Gallatin's goal to extinguish the debt by 1816, but Gallatin's successor Alexander J. Dallas, who provided the numbers for Madison's report on public credit, did not consider this an insuperable hurdle. The national debt was estimated at $120 million, including the $39 million remaining from the Hamilton-Adams debt that Gallatin had been whittling away from 1801 until 1812. Madison even argued that the continuing debt would be more tolerable because expenditures would "long be visible in the number and equipments of the American Navy, in the military works for the defense of our harbors and our frontiers and in the supplies of our arsenals and magazines." He found great satisfaction in the "revival of the public credit and the efficiency of the public resources." But if the state banks proved unable to meet the need for a uniform national currency "the probable operation of a national bank will merit consideration."[16]

This passing reference to a national bank was ironic coming from the pen of the statesman who preceded Jefferson in arguing the unconstitutionality of Hamilton's Bank of the United States in 1791. Next he led the United States to war without an adequate banking structure because he allowed a renewed charter

[16] Ibid., pp. 335-340.

to be prevented by a tie vote in Congress rather than admit publicly that he had been in error two decades earlier and that by 1811 he wanted the bank to survive. Then in January 1815, he had exercised one of his rare vetoes to negate a new national bank, after explicitly *justifying* it as constitutional. Rather than the fearsome engine of Hamilton, the 1814 "act to incorporate the subscribers to the Bank of the United States of America" seemed to benefit only the investors while the United States gained far too little. "The question of the constitutional authority of the Legislature to establish an incorporated bank" was precluded in his "judgment by repeated recognitions under varied circumstances of the validity of such an institution in acts of the legislative, executive, and judicial branches of the Government, accompanied by indications, in different modes, of the concurrence of the general will of the nation." With the constitutional issue set to rest, he finished this interminable sentence by ruling that "the proposed bank does not appear to be calculated to answer the purposes of reviving the public credit, of providing a national medium of circulation, and of aiding the Treasury by facilitating the indispensable anticipation of the revenue and by affording to the public more durable loans." In short, this bank was constitutional but inadequate. He then argued at length that public credit would be improved little if any by the bank legislation.

Madison was unaware when he wrote this veto message that the war had already ended, so he placed heavy emphasis on its inability to meet the wartime needs of the nation. If he had known of the peace he might have argued instead that there was no need of such a weak reed in peacetime. He concluded that while it was painful to confront Congress on such an issue, he was consoled by the fact that if his reservations were not persuasive "they can be constitutionally overruled" and otherwise "the wisdom of Congress will hasten to substitute a more commensurate and certain provision for the public exigencies."[17] Early in 1816 Congress would accept the challenge and Madison would join Representative John C. Calhoun as unlikely "fathers" of the Second Bank of the United States that would succumb two decades later in another constitutional battle with the attack led by President Andrew Jackson and Attorney General Roger B. Taney (later Chief Justice) against the Bank's supporters, Chief Justice John Marshall and Senator Henry Clay.

Madison's comments on protective tariffs represented a change that had been developing gradually throughout his political career. As early as 1789 in Congress he advocated trade taxes designed to force Great Britain to agree to a commercial treaty with the United States; yet shortly thereafter he opposed and defeated

---

[17] Ibid., pp. 327-330.

Alexander Hamilton's plan to utilize tariffs to hasten the development of American manufactures. Madison's early tariff policies were designed instead to increase markets for American agricultural produce. In a series of presidential messages he had highlighted the value of American manufactures. In 1815 he urged Congress to adjust duties on imported goods so that "the influence of the tariff on manufactures" should be an important consideration along with the customary need for government revenue. He never put the buzz word "protective" in front of "tariff" but he made it clear that there were circumstances where government aid was appropriate for the development of American industries. Public support was especially appropriate for products that would "relieve the United States from a dependence on foreign supplies, ever subject to casual failures, for articles necessary for the public defense or connected with the primary wants of individuals." Obviously the last category was very broad. Finally he returned partially to his agrarian roots by adding special approval for manufactures that were "extensively drawn from agriculture," such as tobacco and cotton in his view.

Madison next called the attention of Congress to the "great importance of establishing throughout our country the roads and canals which can best be executed under the national authority" with such enthusiasm that too little attention was given to his concluding sentence. Comments such as "No objects…so richly repay the expense bestowed on them; there is none the utility of which is more universally ascertained and acknowledged; none that do more honor to the governments whose wise and enlarged patriotism duly appreciates them" sounded to Congress like an invitation to start building. After praising the role of the states in such projects, he added that "the General Government is the more urged to similar undertakings." After such encouragement too little attention was paid to Madison's "happy reflection that any defect of constitutional authority which may be encountered can be supplied in a mode which the Constitution itself has providently pointed out." This reminder of the amending process was overlooked by Congress as much as the perennial presidential call since John Adams for "a national seminary of learning within the District of Columbia."[18]

FINALLY A MORE COOPERATIVE CONGRESS

Upon their return to Washington, the President moved to new lodgings at the corner of 19th Street and Pennsylvania Avenue, three blocks west of the

---

[18] Ibid., pp. 341-343.

presidential mansion, while government buildings were under repairs. The painting that followed repairs was gradually converting the presidential mansion into the "White House," in which James Monroe would be the first occupant. The Capitol Building also became more sturdy and impressive, though it would not achieve its true grandeur until well after the Civil War when its magnificent dome made it the pattern for state capitol buildings throughout the United States. The senators and representatives who occupied this building were much more attractive as well to President Madison. Republican majorities grew steadily during the post-war euphoria, coming in considerable numbers even from New England due to the disintegration of the Federalist Party. Legislative foes from within Madison's own party also lost their influence. Virginian William Branch Giles and Pennsylvanian Michael Leib, both leaders of the troublesome "Invisibles," lost their Senate seats and the leader of these dissidents, William Smith of Maryland, was relegated to the House of Representatives where his influence was diminished. John Randolph of Roanoke was back in the House but even his rhetoric against the leader of unexpected victory (or at least peace) was muted. He complained that the legislative program of 1816 demonstrated that Madison "out-Hamilton's Alexander Hamilton" but as Madison departed finally from Washington, Randolph grudgingly conceded that Madison "was a great man—for unquestionably he was in some respects—and he sincerely wished him all happiness in his retirement.[19]

Congress responded quickly and supportively to Madison's legislative agenda. Treasury Secretary Dallas had long been an advocate for a bank that could establish the uniform national currency that had been so severely lacking in the recent war, when specie (gold and silver) was nearly impossible to acquire. Thus he could respond rapidly to Rep. John C. Calhoun's request for a proposal for the Second Bank of the United States. Calhoun then hustled it through his committee and gained approval by the House of Representatives. Madison signed the bank legislation on April 10, and it would begin business in Philadelphia (the home also of the First Bank) in January 1817. The first president of the Bank was also a member of Madison's war cabinet: William Jones had been successful Secretary of the Navy as well as Acting Secretary of the Treasury during much of Albert Gallatin's extended diplomatic leave in Europe. It would establish the uniform national currency that was so sorely lacking in the war and would continue to do so until it was drawn into presidential politics by Henry Clay and, in retaliation, decimated by Andrew Jackson while Madison lay dying. Even though his reading of the "necessary and proper clause" of Article I Section 8 of

---

[19] Brant, *James Madison: Commander in Chief,* pp. 415-416; Ketcham, *James Madison,* p. 603.

the U.S. Constitution had changed from his powerful opposition to Hamilton's broad interpretation of that clause, Madison could never quite bring himself to admit that he may have been wrong when he opposed the First Bank. It was even harder to admit that Hamilton was right, but decades of precedent and public acquiescence had expanded the reach of the "necessary and proper clause," for he regarded the American people as the ultimate interpreter of the Constitution.

The Senate quickly approved the commercial treaty with Great Britain but then Congress spent two months wrestling with the related legislation that it mandated. To get them over this hurdle Madison declared the treaty in effect, ruling that by agreeing to the treaty Great Britain had in effect retreated from any discriminations against American commerce, and then waited and hoped that the British ministry would respond in kind. He met a very different British response than that of June 1812 when his more daring gamble led to war. Fortunately Viscount Castlereagh, who had become Foreign Secretary in 1812 a few weeks too late, and too far away across the Atlantic, to prevent the War of 1812, would remain in that same office for a decade. In 1816 Castlereagh stated publicly that the United States and Great Britain were natural friends rather than enemies, and his policies helped to make this opinion a fact, which led to successes for President Madison and even more for President Monroe and his principal diplomat John Quincy Adams. Madison contributed to this "era of good diplomatic feelings" by following his call for the funding of a fleet to match that of Great Britain on the Great Lakes with his assurance to Lord Castlereagh that he would follow Britain's lead and would match any steps to neutralize the Lakes. The non-militarization of the Lakes that followed provided the core of the peaceful border that still exists between Canada and the United States.

By the end of 1816 Madison would still be disillusioned that the British were a less gracious trade partner than he had envisioned, but all the trends were positive. In a busy session, Congress also established tariffs that were moderately protective of American industry, while providing sufficient revenue to continue diminishing the national debt to the point where it appeared in the second Adams administration that the debt would finally be extinguished. Reorganization of the army command and some improvement of militia operations were approved along with funding for military fortifications. Madison's proposal to require that only American citizens serve on American merchant ships was approved by the Senate but died in the House. Fortunately the century of peace with Great Britain that followed made this defeat irrelevant since there was no need for the Royal Navy to prey on American merchantmen. Even Madison's persistent advocacy for a national university was reported out of committee but it died almost immediately in the House.[20]

Choosing a Successor

The legislative caucus that James Monroe had earlier resented when it nominated James Madison for president while Monroe was in England, finally granted Monroe the reward that he craved in mid-March 1816, after an earlier caucus had failed because of poor attendance. Monroe had waited his time somewhat petulantly in 1810 but now it was young William H. Crawford who was told to wait when Monroe prevailed by only nine votes. Madison played no obvious role in this decision but he was delighted by the outcome, both the spring nomination and the autumn election. Monroe easily surpassed Rufus King, who had finally won Federalist nomination in his third attempt to become president. After Monroe won the electoral votes of every state but Massachusetts, Connecticut and Delaware, John Adams speculated that if Madison had been the nominee New England would have unanimously supported him! Since John Quincy Adams was reported in September 1815 in support of Madison for a third term if he were willing, the only two presidents among the first seven who were defeated for a second term seemed content to see Madison become the first three-term president. It is ironic then that their great-grandson (of John Adams) and grandson (of John Quincy Adams), Henry Adams, consistently voted against President Madison throughout his magisterial, nine-volume *History of the United States during the Administrations of Jefferson and Madison* nearly a century later. As further evidence of Good Feelings the last Federalist aspirant for the presidency would serve briefly as American minister to Great Britain during Monroe's presidency as he had during in the first Adams administration and during the first three years of Jefferson's. [21]

Since the United States had thrived during Madison's long hiatus from Washington in 1815, he risked what would be a record vacation in the following year. He left for Montpelier on June 5, not to return until October 9. Although he had ample time to work on his final State of the Union Message, it fell far short of that of 1815, which had encouraged significant legislative responses. One historian of his presidency described it with faint praise as close to "downright

[20] Brant, *James Madison: Commander in Chief,* pp. 401-403, 406.
[21] Ibid., pp. 412, 398.

dull."[22] The annual message of December 3, 1816 accorded with the consistent pattern of his troubled presidency by focusing first on diplomatic concerns and successes. Despite progress following peace with Great Britain, "a depression is experienced by particular branches of our manufactures and by a portion of our navigation." Both resulted from problems still unresolved with the British. He did not specifically blame the British for the "excess of imported merchandise" that hindered some American industry, but that nation had long been the principal exporter to the United States and was eager to regain its markets and priced its goods sufficiently low to undercut many American competitors. While he was sure that this evil could not long continue, he warned Congress to be aware that American industries "suffered to sink too low or languish too long, may not revive after the causes shall have ceased." Losses in American shipping were not so easily resolved. Exclusion of American ships from many British colonies, most importantly the West Indies, must be ended and he urged Congress to pursue a "rule of reciprocity." He said the United States was being "in amity with foreign powers" but then proceeded to express concern about a naval skirmish with Spain over American interests in Florida, and a resumed threat of war by the Dey of Algiers, to which Madison tartly responded that while the United States prefers peace to war it also prefers war to tribute. He was pleased by extensive negotiations with Indian tribes but unknowingly foreshadowed the sad history of American-Indian relationships as he parroted the Jeffersonian doctrine of "civilization" that would draw the original Americans "from the habits of the savage to the arts and comforts of social life." The fate of the original American inhabitants was hinted by the admission of Louisiana and Indiana as the eighteenth and nineteenth states during Madison's administration. While some progress had been made in the previous legislative session regarding the militia, Madison asked for still more efficiency, a reorganization of the militia "into classes according to the periods of life more or less adapted to military services." He argued that reform was most possible in peacetime, especially if it was based on the experience of recent war, but that argument carried little weight in a Congress that wanted to separate itself as far from war as possible.

The longest and most important part of his message heralded the financial success of the Treasury department, its recently retired Secretary Dallas, and the economy in general. Thanks to the return of peace "the revenue has far exceeded all the current demands upon the Treasury" and should soon lead to the "effectual and early extinguishment of the public debt." He anticipated a surplus of about $9 million in 1816. Even though the "local currency of most of the States" had

[22] Rutland, *The Presidency of James Madison,* p. 203.

sufficed to meet most needs, "the restoration of an uniform medium of exchange" was needed for fiscal prosperity. The reference to its "restoration" was a subtle admission of the importance of the national bank that was allowed to die in 1811. He was quite open in praise of the Second Bank: The Constitution has "intrusted Congress exclusively with the power of creating and regulating" a uniform currency. "The Bank of the United States has been organized under auspices the most favorable, and can not fail to be an important auxiliary to those measures." This was praise for what Congress accomplished in 1816.

The only national legislation in 1817 that can be linked to Madison's December 1816 message stems from this comment: "And I particularly invite again their attention to the expediency of exercising their existing powers, and, where necessary, of resorting to the prescribed mode of enlarging them, in order to effectuate a comprehensive system of roads and canals, such as will have the effect of drawing more closely together every part of our country by promoting intercourse and improvements and by increasing the share of every part in the common stock of national prosperity." As will soon be seen, Congress gave Madison just what he wanted, except for the hinted constitutional amendment because they did not regard it as necessary.

A "grab bag" of recommendations that were ignored by Congress included "uniformity of weights and measures," "a University within this District," "revisal of the criminal code," "re-modification of the judiciary establishment" to relieve Supreme Court justices of the obligation to travel great distances to serve on circuit courts, and "an additional department in the executive branch of the Government." He was not specific about what that department would be, other than that it would "be charged with duties now overburdening other departments and with such as have not been annexed to any department." This recommendation was followed by a request that the Attorney General be better paid and be provided "the usual appurtenances to a public office," but he calls this "another improvement in the executive establishment" so presumably the proposed new department would not be a Department of Justice. After boasting of world leadership in attempts to abolish the African slave trade, Madison urged Congress to take action against "unworthy citizens" persisting in "collusive importations of slaves," as well as more humane treatment of "the trade between the several States," an embarrassing reminder that a very active slave trade continued *within* the United States of America.

Madison properly chose this message for his farewell to his "fellow-citizens," thanking them for their "continued confidence and kind support" which convinced him that "If I have not served my country with greater ability, I have served it with a sincere devotion." He had the "proud reflection" that the nation had not only existed for four decades as an independent nation but had thrived for "nearly an entire generation" under the Constitution in which he took such pride. Surely Madison would have winked at his predecessor if Jefferson had been present, for Madison had persuaded him to retreat from his early view that every generation should review and develop a Constitution to meet the needs of a new day. The Constitution had survived through war without severe dislocation. When he listed "the great principles consecrated in its charter and by those moral principles to which they are so well allied," he started with "a Government which watches over the purity of elections, the freedom of speech and of the press, the trial by jury, and the equal interdict against encroachments and compacts between religion and the state." After a lengthy chain of lengthy clauses, this sentence concluded, "a Government, in a word, whose conduct within and without may bespeak the most noble of all ambitions—that of promoting peace on earth and good will to men."[23]

ONE FINAL CONSTITUTIONAL LECTURE

The Madisons, and especially their slaves and servants, spent the first two months of 1817 busily packing for their final departure from Washington. On March 3, though, the departing president delivered a surprising constitutional lecture as his final official action as President. Based on the supportive words Madison had often stated on the benefits of internal improvements at national expense, Congress had adopted "An act to set apart and pledge certain funds for internal improvements" without paying sufficient attention to Madison's reminders that a constitutional amendment might be required to allow federal action on what the legislation called "roads and canals, and improving the navigation of water courses, in order to facilitate, promote, and give security to internal commerce among the several States, and to render more easy and less expensive the means and provisions for the common defense." It was also called the "bonus bill" because the $1.5 million to be expended was one of the terms for approval of the charter of the National Bank. It was adopted with scant questioning of its constitutionality. On March 3 congressmen learned that constitutionality was indeed an issue to the President. Because the legislation was justified by Rep. Calhoun under the general welfare clause at the beginning of Article I, Section 8 of the Constitution, rather than the necessary and proper clause at the end of that section, Madison was carried back to a different dispute with Alexander Hamilton. In both cases Hamilton had argued for a broad

[23] Hunt, *Writings of James Madison,* VIII, pp. 375-385.

construction, while Madison insisted on a limited reading. This time he could not find the string of precedents that he had used to justify his Bank decision, even though he himself had in 1815 signed off on federal funding for the National Road, also called the Cumberland Road because its original segment was to proceed from Cumberland, Maryland, along the Potomac River to Wheeling in what is now West Virginia.

Madison was not secretive about his reservations regarding this legislation but Speaker Clay was astonished that Madison would veto popular legislation at this late stage of his official life. The statesman who would become the nation's leading advocate of such federal projects delicately asked if Madison would "excuse me for respectfully suggesting whether you could not leave the bill to your successor?"[24] Because he could not reconcile the legislation with the Constitution, Madison replied that he was compelled to return it unsigned to the House of Representatives. Five paragraphs of explication of Section 8 followed, in which he ruled out the so-called "elastic" constitutional clauses as justification. If enacted the legislation would "have the effect of giving to Congress a general power of legislation instead of the defined and limited one hitherto understood to belong to them." He argued that such latitude would allow Congress to supplant the Constitution as "the supreme law of the land."

Thus Madison's last official words as President were "I am not unaware of the great importance of roads and canals and the improved navigation of water courses, and that a power in the National Legislature to provide for them might be exercised with signal advantage to the general prosperity. But seeing that such a power is not expressly given by the Constitution, and believing that it can not be deduced from any part of it without an inadmissible latitude of construction and a reliance on insufficient precedents; believing also that the permanent success of the Constitution depends on a definite partition of powers between the General and the State Governments, and that no adequate landmarks would be left by the constructive extension of the powers of Congress as proposed in the bill, I have no option but to withhold my signature from it, and to cherishing the hope that its beneficial objects may be attained by a resort for the necessary powers to the same wisdom and virtue in the nation which established the Constitution in its actual form and providently marked out in the instrument itself a safe and practicable mode of improving it as experience might suggest."[25] Madison's last two sentences of farewell to Congress were extremely long ones!

---

[24] James F. Hopkins, ed., *The Papers of Henry Clay* (Lexington: University of Kentucky Press, 1959), II, p. 322.

[25] Hunt, *Writings of James Madison,* VIII, pp. 386-388.

Madison would indeed have the last word but not for long. Perhaps as solace to their departing "war hero," Congress did not muster the two thirds vote required to override a presidential veto. However Congress would soon fund such projects—and it still does--without ever being required to adopt the amendment that Madison hinted about so often but never stated explicitly. When Monroe consulted his predecessor regarding the veto of the next extension of the National Road, Madison speculated that when this project was initially approved in 1806, "the question of Constitutionality was but slightly if at all examined" by President Jefferson and his "assent was doubtingly or hastily given." Succeeding appropriations under Jefferson led the "succeeding" administration (and Madison chose not name its leader) to continue with "less of critical investigation perhaps than was due to the case." Monroe would soon open the floodgates by conceding that internal improvements at national expense would be constitutional if the states approved.[26]

Eight years as president ended for James Madison at noon on March 4 when James Monroe was inaugurated. Madison hoped to leave soon for Virginia but was retained for more than a month by continued packing but most of all by rounds of honors and celebrations of the two presidents. He was honored by public addresses and letters from admirers, some of whom had only belatedly been able to say anything good about him. On April 6 he and Dolley left Washington on a steamboat that carried them down the Potomac to where carriages awaited in the Virginia side. James Madison never again left Virginia and despite her dream of seeing Europe and at least Philadelphia again, Dolley was also confined to Virginia until her husband died. A companion on the vessel wrote that "if ever man rejoiced sincerely in being freed from the cares of public life it was him. During the voyage he was as playful as a child; talked and joked with everybody on board, and reminded me of a schoolboy on a long vacation."[27]

---

[26] James Madison to James Monroe, December 23, 1817, ibid., VIII, 404-405; Brant, *James Madison: Commander in Chief,* p. 426.

[27] Ralph L. Ketcham, "An Unpublished Sketch of James Madison," *Virginia Magazine of History and Biography,* LVII (October 1959), p. 453.

Chapter 13

TWO BUSY DECADES OF RETIREMENT

The retired President's final journey in April 1817 from Washington, D.C., to his Virginia estate of Montpelier in Orange County was only a hundred miles. Yet he never intended to return, nor did he ever again travel beyond the boundaries of Virginia. Jefferson wrote John Adams on May 5 that "I do not entertain your apprehensions for the happiness of our brother Madison in a state of retirement. Such a mind as his, fraught with information, and with matter for reflection, can never know ennui. Besides, there will always be work enough cut out for him to continue his active usefulness to his country."[1] His expectations for Madison's retirement would be prophetic for the next nineteen years. The farthest that Madison ever ventured from his beloved home was in the winter of 1829-1830 when he was elected as a delegate to his final constitutional convention in Richmond, which had become the capitol city in 1779. There he played a surprisingly active role in the proposed revisions of the Virginia constitution to which he had made a small but significant contribution more than a half-century earlier. Although frail and weak of voice, the 78-year-old retired President participated actively in debates but was disappointed with the resolution of the issue to which he dedicated his greatest efforts. In the meanwhile he had devoted his years of retirement to diplomatic and political counsel to his successors in Washington, D.C., to frustrating efforts to apply his scientific study of farming to a declining Virginia agrarian economy, to the establishment of a great public university, to safeguarding his own political reputation and that of his great friend and mentor Thomas Jefferson, and most important of all to an ardent defense of

---

[1] Cappon, *Adams-Jefferson Letters,* II, p. 513.

the United States Constitution of 1787, and the federal union that it established. Of course these varied goals often intersected.[2]

James and Dolley Madison had withdrawn geographically but they were by no means isolated from the world, either culturally or intellectually. For many years Montpelier and Jefferson's Monticello, just thirty-two miles to the south, were common gathering places for American and European travelers. Inveterate socialite though she was, it sometimes seemed to Mrs. Madison that the parade of visitors never ceased. The only permanent residents of the mansion were the retired President and First Lady and his aged mother who survived until the age of ninety-eight in the separate wing of Montpelier that had been built as nearly a private home. She died in 1829, twenty-eight years after the death of James Madison, Sr., and only seven years before that of James Madison, Jr. The only direct family descendant of James *or* Dolley Madison was the wastrel John Payne Todd, who was usually off gambling and womanizing in the cities he loved, and seldom in contact with his family other than when he needed relief from gambling debts that were sometimes known to his mother but more often paid secretively by his step-father to protect Dolley from embarrassment due to her son's excesses. Both Payne Todd and his parents would surely have been better off if he had remained in Virginia where some restraint could be applied to him. Despite the few permanent residents at Montpelier, visitors seldom arrived at an empty house because there was usually a multitude of Orange County relatives as well as family members of Dolley visiting from greater distances. Montpelier was often shared unofficially by siblings of both James and Dolley, and much larger numbers of nieces and nephews and great-nieces and great-nephews. Historian Ralph Ketcham provides an extraordinarily detailed account of the omnipresent families of Madison's brothers, sisters and in-laws.[3] Thus there was ample company for the many visitors who arrived sometimes with prior notice but all too often by surprise. One of the former President's celebrations of American independence was shared by nearly a hundred guests, primarily men. Vacationing and traveling statesmen, including many presidential candidates, and European diplomats and generals, mingled with general citizens as they gathered to pay their respects and seek the advice and wisdom of the retired presidents, neither of whom could really afford the hospitality that they willingly but often painfully provided. Like countless other Virginians, Madison and Jefferson and Monroe as well were "land poor." Jefferson died nearly bankrupt while the legislature was

---

[2] This chapter draws extensively upon Donald O. Dewey, "The Sage of Montpelier: The Constitutional and Political Thought of James Madison, 1817-1836," doctoral dissertation, University of Chicago, September, 1960.

planning a state lottery that was designed to allow him to live out his days at his beloved Monticello. Monroe had to sell his Virginia home and move to New York shortly before his death in 1831. Madison's economic plight was less extreme than theirs but his final years presented a constant juggling act because of poor weather and poor crops and, to his credit, because of his conscientious unwillingness to follow so many of his peers by selling slaves down-river to the Deep South.

It should be no surprise that the retired President would be frequently consulted regarding the diplomacy of the Monroe administration. The teamwork of Madison and Monroe that had dominated the previous six years of American history continued unabated when Monroe succeeded to the presidency. Two other admiring allies of Madison exchanged diplomatic portfolios at that same time to influence the decades of world peace often called Pax Britannica that allowed the United States finally to escape the European wars that had plagued both Madison administrations, and instead to concentrate on occupying its continent. Richard Rush, Madison's long-time personal friend, his Attorney General since 1814, and briefly Secretary of State in 1817 pending the return of John Quincy Adams to assume that position, was dispatched by Monroe as United States ambassador to Great Britain in place of Adams. In their new official positions Rush and Adams would be instrumental in the development of the Monroe Doctrine, which long discouraged European nations from seizing the colonies that were rapidly breaking free from Spain as it became steadily more incapable of defending them, or even itself. One of Madison's cherished ambitions was achieved in 1819 when Florida was purchased by treaty. Fortunately for the United States, Great Britain was so fully committed to free trade with Mexico and Central and South America as they achieved freedom, that it had not taken offense at previous American bluster that France and Great Britain must keep hands off of Florida. It was never regarded by Americans as a colony, although it would not be organized as a territory until 1822 and as the twenty-seventh state until 1845, when it entered the Union as a slave state.

In July 1823 Madison wrote Rush to propose that Great Britain should cooperate with the United States to protect the independence of Mexico, Central America and South America as they broke away from Spain. Madison and Jefferson had long regarded the Spanish colonies as fitting disciples of republican government as it had developed in the United States. Although the return of the decrepit Spain was nothing to fear, more viable European nations were eager to assume its position as a colonial power. Well before Madison's advice arrived,

[3] Ketcham, *James Madison,* pp. 614-620.

Rush on his own initiative proposed to Madison's longtime antagonist British Foreign Minister George Canning that their two nations should cooperate to declare Latin America off-limits to further European colonialism. Shortly after Canning responded with interest, Rush and Monroe sought advice from Madison and Jefferson regarding Canning's proposal that the two nations combine forces to keep European colonialism out of "their" hemisphere. Of course both former presidents enthusiastically welcomed this cooperative relationship with their recent enemy to spread and protect nascent republicanism. Monroe would probably have agreed with his two predecessors if not for the insistence of his nationalistic Secretary of State Adams that the United States must act independently and forcefully rather than appear to "come in as a cock-boat in the wake of the British man-of-war." When Monroe briefly worried that the United States might have missed its opportunity, he considered asking Madison to sail to London as a special envoy to negotiate their respective roles. Adams readily agreed that Madison was ideal for the task, but silence from the British convinced Monroe that they could safely proceed with an entirely American assertion that independence from Europe must prevail throughout the western hemisphere. This was fortunate for the United States because at this age Madison was even less likely to consent to a foreign mission than he had been on all the previous occasions when he was asked to venture across the Atlantic. The assertion of separation from Europe was the highlight of President Monroe's annual message of December 1823 and has become justly famous in American history as the Monroe Doctrine, even though it would long be enforced by British naval supremacy more than by American power or influence. If not for Adams's forceful insistence on American independence, a "Madison Doctrine" would surely have been a minor feature of a "Canning Doctrine."[4]

Constitutional Historian and Archivist

Madison surely spent more of his early years of retirement than he could have anticipated in preserving the history of 1787 and 1788. He had devoted enormous efforts to bring together the fifty-five men who proposed the Constitution of the United States in the summer of 1787. He arrived in Philadelphia with a plan of union that guided the Convention through its early stages and was influential until the document was completed. He had no doubt from the outset that this was an important moment in world history and took appropriate steps to see that its

4 Brant, *James Madison: Commander in Chief,* pp. 437-439.

history would be presented accurately. He recorded in shorthand nearly every speech and vote in this highly secret convention, with a guarantee that members' frank comments could never be used against them because secrecy would be maintained during the lives of all of its members. The largely uninformative official journal published by Secretary of State John Quincy Adams highlights the importance of Madison's decision. Because of the journal's lack of substantive information, the Convention's secrecy was maintained to an astonishing degree more than two decades after the event. We would have extremely limited knowledge of this crucial event in American history without Madison' notes. He lived on for seven years after all others had fallen to carry out his pledge of secrecy. He appears to have first reviewed these records with care as he assisted Adams's publication in 1818-1819.

Pressures for Madison to release his Convention notes increased in 1821 with the publication of sketchy notes by another delegate who was present for only five weeks and strongly opposed what he observed. Throughout the 1820s Madison consistently argued that the views of the state conventions that ratified the U.S. Constitution were more significant than those of the Convention that created the document. By this standard his debates recorded in 1788 by an independent reporter at Richmond, to the extent that he could properly hear Madison's low voice, were of more constitutional significance than his personal notes on his own speeches delivered the previous year in Philadelphia. Yet when Jonathan Elliot invited him to correct the record of his comments in the Virginia ratifying convention prior to their publication in his five-volume edition of *Debates in the Several State Conventions on the Federal Constitution,* Madison declined. He feared that "it might not be safe, nor deemed fair, after a lapse of 40 years, lacking a few months, and without having in the meantime ever revised them, to undertake to make them what it might be believed they ought to be. If I did not confound subsequent ideas, and varied expressions, with the real ones, I might be supposed to do so."[1] Despite nearly as great a lapse of time since 1787, he had been carefully reviewing his notes from the Constitutional Convention, making small corrections that led to an accusation in 1955 that he had distorted the records to disguise his own political inconsistencies.[2]

The public would not see his notes of the Convention debates until they were published in 1840 by the federal government, four years after Madison's death. Thus the great decisions of Marshall Supreme Court, President Jackson's

[1] November 1827, Hunt, *Writings of James Madison,* IX, p. 292.

[2] For more information on Madison's notes and on the resulting controversy and its refutation, see Chapter Four of this volume.

dismantling of the Bank of the United States (which had been established in 1816 with Madison's blessings), and the powerful debates of Senators Daniel Webster (Massachusetts) and Robert Y. Hayne (South Carolina) over the constitutionality of South Carolina's nullification of acts of Congress all occurred before accurate knowledge of the debates that led to the United States Constitution was available. This delay resulted from the failure of Congress to agree that this final legacy, which Madison believed would assure funds that would enable his widow to remain in their Orange County home after his death, was worth what Madison had believed. Sadly she was forced to sell Montpelier and live her final years in Washington, D.C., where she died in 1849.[3]

A new edition of *The Federalist Papers* as he was retiring from the presidency drew Madison into another important, but much less time-consuming, explication of his early and anonymous constitutional writings. Earlier editions had assigned authorship based presumably on a lapse of memory by the principal author, Alexander Hamilton.

Word of a differing account by Madison had recently surfaced and he was asked to clarify the disparity. He provided his own list which resulted in "conflicting" editions based on Madison's or Hamilton's claims but often compromising by listing both. Hamilton wrote a clear majority of the Publius essays, the only dispute being whether it was only a considerable majority or a huge majority.[4]

An historian's delight, Madison in that same period actively reclaimed many letters that he had written decades earlier to prominent colleagues such as Washington, Jefferson, Monroe, and many other prominent statesmen who served with him in national and state government. Because he was less innovative than Jefferson, who invented clever devices to preserve copies of his correspondence, Madison sought the originals with considerable success. He arranged his papers through the Federal Convention and even wrote an introduction, fully justifying Historian Ketcham's assertion that Madison was in effect editor of the first edition of his papers, the three volumes generally known as the Congress Edition of *The Papers of James Madison*, that were published in 1840 and that finally introduced to the public the long-awaited Notes of the Debates. In 1827 and 1830 he also talked at length with Jared Sparks, later President of Harvard University, and allowed Sparks to search through his papers to enhance his historical writings on George Washington.[5]

---

[3] Zall, *Dolley Madison*, pp. 97-107.

[4] For more information on the "*Federalist* dispute" see Chapter Five of this volume.

[5] Brant, *James Madison: Commander in Chief*, pp. 462-464.

In addition to preserving historical records of the Constitution he also contended frequently that historic events were basic to its correct interpretation. Considering that his busy summer of 1787 was the high mark of his long life, his frequent down-playing of the significance of the Convention and his notes on it comes as something of a surprise. While he insisted that original intent was the key to interpretation of the Constitution, this did not necessarily mean the intent of those, including himself, who proposed the document in 1787. The true meaning of the Constitution or laws should be found in knowledge of the evils they were intended to prevent and the benefits they were designed to achieve. When such questions could not be resolved by careful reading of the Constitution itself, then answers should be sought first through study of the debates of the state conventions that had by ratification made it the law of the land. Thus ratification debates were Madison's preferred starting points, abetted by discussions published in 1787 and 1788 by newspapers and pamphlets, by legislation enacted in the earliest Congresses as they implemented the new Constitution, and only then by the views of the Founding Fathers of the Federal Convention, to the limited extent that they could be determined.[6] Madison's emphasis on the state conventions was not mere speculation of an aging statesman. As early as 1796 he argued in Congress that

> "...whatever veneration might be entertained for the body of men who formed our Constitution, the sense of that body could never be regarded as the oracular guide in expounding the Constitution. As the instrument came from them it was nothing more than the draft of a plan, nothing but a dead letter, until life and validity were breathed into it by the voice of the people, speaking through the several State Conventions. If we were to look, therefore, for the meaning of the instrument beyond the face of the instrument, we must look for it not in the General Convention, which proposed, but in the State Conventions, which accepted and ratified the Constitution."[7]

Ironically he was in 1796 challenging information slipped beyond the secrecy of the Federal Convention when President Washington referred to his personal recollection of 1787 debates with the goal of undercutting Madison's efforts in the U.S. House of Representatives to deny the funding of commissions that were essential to implementation of the Jay Treaty of 1794. Madison seldom

---

[6] Donald O. Dewey, "James Madison Helps Clio Interpret the Constitution," *The American Journal of Legal History*, XV, (October 1971), p. 39.

[7] *The Debates and Proceedings in the Congress of the United States (1825-1837),* 4th Congress, 1st Session, V, p. 776.

demonstrated how constitutional interpretation based on ratifications could be accomplished. Who would decide which delegates in which state conventions should prevail? Even though he possessed records from some other states, he referred primarily to those of Virginia and even there he wrote generically without reference to specific commentary. Information on ratification debates of 1788 could be more easily reviewed than those of 1787 that occurred during the Federal Convention, but full and accurate information was difficult to obtain. It was only in 1827 that Madison viewed advance copies of the first of the proposed volumes of published debates from state ratification conventions. Even then he was still providing for the editor pamphlets that he possessed on state debates. The published debates would not be readily available to the public for several more years, and even then only to those with access to excellent libraries.

In the era before the internet, early newspapers were equally difficult to research. Published essays supporting the Constitution were of course more readily available and Madison used them freely, including his own and Hamilton's contributions to *The Federalist.* As for the views of early legislation, which laws would be so honored? Surely not the programs proposed by Alexander Hamilton and readily enacted by a Federalist-dominated Congress, often over Representative Madison's objections. Some later legislation would be much more fruitful. Even while refusing to concede that authority to establish a National Bank was hidden somewhere in the Constitution, Madison agreed that twenty years of acceptance by the American people, the true founders of the Constitution, had made it constitutional in 1811 if it had been renewed: in 1816 when he signed the Second Bank into law: and even in 1832 when President Andrew Jackson vetoed its renewal because he denied its constitutionality. While Madison disapproved of some of the nationalistic peripheral comments (*obiter dicta)* in Chief Justice John Marshall's monumental *McCulloch v. Maryland* decision upholding the Bank in 1819, he supported the basic decision. On the other hand he persistently denied constitutional justification for internal improvements at national expense (roads, canals, etc.) despite frequent evidence that they were desired by the public. He would spend his last years suggesting a constitutional amendment to meet this need. Madison parted company with Virginia critics such as John Taylor of Caroline, Spencer Roane and even Thomas Jefferson, who contended that the Marshall Court exceeded its authority, gently admonishing Jefferson that the Constitution could not survive if the Supreme

Court was prevented from ruling with finality, even when the results were resented by some Virginians.[12]

Madison made his strongest argument against relying on the Federal Convention to understand the Constitution in 1821 when he was challenged by the powerful editor of the *Richmond Enquirer* to release his own notes to counter the recently published records of another delegate:

> "As a guide in expounding and applying the provisions of the Constitution the debates and incidental decisions of the Convention can have no authoritative character. However desirable it be that they should be preserved as a gratification to the laudable curiosity felt by every people to trace the origin and progress of their political institution, & as a source perhaps of some lights on the Science of Govt. the legitimate meaning of the instrument must be derived from the text itself; or if a ray is to be sought elsewhere it must be not in the opinions or intentions of the Body which planned & proposed the Constitution, but in the sense attached to it by the people in their respective State Conventions when it recd. all the authority which it possesses."[13]

Mere gratification to laudable curiosity? Yet Madison would contend years later that he had risked his life with the night and day labors of this project. And he also felt that these notes and related papers would be the most valuable legacy that he could bequeath to his widow. While he did not directly cite his Notes of Debates, he used them to research corrections to the sporadic and sometimes emotional notes of Robert Yates and Luther Martin. Whenever possible he used the limited published resources that were available. But he would on occasion refer to the Convention without specific reference to what he often called the *"telum imbelle"* (peaceful weapon) that he regarded himself as too principled to wield. On one such occasion he went so far as to identify another delegate when

---

[12] Dewey, "James Madison Helps Clio Interpret the Constitution," pp. 40-43, 48-55; Hunt, *Writings of James Madison,* IX, pp. 142-143, 270-271, 291-292.

[13] To Thomas Ritchie, September 15, 1821, Hunt, *Writings of James Madison,* IX, pp. 71-73. It must be conceded that Madison looked at his notes quite differently when he signed his will on April 18, 1835. Then he thought that "Considering the peculiarity and magnitude of the occasion which produced the convention at Philadelphia in 1787, the Characters who composed it, the Constitution which resulted from their deliberations, it's effects during a trial of so many years on the prosperity of the people living under it, and the interest it has inspired among friends of free Government, it is not an unreasonable inference that a careful and extended report of the proceedings and discussions of that body, which was with closed doors, by a member who was constant in his attendance, will be particularly gratifying to the people of the United States, and to all who take an interest in the progress of political science and the cause of true liberty." Ibid., p. 549.

he revealed that even a nationalist such as Alexander Hamilton had opposed authority to build roads and canals at national expense because its inclusion would likely have caused rejection of the Constitution by state conventions.[14] Such usage would increase when he feared the Union was threatened by South Carolina's assertion of *constitutional* authority to nullify acts of Congress.

PROTECTING JEFFERSON AND THE UNION

Less than five months before he died, Jefferson wrote plaintively to his lifelong friend, "To myself you have been a pillar of support through life. Take care of me when dead, and be assured that I shall leave with you my last affections." Little realizing how near the time was when he must assume this responsibility, Madison ended a lengthy letter with his heart-felt acceptance:

> "You cannot look back to the long period of our private friendship & political harmony, with more affecting recollections than I do. If they are a source of pleasure to you, what ought they not to be to me? We cannot be deprived of the happy consciousness of the pure devotion to the public good with which we discharged the trusts committed to us. And I indulge a confidence that sufficient evidence will find its way to another generation, to ensure, after we are gone, whatever of justice may be withheld whilst we are here. The political horizon is already yielding in your case at least, the surest auguries of it. Wishing & hoping that you may yet live to increase the debt which our Country owes you, and to witness the increasing gratitude, which alone can pay it, I offer you the fullest return of affectionate assurances."[15]

The embarrassing word "nullify" that Jefferson had used in the Kentucky Resolutions, which were no longer as anonymous as they had been in 1798-1799, came back to haunt supporters of the federal union such as Madison during the nullification crisis of 1828-1833. When a protective tariff that was branded the "Tariff of Abominations" by its Jacksonian opponents was approved by President John Quincy Adams in 1828, his Vice President John C. Calhoun asserted in his anonymous "Exposition" the contention that a single state possessed

[14] Dewey, "James Madison Helps Clio Interpret the Constitution," pp. 43-47; James Madison to Edward Livingston, April 17, 1824, Hunt, *Writings of James Madison,* IX, p. 188.

[15] Thomas Jefferson to James Madison, February 17, 1826, Paul L. Ford, ed., *The Writings of Thomas Jefferson,* 10 Volumes, (New York: G. P. Putnam's Sons, 1892-1909), X, pp. 377-378; James Madison to Thomas Jefferson, February 24, Hunt, *Writings of James Madison*, IX, pp. 245-246.

constitutional authority to nullify federal legislation and thus make it null and void within that state. Even though the succeeding tariff of 1832 was considerably less "abominable," Calhoun resigned as Jackson's Vice President, the first of only two Vice Presidents to do so. Then as a U.S. Senator from South Carolina he assumed open leadership of the nullification movement. The South Carolina legislature promptly summoned a convention to nullify that tariff. When a reform tariff of 1833 briefly defused the tariff issue, the same convention nullified the Force Act that had authorized President Jackson to use force to collect tariffs in South Carolina.

Madison found it more difficult to distance Jefferson entirely from nullification than he had anticipated, because the Kentucky Resolutions were "less guarded" than those of Virginia. While suffering from a fever as well as his painful rheumatism in May 1832, he dictated a defense that "allowances also ought to be made for a habit in Mr. Jefferson as in others of great genius, of expressing in strong and round terms, impressions of the moment."[16] He neglected to add that a less brilliant but more circumspect man such as Mr. Madison instead would use the word "interpose," as he had in the Virginia Resolutions. He contended that Virginia and Kentucky had been merely seeking the views of the other states, certainly not planning to violate or nullify the detested laws. Calhoun's spokesman in the Senate responded that the Virginia Resolutions were as supportive of his doctrine as the Kentucky Resolutions and even promised to prove to Madison that he had not properly understood his own arguments in the Virginia Resolutions more than three decades earlier. This promise was never kept.[17]

Defending Jefferson's reputation was important to Madison. Defending the Union was infinitely more so, and he devoted a huge amount of his waning energies to rejecting the threat to the Union that was generated through Calhoun's philosophy of state sovereignty. Calhoun and his followers, including some influential Virginians, were convinced that the economic problems of the South resulted from artificial commercial advantages of northern states rather than from slavery. If the federal government could be denied authority to assist northern commerce and industry, surely it would likewise be prevented from interfering with the South's "peculiar institution." Madison remained behind the scenes for as long as possible. He mailed lengthy essays to Joseph C. Cabell to strengthen his opposition in the Virginia legislature, including even notes for a proposed speech.

---

[16] To Nicholas P. Trist, May 1832, ibid., IX, p. 479 in Brant, *James Madison: Commander in Chief*, pp. 487-491.

Similar advocacy was submitted to Nicholas P. Trist, Jefferson's son-in-law who had advanced from a clerk in the State Department to President Jackson's personal secretary. Through Trist, a friend for nearly a half-century, Madison again had a direct pipeline to the White House.[18] The leaders of Senate debates on South Carolina's dangerous experiment, Daniel Webster and Robert Y. Hayne, each claimed Madison's support. Madison replied politely to both, expressing support for Webster and dissenting from Hayne, but requesting that his statements not be made public.

Years before Calhoun even thought of nullification Madison had expressed surprise that the protective tariff had become so heated a constitutional issue, because there had *never* been a question in his mind regarding its constitutionality. He felt that regulation of commerce in the national interest was one of the principal reasons for convening the Federal Convention. One of his earliest goals in the First Congress was the establishment of tariffs on importations. Although they were primarily for desperately needed revenue, mild support for industry was to him clearly constitutional. For him the only problem was what level of protection was allowed. Madison could not support the full extent of Henry Clay's American System, but in April 1824 he sent him a lengthy letter asserting that "a moderate tariff" would "answer the purpose of revenue and foster domestic manufactures." He especially encouraged protection of "1. the case of articles necessary for national defense; 2. articles of a use too indispensable to be subjected to foreign contingencies; 3. cases where there may be sufficient certainty, that a *temporary* encouragement will introduce a particular manufacture, which once introduced will flourish without that encouragement."[19] This is one of the rare early occasions when he referred specifically to the views of a state convention as it ratified the Constitution. By 1828 when he was preparing Cabell for Virginia's defense against South Carolina, he had viewed the records that would be published in the first volume of Jonathan Elliot's *Debates of the Several State Conventions* and could declare with more certainty that "the power to regulate trade with foreign nations" that was delegated to Congress in Article I "has been understood and used by all commercial & manufacturing Nations as embracing the object of encouraging manufactures. It is believed that

[17] Robert Y. Hayne to James Madison, July 22, 1830, Dewey, "The Sage of Montpelier: The Constitutional and Political Thought of James Madison," p. 178.

[18] The extent and intensity of this correspondence is graphically demonstrated in Hunt, *Writings of James Madison,* IX, pp. 316-364, 471-482, and 489-497. There are occasional brief letters to others interspersed within these pages, but they too focus largely on nullification.

[19] Ibid., p. 184.

not a single exception can be named." He concluded that "this was the aim of Virginia herself."[20]

From the outset Madison rejected the idea that there could be a constitutional right for a single state convention to nullify an act of Congress. A state confronted by serious violations might have a *natural right* of revolution, so both nullification and its hidden threat of secession would be revolution. He argued that the protective tariff, even if it had been an offense, did not justify revolution. For him it was far short of the Alien and Sedition Acts that prompted the Virginia and Kentucky Resolutions. Despite severe illness, when his private comments became semi-public he finally agreed to prepare a frontal attack for publication in the *North American Review* of October 1830. A private recipient of similar comments on nullification since 1827, Cabell declared that the effect of this article was "as great as ever was produced by any document in any age or country." Chief Justice Marshall wrote of his "peculiar pleasure" to see Madison again expressing "the opinions of his best days." Associate Justice Joseph Story concluded that "the general structure of the argument stands on immovable foundations, and can scarcely perish but with the Constitution that it seeks to uphold." South Carolinians and some Virginians, however, treated Madison with vicious contempt that he had not encountered since the unhappy days of New England attacks on "Mr. Madison's War."[21] Madison responded with language that was far stronger than might be expected of an octogenarian former President. He described nullification as "equally unconstitutional, preposterous, and anti-republican." It was "variously described as ruinous, hideous, fatal, stupid, poisonous, absurd, rash, insidious, humiliating, and heretical—a veritable thesaurus of vituperation."[22]

While Madison never contended that the government to which he had contributed so much was perfect, there was no question in his mind that American federalism provided the best system ever created, and extreme care should be taken in revising it. Maintaining the proper balance between the union and the states was a delicate balancing act. He was offended by Calhoun's contention that a single state could negate an act of Congress, unless the act was supported by three-fourths of the states—a weird reversal of Article V which instead required

---

[20] Ibid., pp. 328-329.

[21] James Madison to Edward Everett, August 28, 1830, ibid., IX, pp. 383-403; Everett was a Massachusetts congressman as well as editor of the *North American Review*; Ketcham, *James Madison,* pp. 642-643.

[22] Joseph Story, *Commentaries on the Constitution of the United States,* 4th ed. (Boston: Little Brown, 1873), I, p. 289; Dewey, "The Sage of Montpelier: The Constitutional and Political Thought of James Madison," p. 175.

three fourths of the states in order to *amend* the Constitution. He scoffed at the basis of Calhoun's doctrine, that individual states retained their sovereignty when they ratified the Constitution, because sovereignty cannot be divided. "If sovereignty or the supreme powers composing it can not be divided and placed in different depositories, the political System of the U.S. is a meteor or a mockery."[23] After helping to beat back the threat of nullification, Madison correctly gauged the greater danger that would be Calhoun's next major thrust, sectionalism and secession. Madison predicted that the union could not survive if political parties became regional parties. While criticizing fears that northern states would interfere with the South's "peculiar institution," because it was against their own interests, he added "what *madness* in the South, to look for greater safety in disunion. It would be worse than jumping out of the Frying-pan into the fire. It wd. be jumping into the fire for fear of the Frying-pan."[24]

His continuing fears for survival of the Union even after the failure of nullification were resented by some of his recent allies who now insisted that he must enlist in Whig campaigns against the alleged executive despotism of Andrew Jackson, only two years before his presidency would end. Dolley's Madison's cousin Edward Coles, who had been the second Governor of the new state of Illinois only three years after his arrival from Virginia with slaves whom he promptly freed, irritated Madison by his insistent demands that Madison was obligated to devote the same energy and passion against Jackson that he had against Calhoun. Especially offensive was Coles' complaint that nullification was "harmless compared to the Executive powers and prerogatives now claimed by the President of the U.S." As a life-long friend and Madison's personal secretary from 1809 to 1815 when he was appointed to a special mission to Russia, Coles should have known better than to argue that South Carolina's "Nullification only endangered the Union." In addition to welcoming President Jackson as an essential ally in the defense of the Union, Madison was critical of Whig efforts to impose on the President interference with appointments and especially dismissals. When a Senate committee had sought to meet with President Madison in 1813 to object to recess appointment of a peace commission to negotiate an end to the war, he flatly refused even to meet with them because he regarded them as intruding on executive authority. While Madison was not enthusiastic about some

23 James Madison on Sovereignty, 1835, Hunt, *Writings of James Madison,* IX, pp. 568-573.

24 James Madison to Henry Clay, June 1833, Hunt, *Writings of James Madison,* IX, pp. 184-185.

aspects of Andrew Jackson as President he recognized the old soldier as a vital ally in the more important campaign to preserve the Union.[25]

While the one proposed constitutional amendment that Madison discussed in extensive detail concerned the presidency, it was a complex proposal to change the system of elections, and it was suggested five years before Jackson became President. He proposed to strengthen the Electoral College by abandoning the winner-take-all system that ironically he and Virginia had helped to impose on the United States in 1800 to assure Jefferson's triumph, and to adopt instead an intricate system of double votes to lessen the likelihood of Congress becoming involved in elections where there was no clear majority. While this possible amendment was presented with precision in letters of August 1823 and January 1824, just before the famed conflict of Adams, Jackson, Crawford and Clay to succeed Monroe, it was not further pursued.

Although in his last act as President Madison challenged Congress to propose an amendment to make constitutional the internal improvements legislation that he had just vetoed, he made only occasional suggestions to Senator Martin Van Buren from New York while dissuading Jefferson from pressuring Virginia to take the lead on the issue.[26]

Madison's lengthy correspondence in November 1830 with Virginia Speaker Andrew Stevenson criticizing the general welfare clause in the introductory paragraph of the Constitution's Congressional powers clause, Article I, Section 8, was aimed indirectly at the internal improvements issue. When these letters became public, retired President John Quincy Adams retreated from his broad advocacy of general powers due to his respect for his predecessor and friend.[27]

FATHERS OF THE UNIVERSITY OF VIRGINIA

Madison was never able to bring into existence the national university that was the dream of the Virginia presidents as well as both Adamses, but he would rank second only to Thomas Jefferson as "father" of the nation's first *state* university, the University of Virginia. Jefferson provided the inspiration and the philosophy for this grand experiment in public education, but as usual Madison

[25] Donald O. Dewey, "Madison's Response to Jackson's Foes," *Tennessee Historical Quarterly,* (June 1961), pp. 167-176; Hunt, *Writings of James Madison,* VIII, pp. 250-251 and IX, 534-36.

[26] Donald O. Dewey, "Madison's Views on Electoral Reform, *Western Political Quarterly,* XV (March 1962), pp. 140-145; Hunt, *Writings of James Madison,* IX, pp. 147-155, 236-240, 251-255, 576-583.

[27] Ibid., IX, pp. 411-437.

was the first ally that was recruited for the project and he was required to do much of the hard work. Since Jefferson died only a year after the first obstreperous student enrolled, his successor as rector, Madison, was chief administrator for most of the University's first decade. The awesome board of visitors, in effect trustees, for a new Central College at Charlottesville that was authorized in 1816 included Presidents Jefferson, Madison, and Monroe, as well as several younger Virginia luminaries. By the time the small faculty recruited for Central College met their first students Jefferson's plan to convert it to the University of Virginia had been implemented. The college was formally disbanded by the visitors in February 1819 at a meeting hosted by Madison at Montpelier. State funds for college buildings that were authorized by the legislature strengthened Charlottesville's successful competition against two competitive towns. The College of William and Mary, where Jefferson was an undergraduate, was a third unsuccessful claimant for this honor. Supporters of Central College also donated $50,000 in start-up funds, $1,000 of it directly from Madison. Jefferson was given charge of all aspects of the planning commission during four days at a small inn in the Blue Ridge Mountains; the lone exception was selection of the site, because of his obvious conflict of interest. At his age it was essential that the campus be at Charlottesville or he would never be able to oversee the development of his pet project. Fortunately for him Lexington overplayed its hand when it insisted that the faculty of its already existing Washington College become the faculty of the new university. This would prevent the recruitment of the outstanding faculty envisioned, and basically achieved, by Jefferson and Madison. Jefferson prevailed on the site as well as the overall plan and was able to monitor the development of the campus through telescopes set up permanently at Monticello. Madison missed the first meeting of the Central College trustees because he had not yet arrived back in Virginia but he rarely was absent from another meeting of the college or the university, several of which he hosted at Montpelier.[28]

The legislature approved Jefferson's innovative plan for a practical educational system based on public supported schools that would provide the elements of good citizenship and on a number of academies throughout the state responsible for preparing students for the truly *higher* education at Charlottesville. The university would be patterned after academic communities in Europe. His university promised the best of education without the regulations, requirements and discipline prevailing then at most colleges and universities. With one notable exception, the faculty would have remarkable academic freedom to teach what they felt their students needed and the students were in turn allowed a unique

[28] Ketcham, *James Madison,* pp. 649-650.

degree of self-governance. Toward the end of his years as rector Jefferson would be in tears when he learned how little some of the sons of wealthy landowners merited that trust, when they rioted against the faculty so carefully selected by Jefferson and Madison.

Madison faithfully supported Jefferson's ideas and devoted his principal efforts to finding the faculty who would make the system work. Unwilling to hire presumed second-raters who had not found a teaching position, yet too conscientious to steal many faculty from other American universities, they concentrated on bright young scholars from Europe. The few established American faculty members to whom they made an offer soon convinced them that the salaries they offered were not competitive. The land-locked Madison of course did not go to Europe, or even to New England, but he was very explicit in instructing his agent regarding the kind and level of scholarship that was required. The faculty brought from Europe were impressive, although Jefferson showed sufficient surprise at their youth that one felt obliged to assure him that "I shall grow older, sir." Madison however was pleased by their youth: "They will be the less inflexible in their habits, the more improvable in their qualifications, and will last the longer."[29]

Jefferson and Madison agreed that law and government must be taught by Americans who would be conscious and respectful of the unique governmental systems that these two "visitors" had been so influential in developing. Jefferson took a large step further by recommending required reading in which they had also played a pivotal role: the Declaration of Independence, *The Federalist,* and the Virginia Report of 1799 which replied to the antagonistic responses of other states to their Virginia and Kentucky Resolutions. From England he added the writings of John Locke and Algernon Sidney. Madison converted Jefferson's mandates to "best guides" to the "distinctive principles of the Government of our own State, and of that of the U. States" and for balance added "the Inaugural Speech & Farewell Address of President Washington" without adding that he had written the draft of the inaugural and a preliminary draft of the Farewell Address. He warned against mandating documents that were personal as well as controversial to some Virginians. Care was taken, nevertheless, to see that chosen faculty would be properly respectful of the American experiment with republican government. He wrote Jefferson that "The most effectual safeguard against heretical intrusions into the School of Politics will be an Able and Orthodox Professor, whose course of instruction will be an example to his successors"[30]

---

[29] Brant, *James Madison: Commander in Chief,* p. 453.

[30] February 8, 1825, Hunt, *Writings of James Madison,* IX, pp. 218-221.

Biographer Ralph Ketcham wisely observes that this was not as violative of academic freedom as it might at first appear. Since there would be only one professor of "Politics" it was not unreasonable to require that he support the American experiment in government.[31]

Of course religion was another major concern to these two world leaders on the issue of separation of church and state. It was a balancing act to assure that Anglican leaders and ministry, who still were highly influential in Virginia politics despite Madison's and Jefferson's success in heading off an established church, not turn against the fledgling university as a secular institution. The Unitarianism of an outstanding scientist in the now disbanded Central College, who was also a close personal friend of Madison, presented a red flag that nearly prevented his retention at the University. They were adamant against appointing a professor of theology, calming the issue by proposing subordinate seminaries where religion could be studied at the University. The study of religions without a focus on any single sect and placing doctrinaire churchmen off limits was quite unique for American universities. Madison personally selected religious books for the library with care that the emphasis would be on morality and metaphysical studies rather than church doctrine. It could not be guaranteed then but the early acquisitions were expanded significantly by major donations from Madison's own library when he died. The bulk of Jefferson's library had already been donated to the Library of Congress in Washington, D.C.

The University of Virginia opened its doors to students in March 1825 and by September they numbered 100. Unfortunately, before that month ended a considerable majority of students had rioted against the European professors, wielding first a stink bomb and then greater violence with a brick and cane. The visitors happened to be in Charlottesville and a meeting was convened the next day. The inability of the disillusioned Jefferson to finish his admonition of the rioters, as he burst into tears at the conduct of students in whom he held such high hopes, may have had better effect than a severe lecture would have had. The students were shamed, faculty were persuaded to withdraw their resignations, and Jefferson personally developed a more rigid disciplinary program for students. Four students were expelled and the survivors changed their ways. This painful administrative action was one of Jefferson's last as rector. He soon found it increasingly difficult to ride to the campus and he died on July 4, 1826, ironically on the same day as his frequent correspondent, John Adams. Madison was elected rector at the age of seventy-five and continued to serve for eight years, with more rigorous controls than Jefferson had felt was necessary. He seldom missed a

[31] Ketcham, *James Madison,* p. 655.

meeting of the visitors, usually arriving by carriage with Mrs. Madison, who loved the rare opportunity to travel. He retired only two years prior to his own death.[32]

One More Constitution, One More Presidency

When Madison journeyed to Richmond in October 1829 to attend a convention to propose revisions of the Virginia constitution that he had helped to craft in 1776, it was the first time that the Madisons had ventured farther from home than their frequent visits to Jefferson and the University. Dolley was in her glory throughout the thirteen weeks and delighted Richmond society. She dressed with her accustomed flair and was said to be "as active on her feet as a girl" who appeared more the daughter than the wife of the aged President. It was "impossible not to admire her."[33] By comparison James Madison appeared aged, wrinkled and drab in his customary black and old-fashioned clothing. As in 1787 he sat at the front of the meeting room where he could hear and hopefully be heard, and he attended every session. This convention would mark a final gathering of old friends and former foes. Partly to head off his own election Madison nominated President James Monroe to preside, after which he and Chief Justice John Marshall escorted Monroe to the chair. Unfortunately Monroe soon proved inadequate for the task because of illness. Long-standing political opponents in Congress from within Madison's own party were there as well, most notably John Randolph of Roanoke and William Branch Giles.

As might be expected at the dawn of "Jacksonian democracy" voting rights caused the most heated debates. As chair of the Legislative Committee, Madison struggled to achieve compromise between eastern and western interests. The Tidewater counties had been dominant in Virginia for more than five decades and had come to regard this dominance as their right, even though they were declining in population while western counties increased. Madison's committee lessened the influence of large land owners by adding home owners and heads of families who paid taxes to the voter lists. Thus residents of towns and cities would finally have some political influence in Virginia, one of the last states to make this concession.

---

[32] Philip A. Bruce, *History of the University of Virginia* (New York: Macmillan Co., 1920), II, pp. 298-301; Adrienne Koch, *Jefferson and Madison: The Great Collaboration* (New York: Oxford University Press, 1964), pp. 261-280.

[33] Katharine Anthony, *Dolly Madison, Her Life and Times* (Garden City, NY: Doubleday, 1949), pp. 315-316.

Madison's contention that owning land was not the only way for a citizen to demonstrate a "stake in society" and thus to act responsibly was persuasive.

It was his attempt to lessen the political dominance of eastern slave owners that unleashed a storm of controversy. The political influence of plantation owners was in effect doubled so long as representation was based on the number of slaves whom they owned to work their land, but who of course would never be allowed to cast a vote. African-American slaves comprised more than half of the population of counties east of the Blue Ridge, whereas they were only a tenth of the population west of the mountains. Although Montpelier was in the eastern shadow of the Blue Ridge, it was close enough to the west that Madison had long comprehended and sympathized with western interests. As a concession to the west, his committee proposed that representation in the House of Delegates be based on white population, though by the narrowest possible margin, 13 to 11. This would have left the Tidewater still over-represented, but at least less drastically. In vain hopes of winning eastern support, Madison voted to maintain slaves as a basis of representation for the Senate, causing the "white basis" to fail by a tie vote. Eastern delegates were outraged at the prospect of losing influence in even one house and muttered threats of disunion and violence. They regarded Madison a traitor to his class and expressed disgust with the interference of old men in governance. Madison next proposed a compromise similar to the one that he achieved in 1787. His recommendation that Virginia borrow the clause in the fifth paragraph of the U.S. Constitution that based representation for the House of Representatives on "the whole number of free persons" plus "three fifths of all other persons" (a circumlocution for slaves) was instead rejected in Virginia for both houses. Northern and southern states had compromised in 1787 to count 60 per cent of slave population as a concession to protect the southern minority against the growing northern majority. In 1830, though, eastern Virginians insisted that *all* slaves be counted for representation even though they were adamant that none would ever cast a vote. Madison had optimistically predicted early in the brief convention that the constitution on which they were laboring would survive for a century but it would last for barely three decades—ended by the Civil War.[34]

On December 2, passions were held in reserve as delegates clustered around Madison to listen to the last public speech of their greatest living statesman. His presentation was described as distinct "to those who heard him." By then he was firmly committed to the three fifths guideline as a useful and widely accepted basis for protecting the rights of the minority as well as the majority. He

[34] Brant, *James Madison: Commander in Chief,* pp. 462-467; Ketcham, *James Madison,* pp. 636-640.

contended that "the rights of persons, and the rights of property, are the objects, for the protection of which Government was instituted." He wrestled especially with that unique form of "property" who were also people, and who were the reason for the proposed three fifths compromise:

> "It is due to justice; due to humanity; due to truth; to the sympathies of our nature; in fine, to our character as a people, both abroad and at home, that they should be considered as much as possible in the light of human beings, and not as mere property. As such they are acted upon by our laws, and have an interest in our laws. They may be considered as making a part, though a degraded part, of the families to which they belong.... [I]f they were of our own complexion, much of the difficulty would be removed. But the mere circumstance of complexion cannot deprive them of the character of men. The Federal number, as it is called, is particularly recommended to attention in forming a basis of Representation by its simplicity, its certainty, its stability, and its permanency.
>
> The Convention is now arrived at a point where we must agree on some common ground, all sides relaxing in their opinions, not changing, but mutually surrendering a part of them. In framing a Constitution, great difficulties are necessary to be overcome; and nothing can overcome them, but a spirit of compromise....I never have despaired, notwithstanding all the threatening experiences we have passed through. I have now more than a hope—a consoling confidence, that we shall at last find, that our labours have not been in vain."[35]

Three or four years later Madison described the frustrating events of Richmond in autobiographical notes written in the third person. "His preference would have been the white basis for one branch and the mixed or federal basis for the other. Tho' aware of the danger of universal suffrage in a future state of Society such as the present state in Europe he would have extended it so far as to secure in every event and change in the state of Society a majority of people on the side of power. A Government resting on a minority, is an aristocracy, not a Republic, and could not be safe with a numerical & physical force against it, without a standing Army, and enslaved press, and a disarmed populace."[36]

Madison's description of African-American slaves as a degraded branch of their family sets the scene for Madison's final presidency. As a young man he yearned to move from Virginia because he did not wish to depend on slave labor as appeared inevitable for a Southern statesman. He shared the views of many

---

[35] Hunt, *Writings of James Madison,* IX, pp. 360-361.

[36] Douglass Adair, ed., "James Madison's Autobiography," *William and Mary Quarterly,* Series 3, II (1945), pp. 206-209.

liberal southerners—liberal Americans for that matter—that slavery was an immoral and shocking embarrassment to American republican principles. Surely it must die of its own weight. Madison was pained to see the sectional conflict harden as slave and free states during the time of the Missouri Compromise. Territories had developed side by side naturally and advanced to statehood during western advancement, until 1819 when Americans became painfully aware of this balance as Missouri was primed for statehood when there was no potential northern state waiting in the wings. Maine was separated from Massachusetts to maintain an artificial equality but the genie of sectionalism based on slavery was out of the bottle. The cotton economy of the Deep South gradually converted the conception of America's "peculiar institution" from a "necessary evil" that was ill suited to American republicanism to a "positive good" that needed and demanded protection from the federal government. Virginia did not share in this expanding economy other than as a source of labor replacement as it became increasingly necessary because of American and British restraints against an international slave trade. Madison was widely and justly recognized as a kindly owner, who was appreciated by his slaves, some of whom lived with him in retirement to very old ages. Yet even kind owners were eventually forced to sell slaves when they could not afford to manumit them, and Madison during his final years was among them, although selling only a small number of slaves who were content to go to nearby owners who also had kindly reputations.

Because Madison was repelled by the institution of slavery, yet at the same time a segregationist who was convinced that the two races could not live together as equals, the American Colonization Society was a convenient institutional home for him. He joined the society when it was founded in 1816, with many others from border slave states. The ACS offered a way to free American slaves, while avoiding the conflicts that he considered inevitable if former owners and former slaves were compelled to live side by side. In 1819 he proposed that "a general emancipation of slaves ought to be 1. gradual. 2. equitable & satisfactory to the individuals immediately concerned. 3. consistent with the existing & durable prejudices of the nation." He clarified the third point with considerable discussion in this vein: "the freed blacks ought to be permanently moved beyond the region occupied by or allotted to a White population." He even suggested that the Colonization Society should be made a branch of the federal executive by a constitutional amendment if necessary.[37] He considered various refuges in the west—the *far* west—and readily supported the purchase of land in Africa for the

[37] James Madison to Robert J. Evans, June 15, 1819, Hunt, *Writings of James Madison,* VIII, pp. 439-446.

establishment of Liberia as a haven for manumitted slaves. The west would remain essential to his plans for he expected the financing to come through the sale of public land. Nearly a decade after the establishment of Liberia, Madison received a proposal that the Oregon Territory become a haven for freed slaves, even though in 1831 it was territory still shared with Great Britain. This was not as preposterous an idea as it might sound because it had proven inordinately expensive to transport the few slaves who desired to move to Africa and were allowed to do so, and slave population grew much more rapidly through natural means than it was being colonized. Madison accepted the presidency of the ACS in February 1833 declaring an "earnest prayer, that every success may reward the labors of an Institution…so noble in its object of removing a great evil." He succeeded Charles Carroll of Carrollton, a Maryland signer of the Declaration of Independence.[38]

There is general agreement that Madison was a kind master, but he remained a slave owner for a half-century after his momentary rejection of the South. Like other enlightened and humane plantation owners he intended to free his work force some day—but it never quite happened. In 1836 he died still a slave owner and those who were intended by his will to become freedmen were instead sold to new owners, fortunately to nearby plantations rather than the Deep South.[39]

Despite a lifetime of anticipating an early death, Madison lived to an old age without suffering the major illnesses that took the lives and health of many of his contemporaries. He was in good health when he left Washington and remained so for more than a decade with only occasional illnesses. Beginning in 1828 he began to complain of "bilious indisposition" and by 1831 rheumatism imposed on him the tiny and awkward handwriting that would continue to the end, with increasing reliance on clerical help from Dolley's brother John C. Payne and from Dolley herself, when her poor eyesight permitted. He became very ill in the winter of 1831-1832 and for the first time began to miss important meetings. By the next year he was often confined to bed. Even though he required nearly constant care in 1835 and 1836, his several visitors described him as bright and alert. He thought of Jefferson during his last hours and struggled to acknowledge a dedication to Madison from the author of a biography on his lifelong political ally.

James Madison died during breakfast on June 28, 1836. He had earlier rejected proposals for stimulants to keep him alive until July 4, so that he could

---

[38] P. J. Staudenraus, *The African Colonial Movement, 1816-1865* (New York: Columbia University 1961), pp. 183-184, 287.

expire on the same day as Presidents Jefferson and Adams (in 1826) and Monroe (in 1831). It is possible that if it had been that close to September 17, the anniversary of the completion of the Constitutional Convention, he would have found the possibility of extending his life for another week more difficult to resist. His personal servant reported that his last words before he died, were in response to this question of his niece: "What is the matter, Uncle James?" He replied "Nothing more than a change of *mind* my dear."[40] His wit remained with him to the end. The next day he was buried a half-mile from the home where he had always lived with a plain marker over his grave.

MADISON'S FINAL CONTRIBUTION TO THE UNION

The final words that Madison left for the American people provided a brief outline of his legacy. It would first be published in 1850, when the sectionalist and secessionist ambitions of John C. Calhoun again threatened the Union. In 1834 Madison wrote this "Advice to my Country:"

> "As this advice, if it ever see the light will not do it till I am no more it may be considered as issuing from the tomb, where truth alone can be respected, and the happiness of man alone consulted. It will be entitled therefore to whatever weight can be derived from good intentions, and from the experience of one who has served his country in various stations through a period of forty years, who espoused in his youth and adhered through his life to the cause of its liberty, and who has borne a part in most of the great transactions which will constitute epochs of its destiny.
>
> "The advice nearest to my heart and deepest in my convictions is that the Union of the States be cherished and perpetuated. Let the open enemy to it be regarded as a Pandora with her box opened; and the disguised one, as the Serpent creeping with his deadly wiles into Paradise."

This injunction was published fourteen years after his death when John C. Calhoun and Daniel Webster were again waging oratorical battle in the Senate over the meaning and survival of the Federal Union, and Henry Clay was crafting one last political compromise to preserve that Union. Madison's former secretary Edward Coles, a firm Whig supporter of Clay, produced the document in Dolley Madison's hand but secessionists challenged its validity. Many years later a copy

---

[39] Ketcham, *James Madison,* pp. 625-630; Donald O. Dewey, "An American Liberia," *Pacific Historical Review,* May 1962, pp. 179-182; Zall, *Dolley Madison,* p. 97.

[40] Brant, *James Madison: Commander in Chief,* pp. 518-520.

in James Madison's own tiny handwriting was found in his papers. Adrienne Koch chose a few key words from this "Advice" as the basis of a brief but powerful history of Madison's political thought: "Liberty," "great transactions," and "Union."[41]

[41] A facsimile of Madison's "Advice" in his own tiny writing is printed in ibid. between pp. 530 and 531 and a facsimile of Dolley's copy is in Hunt, *Writings of James Madison,* IX, between pp. 610 and 611. Both versions use "see" rather than "sees" in the first sentence; Adrienne Koch, *Madison's "Advice To My Country"* (Princeton: Princeton University Press, 1966); Facsimiles of pages from Madison's will are in Rutland, *James Madison Encyclopedia,* pp. 285-287.

Chapter 14

LEGACY OF PRESIDENT JAMES MADISON

The *liberty* and *union* cited in Madison's final advice to his country perfectly frame his lifetime, with very *great transactions* in between. In his first venture into statesmanship beyond the Orange County level in 1776, he added significant words to the Virginia Declaration of Rights that converted a proposal for religious toleration into a right of religious freedom. In 1789 he expanded the issue of religious freedom to include freedom of speech, press, assembly and petition in a mere 45 words in the magnificent First Amendment of the Bill or Rights. In between those landmarks he had provided the legislative leadership that finally won Virginia's approval of Thomas Jefferson's proposed Statute for Religious Freedom. Jefferson considered this legislation so significant that he insisted that it be engraved on his tombstone along with the Declaration of Independence and establishment of the University of Virginia as his three most memorable contributions, without any mention of his presidency. Madison thus had a direct hand in two of what Jefferson regarded as his greatest personal achievements. The Statute for Religious Freedom and Madison's own "Memorial and Remonstrance against Religious Assessment," guided through the legislature in November 1785, mark a then-rare victory over Patrick Henry and the dominant Virginia Anglican Church. More than two centuries after Madison's epic contributions to religious freedom, they provide the centerpiece of an inspiring new book on religious freedom.[1]

Madison's commitment to preserving the Union was amply demonstrated when he overcame pain and age to compose extensive constitutional essays and correspondence in opposition to state nullification of legislation that had been

---

[1] Hunt, *Writings of James Madison*, I:, pp. 183-191; Steven Waldman, *Founding Faith: Providence, Politics and the Birth of Religious Freedom in America* (New York: Random House, 2008).

approved by Congress and enacted by the President. "The great transactions" hinted at in Madison's advice included his unquestioned leadership in preparing the United States Constitution, winning its ratification by the states, guiding the Bill of Rights through the first Congress, other major legislation in the early Congresses, establishment and leadership of the first national opposition party that would be called "Madisonian" before it became "Jeffersonian" and finally "Republican" and, oh, yes, eight years as Secretary of State and eight more years as President.

Had he not been too modest to request anything more than "James Madison, 1751-1836" on his tombstone a half mile from his Montpelier home, he too would likely have excluded the presidency. This would be entirely appropriate because Madison's years as President were not foremost among those "transactions." Despite his diminutive size he was a truly great man who became President, but his extraordinary achievements in the 1780s and 1790s have not won him a place among the Great Presidents. He was certainly a better President than he has been regarded throughout much of American history, but he is always placed in the second tier. Historian Henry Adams was long the arbiter of the Madison presidency. The disdain for Madison's role as President and as Commander in Chief that pervades Henry Adams's magisterial ten-volume *History of the United States during the Administrations of Jefferson and Madison* (published in 1889 to 1891) would provide the standard view of the fourth President for the next seven decades. This first truly scholarly and extensive history of Madison's presidency exemplified the warning of Associate Justice Joseph Story in 1842. After declaring that the wisdom of Madison surpassed that of Jefferson, Story expressed the burning need for "a full and accurate biography of Madison. I fear that it can hardly be done now; for the men who best appreciated his excellence have nearly all passed away." Among those contemporaries was Henry Adams's grandfather, sixth President John Quincy Adams, who questioned during a eulogy for James Madison, "Is it not in a pre-eminent degree by emanations from his mind that we are assembled here as the representatives of the people and the states of this Union? Is it not transcendentally by his exertions that we address each other here by the endearing appellation of countrymen and fellow citizen?" And the historian's great-grandfather, the second President, wrote to the third President as Madison was leaving Washington, D.C. for the last time in 1817 that Madison's successes in the War of 1812 had accomplished more than each of his predecessors, a startling comment considering the ego of John Adams. For all the "thousand Faults and blunders" of the administration of the War of 1812, as Adams so trenchantly stated, President Madison emerged with a peak of popularity and, more important, the United States emerged stronger than it had ever been and with an international respect to approach its own soaring self-image, no mean accomplishment for what was still a very young nation. Madison was beneficiary of a great deal of luck at the end—highlighted by Ghent and by New Orleans, but good luck was certainly the fate of a number of the more celebrated presidents as well.[2]

It was not only contemporaries named Adams, or his greatest admirer Thomas Jefferson, who praised Madison. The language most often used by commentators such as Henry Clay, Daniel Webster, Charles J. Ingersoll, however, expressed the language more of scholarly constitutional precision rather than that of executive command. "Imperturbable patience" is a virtue but more prized in the many legislatures where Madison reigned supreme than it would be in the White House. Jefferson justly described him as "the first of every assembly of which he afterward became a member. Never wandering from his subject into vain declamation, but pursuing it closely, in language pure, classical, and copious, soothing always the feelings of his adversaries by civilities and softness of expression…." Harold Schultz's brief biography accurately summarized contemporaries' common views of Madison in a single sentence: "All saw him as cool, calm, moderate, temperate, dispassionate, cautious, and reserved."[3]

The balanced government of the United States Constitution is reflected in the personal and political life of James Madison. In addition to a balancing act between states and nation as well as the three essential branches of government that composed them, his political career and entire life were focused as well on the difficult balance of majority and minority rights and responsibilities, political philosophy and scholarship while he was deeply involved in day-to-day politics, and even the existence of slavery in the "land of the free." The last was his greatest frustration because the embarrassing anomaly of slavery was the one crisis for which he could not even envisage a solution.[4]

An expanded conception of James Madison emerged when Irving Brant published his six-volume *James Madison* from 1941 to 1961. A retired editor of a strongly liberal Democratic newspaper, he brought to the biography a mission to demonstrate that his subject was a more capable and more nationalistic President and especially statesman than previous historians had believed. While he constantly allows Madison the benefit of the doubt, even Brant does not claim for

---

[2] Brant, *James Madison: Commander in Chief*, pp. 521, 528; Cappon, *Jefferson-Adams Letters*, II, p. 508.

[3] Thomas Jefferson, *Autobiography* (New York: Capricorn, 1959), p. 55; Harold S. Schultz, *James Madison* (New York: Twayne Publishers, Inc. 1970), p. 8.

[4] Jack N. Rakove, *James Madison and the Creation of the American Republic*, 2nd ed. (New York: Longman, 2002), pp. 227-232.

him greatness as President but he certainly seeks to nudge him somewhat closer toward the top. Ralph Ketcham followed in 1971 with a thoroughly researched and highly readable *James Madison: A Biography,* which remains the standard single volume, although Brant boiled down his six volumes to one in 1970, called *James Madison The Fourth President.* Recent historians have tended to place Madison's presidency between the extremes of Adams and Brant. Especially since 1948 scholars have joined the game of ranking presidents according to their "greatness." In these surveys Madison has been ranked as high as No. 8 (ahead of Andrew Jackson, which certainly would have been applauded by John Quincy Adams and Senators Clay and Webster) and as low as No. 18 (behind William McKinley), with an average of 12.6 in ten polls.[5] There will also be much more research and continued evaluations of him as *The Papers of James Madison,* which began publication at the University of Chicago Press in 1962 and have extended well into the Madison presidency now at the University of Virginia Press, with separate series for his two terms as Secretary of State and for his two terms as President, make important documents available in libraries throughout the world. Ketcham was able to conduct some of the research for his Madison biography while an editor for that project, scouring the country in search of Madison materials. Both before and after he became senior editor when the project was moved from Chicago to Charlottesville, Virginia, Robert A. Rutland has produced several useful studies of various aspects of Madison's political career. Significantly, President John F. Kennedy remarked when he was handed the first two volumes of *The Madison Papers* in 1962 that Madison was probably "the most underrated of our Founding Fathers."[6]

As President, Madison is generally faulted for tolerating a weak Cabinet and ineffective generals early in the War of 1812, and especially for the seizure and burning of Washington, D.C. Yet he ended the war with a strong Cabinet and capable military, naval and diplomatic leadership. And the timing of the peace was for him exquisite. The United States came out of the war united as it never had been and it could with some legitimacy describe the recent conflict as its second War for Independence. Americans felt less insecure and Great Britain no longer regarded Americans as fallen-away colonies in need of discipline. They could now look toward the Pacific with optimism rather than warily toward the Atlantic and could fill in "their" continent with relatively little European interference, partly because of the unofficial protection of the British Royal Navy.

---

[5] Robert K. Murray and Tim H. Blessing, *Greatness in the White House* (University Park: Pennsylvania State University Press, 1988).

Whatever else could be said about the War of 1812 it ended beautifully with Ghent and New Orleans, allowing Madison to bask in the glory of seeming victory. One of the miracles of the Civil War was that the Constitution survived such a cataclysm. The threat of English troops and ships was not comparable to a disruptive Civil War, but Mr. Madison's War was the first major test for the Constitution and he contributed importantly to its survival. A President with less respect for and knowledge of limitations on government surely would have been harsher with New England politicians who severely undercut their country in a time of danger. Madison treated them fairly and even gently despite the vicious things said about him and the war effort. He remained conscious and protective of constitutional limitations and civil liberties throughout the war. Indeed his respect for the separation of powers may even advance him up the scale of presidents when historians are creating the next poll regarding the rating of presidents. He is cited frequently by critics of the return of the Imperial Presidency, or unlimited executive, during the early 21st Century. A well drawn "James Madison, Founding Father and Fourth President" even appeared on the comic pages to debate a Democratic presidential candidate, indicating that Madison is most often cited and quoted on his constitutional beliefs and values rather than because of his political party.[7]

At a height of five feet six inches (and some challenge that figure as an exaggeration) and slight build James Madison was by no means monumental. Yet actual monuments do not even live up to his size. To be sure there are scores of counties, towns, rivers, streets and even the capitalist center Madison Avenue in New York City bearing his name. Yet there is a Washington Monument as well as Mount Vernon, a Jefferson Monument as well as Monticello, and even the Adams family is recognized at the charming family home at Braintree, Massachusetts, where they lived and studied, with each generation making its structural addition. Madison's Montpelier, on the other hand, has been a private home for nearly a century and a half. He had to sell off some of its 5,000 acres before he died. His widow was forced to sell more land and even move back to Washington D.C. shortly after his death. Then after seven years of mismanagement by Madison's step-son Payne Todd, Montpelier was sold with its remaining 2,650 acres. It was still later purchased by industrialist William duPont, who greatly enlarged the home. Thus for decades it could be viewed only at a distance and through a fence. In 1984 his daughter, Marion DuPont Scott, bequeathed the estate to the National

[6] Robert A. Rutland in introduction to Merrill D. Peterson, *The Founding Fathers: James Madison, A Biography in His Own Words* (New York: Newsweek Book Division, 1974), p. 6.

Trust for Historic Preservation. Control was turned over to the Montpelier Foundation in 2000, which initiated a major restoration plan in December 2003. The two major wings that were added by the duPonts have been removed and the building will be restored to its appearance in 1809-1836 when President Madison lived there during and after his presidency. This includes the wing that was added by Madison as home for his mother, so it will contain twenty two rooms rather than fifty five. There are frequent tours of the building and its surroundings, including "restoration tours." The Great Collaboration of Madison and Jefferson is renewed architecturally as Montpelier events and tours are routinely announced in conjunction with Monticello events.[8]

Probably it makes best sense considering the life, accomplishments and scholarly nature of James Madison that, whatever happens to Montpelier, what is described officially as "the nation's memorial" to him will always remain the magnificent six-story James Madison Memorial Building of the Library of Congress on Independence Avenue between First and Second streets in Washington, D.C. It is of course next to the Thomas Jefferson and John Adams Buildings of the Library of Congress as well as the Capitol Building. It was dedicated in April 1980 and opened to the public in May.

James Madison University, a public co-educational university located in the Shenandoah Valley in Harrisonburg, Virginia, is celebrating its 100th Anniversary in 2008. Named for the fourth U.S. president, James Madison University was originally founded in 1908 as the State Normal and Industrial School, but was expanded and given the name James Madison University in 1976, the year of the Bi-Centennial. Founded originally by the Virginia General Assembly, this significant research university today remains a fitting monument to James Madison, Defender of the American Republic.

---

[7] A typical example is Robert Scheer, "King George W.: James Madison's Nightmare," *The Nation,* July 30, 2007; Darrin Bell, "Candorville," *Los Angeles Times,* August 12, 2007, p. H 7.

[8] The current status of restorations can be learned at www.Montpelier.org.

ABOUT THE AUTHORS

DR. DONALD ODELL DEWEY

Donald Odell Dewey is emeritus professor of history and emeritus dean of Natural and Social Sciences at California State University, Los Angeles, where he has been a faculty member since 1962. During his retirement he was vice president of Trinity College of Graduate Studies, in Anaheim, California, for five years and he is currently president of the statewide California State University Emeritus and Faculty Association.

Born and raised in Portland, Oregon, he graduated in journalism from the University of Oregon in 1952. He expected to be shipped to Korea after his graduation but when his draft board took an immediate dislike for his glasses he lost the opportunity for heroism and worse in Korea. He then married Charlotte Neuber Dewey to whom he is still married after 56 years. They have three children, Leslie LaVoie (a teacher), Catherine Dewey (a legal administrator) and Scott Dewey (an attorney and history PhD). Don Dewey was managing editor of the *Condon Globe Times* until 1953 when he became city editor of the *Ashland Daily Tidings.* In those days when the great Oregon Shakespearean Festival advertised "Stay four days and see four plays" he reviewed all plays for two years. Then he returned to college to make himself a better newspaperman by studying history.

With an MS degree in history from the University of Utah in 1956, he found that publishers resisted hiring him because "how do we know you'll stay." While returning from such an interview in Indiana in 1957 fortunately he stopped and fell in love with the University of Chicago and made it home for the next five years. Hired first as a typist because of his editing prowess, he soon became a research associate, then assistant editor of *The Papers of James Madison.* When he received his doctorate in 1960 with a dissertation on Madison, he was advanced to associate editor and instructor at the University of Chicago. This was the first time he had ever taught a class, and what a relief for a history PhD to find that he could teach and loved doing it.

In 1962 Dr. Dewey moved to Los Angeles State College of Applied Arts and Sciences, planning to remain for two years but he is still there. He soon became involved in faculty governance, chaired major committees and held every Senate office at what became California State University, Los Angeles. In 1976 he was honored as campus Outstanding Professor. Thirteen years later he was nominated by the faculty committee as the Cal State LA candidate for the statewide Outstanding Professor award.

1970 was a banner year for him. He had declined the senate chairmanship to remain vice chair for the previous two years because of book contracts. With both *Marshall Versus Jefferson: The Political Background of Marbury v. Madison* and *Liberty and Justice: Documents in American Constitutional History* published by June 1970, accompanied by promotion to full professor, he was elected chair of the Senate. While negotiating with the president for increased support for the senate he was asked instead to become dean of Letters and Science, a position for which he was not a candidate. He was asked to promise five years as dean but would commit only to three years. In 1996 Dean Dewey finally retired after fourteen years as dean of Letters and Science and another eleven as dean of Natural and Social Sciences.

In addition to those previously named, his books range from three volumes of *The Papers of James Madison; Invitation to the Dance: An Introduction to Social Dance;* and *That's a Good One: Cal State LA at 50.* Others include *Becoming Informed Citizens: Lessons on the Constitution for Secondary Students, Becoming Informed Citizens: Lessons on the Bill of Right; The Federalist and Antifederalist Papers and The Continuing Dialogue,* 2 volumes. He has published essays in several encyclopedias, most significantly Melvin Urofsky, *Biography of the Supreme Court: The Lives and Philosophies of the Justices* and Robert A. Rutland, *James Madison and the American Nation: An Encyclopedia, 1751-1836.*

He received $650,000 in grants from the National Endowment for the Humanities to offer a series of constitutional history institutes for secondary and middle school teachers. His programs brought distinguished Madison biographers Irving Brant, Ralph Ketcham and Robert A. Rutland to speak to Los Angeles teachers, as well as early American historians Joyce Appleby and Gary Nash. He was also keynote speaker at a Washington, D.C. meeting of the National Institutes for Health.

Dr. Barbara Bennett Peterson

Barbara Bennett Peterson is Emeritus Professor of History, University of Hawaii and former Fellow at the East-West Center, Honolulu. She was also a Research Associate at Bishop Museum and an Adjunct Professor of History at Hawaii Pacific University. Dr. Peterson was a Professor of History by Courtesy at Oregon State University, Corvallis, Oregon, and Adjunct Faculty at Portland State University, Portland, Oregon, where she was the president of the Friends of History. She has had the pleasure of teaching adults at the Osher Institute of Life Long Learning at California State University San Bernardino, Palm Desert in 2004 and 2005. Dr. Peterson has been a Contributing Review Editor for the *Biography* Journal at the University of Hawaii at Manoa for nearly ten years. Currently, she is the Series Editor of the Nova Science Publishers' book series titled *First Men, America's Presidents.*

Born and raised in Portland, Oregon, Barbara Bennett Peterson attended Oregon State University receiving a dual degree B.A. and B.S. in 1964. She attended graduate school at Stanford University where she received her M.A. in American History in 1965. She received her PhD from the University of Hawaii in 1978 in American History specializing in Social, Cultural, and Intellectual History.

She was a Fulbright Scholar to Sophia University, Tokyo, Japan in 1967 and to the People's Republic of China 1988-89. While a Senior Fulbright Scholar in China, she was presented with the Outstanding Teacher of the Year Award (Number 1 Scholar).

While teaching at the University of Hawaii (1967-1997), she served as Assistant Dean of Humanities and Social Sciences in 1973. Dr. Peterson received the University of Hawaii Board of Regent's Medal for Excellence in Teaching for 1993. She taught World Civilization, a two semester course for the University of Hawaii, for four years on Hawaii Public Television. Dr. Peterson has taught American Civilization courses for thirty one years at the University, in addition to graduate courses in Historiography and American Thought and Culture. Dr. Barbara Peterson and her husband, Dr. Frank L. Peterson, Professor of Geology and former Department Chairman at the University of Hawaii at Manoa, during their sabbatical and a university leave, taught on the Semester at Sea program for Chapman University (Spring 1974), University of Colorado at Boulder (Fall 1978), and for University of Pittsburgh (Fall 1999) sailing/teaching three times around the world. The Drs. Peterson have been married for forty years. They donate a portion of their book royalties to local, state, national, and world-wide children's charities. In 1997 Dr. Barbara Bennett Peterson was chosen as a Distinguished Alumni of the University of Hawaii.

Dr. Peterson has earlier published the books *Franklin Delano Roosevelt, Preserver of Spirit and Hope* (A Volume in Nova's First Men series 2006), *George Washington, America's Moral Exemplar* (A Volume in Nova's First Men series 2005), *Emalani, Queen Emma Kaleleonlani* (with Alfons L. Korn 2003), *Sarah Childress Polk, First Lady of Tennessee and Washington* (A Volume in Nova's First Ladies series 2003), *Hawaii in the World* (2000), *Notable Women of China* (2000), *John Bull's Eye on America* (1995), *American History 17th, 18th, and 19th Centuries* (1993), *America 19th and 20th Centuries* (1993), *The Pacific Region: Change and Challenge* (with Wilhelm G. Solheim II (1990), *America In British Eyes* (1988), and *Notable Women of Hawaii* (1984).

Dr. Peterson worked for the federal Department of Education as a grant reviewer for the Teaching American History Grant Awards in 2008 and earlier was a project reviewer for the National Endowment for the Humanities. In 2007 she was a consultant for the U.S. Mint in editing the descriptions of the coins to be minted and issued in the First Spouse (First Ladies) coin series.

Foremost, Barbara Bennett Peterson is a biographer who seeks to write role models for adults as well as young people of 'lives well-lived'. She is the Deputy Director General of the International Biography Centre in Cambridge, United Kingdom, and a Deputy Governor of the American Biographical Institute in Raleigh, North Carolina. She has contributed over 100 biographies of significant people to encyclopedias and various biographical special collections. Dr. Peterson was an Associate Editor working with Drs. John A. Garraty and Mark C. Carnes, General Editors, on the *American National Biography,* a 24 volume series published by Oxford University Press in 1999. This series won the Dartmouth Medal for Best Library Reference from the American Library Association. Three of her authored books have been nominated for Pulitzer Prizes in History and Biography.

BIBLIOGRAPHY

Adair, Douglass, "The Disputed Authorship of the Federalist Papers," *William and Mary Quarterly,* 3rd series, Vol. I, pp. 97-122, 235-264.

______________, ed., "James Madison's Autobiography," *William and Mary Quarterly, 2nd* series 3, Vol. II (1945), pp. 206-209.

Adams, Henry, *The War of 1812,* edited by Major H.A. De Weerd. Introduction by Colonel John R. Elting, reprinted New York: Cooper Square Press, 1999. This book consists of sections from Henry Adams' nine-volume *History of the United States during the Administrations of Jefferson and Madison* (1889-1891).

____________, *History of the United States during the Administrations of Thomas Jefferson and James Madison,* New York: Charles Scribner's Sons, 1889-1891.

____________, *The Papers of Albert Gallatin,* New York: Antiquarian Press, Ltd., 1960.

Annals of Congress 11 Congress, 1 Session, 1; 12 Congress, 1 Session, 1 (1811-1812).

Anthony, Katharine, *Dolly Madison, Her Life and Times,* Garden City, NY: Doubleday, 1949.

Bailey, Thomas A., *A Diplomatic History of the American People,* New York: Appleton-Century-Crofts, 1964.

Banning, Lance, *The Sacred Fire of Liberty: James Madison and the Founding of the Republic,* Ithaca, NY: Cornell University Press, 1995.

Beard, Charles A., *An Economic Interpretation of the Constitution,* New York: Macmillan Company, 1913.

Benn, Carl, *The War of 1812,* New York: Routledge, 2003.

Berkin, Carol, *A Brilliant Solution: Inventing the American Constitution,* New York: Harcourt, 2002.

Bozonelis, Helen Koutras, *Primary Source Accounts of the War of 1812,* Berkeley Heights, NJ: Enslow Publishers, 2006.

Brant, Irving, *James Madison: The Virginia Revolutionist,* Indianapolis: Bobbs-Merrill, 1941.

__________, *James Madison: The Nationalist, 1780-1787,* Indianapolis: Bobbs-Merrill, 1948.

__________, *James Madison: Father of the Constitution,* Indianapolis: Bobbs-Merrill, 1959.

__________, *James Madison: Secretary of State, 1801-1809,* Indianapolis: Bobbs-Merrill, 1950.

__________, *James Madison: The President, 1809-1812,* Indianapolis: Bobbs-Merrill, 1956.

__________, *James Madison: Commander in Chief, 1812-1836,* Indianapolis: Bobbs-Merrill, 1961.

__________, *James Madison: The Fourth President: A Life of James Madison,* Indianapolis, Bobbs-Merrill, 1970.

__________," Dolley Payne Todd Madison," in Edward T. James, et al, eds., *Notable American Women,* Cambridge, MA: Belknap Press of Harvard University, 1971.

Berky, Andrew S. and James P. Shenton, *The Historians' History of the United States,* Vols. I & II, New York: G.P. Putnam's Sons, 1966.

Berton, Pierre, *The Invasion of Canada, 1812-1813,* Boston: and Toronto: McClelland and Stewart, 1980, republished by Anchor Canada, 2001.

__________, *Flames Across the Border: The Canadian-American Tragedy, 1813-1814,* Boston and Toronto: McClelland and Stewart, 1981, republished by Anchor Canada, 2001.

__________, *Capture of Detroit,* Toronto: McClelland and Stewart, 1991.

__________, *Death of Isaac Brock,* Toronto: McClelland and Stewart, 1991.

Borneman, Walter R., *1812: The War That Forged a Nation,* New York: HarperCollins, 2004.

Bozonelis, Helen Koutras, *Primary Sources Accounts of the War of 1812,* Berkeley Heights, NJ: Enslow Publishers, 2006.

Brugger, Robert, and Mary A. Hackett, et al., *The Papers of James Madison, Secretary of State Series,* Charlottesville: University of Virginia Press, 1986---.

Bruce, Philip A., *History of the University of Virginia,* New York: Macmillan Co., 1920.

Burnett, Edmund C., ed., *Letters of Members of the Continental Congress,* 8 volumes, Washington, D.C.: Carnegie Institution, 1921-1936.

Carter, Alden, *The War of 1812: Second Fight for Independence,* New York: F. Watts, 1992.

Cooke, Jacob, ed., *The Federalist,* Middleton, CT: Wesleyan University Press, 1961.

Cappon, Lester J., *The Adams-Jefferson Letters,* Chapel Hill: University of North Carolina Press, 1959.

Debates and Proceedings in the Congress of the United States (1825-1837), 4th Congress, 1st Session, V.

Dewey, Donald O., *Union and Liberty: Documents in American Constitutionalism,* New York: McGraw Hill, 1969.

_________________, *Marshall Versus Jefferson: The Political Background of Marbury v. Madison,* New York: A.A. Knopf, 1970.

_________________, "Democratic-Republican Societies" in Robert A. Rutland, *James Madison and the American Nation, An Encyclopedia*, New York: Simon & Schuster, 1994, pp. 111-112.

_________________, "James Monroe," in Robert A. Rutland, *James Madison and the American Nation, An Encyclopedia,* New York: Simon & Schuster, 1994, pp. 305-308.

_________________, "John Randolph of Roanoke," in Robert A. Rutland, ed., *James Madison and the American Nation, An Encyclopedia,* New York: Simon & Schuster, 1994, pp. 354-355.

_________________, "Supreme Court," in Robert A. Rutland, *James Madison and the American Nation, An Encyclopedia,* New York: Simon & Schuster, 1994, pp. 392-393.

_________________, "Yazoo Land Grab," in Robert A. Rutland, ed., *James Madison and the American Nation, An Encyclopedia,* New York: Simon & Schuster, 1994, pp. 457-458.

_________________, "Crosskey vs. Madison: James Madison and the United States Constitution," *Richmond Law Review,* XIX (Winter 1985), pp. 435-446.

_________________, "Vote of Confidence for the Bill of Rights," *American Journal of Legal History,* VII (April 1963), pp. 137-141.

_________________, "James Madison Helps Clio Interpret the Constitution," *American Journal of Legal History,* XV (October 1971), pp. 38-51.

_________________, "An American Liberia," *Pacific Historical Review,* (May 1962), pp. 179-182.

_________________, "Madison's Response to Jackson's Foes," *Tennessee Historical Quarterly* (June, 1961), pp. 167-176.

_________________, " The Sage of Montpelier: The Constitutional and Political Thought of James Madison, 1817-1836," doctoral dissertation, University of Chicago, September 1960.

Dudley, William S., ed., *The Naval War of 1812: A Documentary History,* Washington, D.C.: Naval History Center, Department of the Navy, 1985.

Elliot, Jonathan, ed. *Debates in the Several State Conventions on the Adoption of the Constitution,* 5 volumes, Philadelphia: Lippincott, 1836-1845.

Elting, John R., *Amateurs to Arms! The Military History of the War of 1812,* New York: Da Capo Press, 1995.

Farrand, Max, ed., *The Records of the Federal Convention of 1787,* 4 volumes, New Haven: Yale University Press, 1911.

Fitz-Enz, Colonel David G., *The Final Invasion, Plattsburgh, the War of 1812's Most Decisive Battle,* New York: Cooper Square Press, 2001.

Forester, C.S., *The Age of Fighting Sail, The Story of The Naval War of 1812,* Sandwich, MA: Chapman Billies, 1956.

Grigsby, Hugh Blair, *The Virginia Convention of 1776,* Richmond, VA: J.W. Randolph, 1855.

_________________, *The History of the Virginia Federal Convention of 1788,* 2 volumes, New York: Da Capo Press, 1969 (reprinted).

Goodman, W.H., "The Origins of the War of 1812: A Survey of Changing Interpretations," *Mississippi Valley Historical Review,* XXVIII (1941), pp.171-186.

Groom, Winston, *Patriotic Fire, Andrew Jackson and Jean Laffite at the Battle of New Orleans,* New York: Alfred A. Knopf, 2006.

Hamilton, Stanislaus, ed., *The Writings of James Monroe,* 7 volumes, New York: G.P. Putnam & Sons, 1898-1903.

Heidler, David Stephen, *The War of 1812,* Westport, CT: Greenwood Press, 2002.

Hickey, Donald R., *War of 1812: A Forgotten Conflict,* Urbana: University of Illinois Press, 1989.

Hitsman, J. Mackay, *The Incredible War of 1812: A Military History,* Toronto: University of Toronto Press, 1965.

Hopkins, James F., ed., *The Papers of Henry Clay,* 10 volumes, Lexington: University of Kentucky Press, 1959-1992.

Horsman, Reginald, *The Causes of the War of 1812,* New York: A.S. Barnes, 1962.

Hunt, Gaillard, ed. *The Writings of James Madison,* 9 volumes, New York: G.P. Putnam & Sons, 1900-1910.

____________, ed., *The First Forty Years of Washington Society in the Family Letters of Margaret Bayard Smith,* New York: Frederick Ungar Publishing Co., 1906.

Hutchinson, William T. and Robert A. Rutland, et al., eds., *The Papers of James Madison, Congressional Series,* 17 volumes, Chicago and Charlottesville: University of Chicago Press and University of Virginia Press, 1964-1991,

Ingersoll, Charles Jared, *Historical Sketches of the Second War Between the United States and Great Britain,* Philadelphia: Lea and Blanchard, 1845-1849.

Jefferson, Thomas, *Autobiography,* New York: Capricorn, 1959.

Kenyon, Cecelia, "Men of Little Faith: The Anti-Federalists on the Nature of Republican Government," *William and Mary Quarterly,* 3rd series, XII (1955), pp. 3-43.

Ketcham, Ralph, *James Madison: A Biography,* Charlottesville: University of Virginia Press, 1971, revised 1990.

____________, "An Unpublished Sketch of James Madison," *Virginia Magazine of History and Biography,* Vol. 67 (1959), pp. 432-447.

Koch, Adrienne, *Jefferson and Madison: The Great Collaboration,* New York: Oxford University Press, 1964.

____________, *Madison's "Advice to My Country,"* Princeton: Princeton University Press, 1966.

Lamb, W.K., *The Hero of Upper Canada,* Toronto: Rous and Mann Press, 1962.

Langguth, A.J., *Union 1812: The Americans Who Fought the Second War of Independence,* New York: Simon & Schuster, 2006.

Latimer, Jon, *1812: War With America,* Cambridge, MA: Belknap Press, 2007.

Levy, Leonard W., "Virginia Report of 1799-1800" in Robert A. Rutland, *James Madison and the American Nation, An Encyclopedia,* New York: Simon & Schuster, 1994, p. 428.

Lipscomb, Andrew A., ed., 20 volumes, *The Writings of Thomas Jefferson,* Washington, D.C.: Thomas Jefferson Memorial Association, 1903-1904.

Lodge, Henry Cabot, *Historical and Political Essays,* Boston: Houghton Mifflin & Co., 1892.

Loizeau, Pierre-Marie, *The Little Magician, Martin Van Buren, Eighth President of the United States,* New York: Nova Science Publishers, 2009.

Looney, J. Jefferson, ed., *The Papers of Thomas Jefferson: Retirement Series,* Princeton: Princeton University Press, 2004---.

Madison, James, *"Advice to My Country,"* edited by David B. Mattern, Charlottesville: University of Virginia Press, 1997.

____________, *Letters and Other Writings of James Madison,* edited by William C. Rives and Philip R. Fendall, 4 volumes, Philadelphia: J. B. Lippincott, 1865.

____________, *The Papers of James Madison, Congressional Series,* edited by William T. Hutchinson, Robert A. Rutland et al., 17 volumes, Chicago and Charlottesville: University of Chicago Press and University of Virginia Press, 1964-1991.

____________, *The Papers of James Madison, Secretary of State Series,* edited by Robert Brugger, Mary A. Hackett, et al., Charlottesville: University of Virginia Press, 1986---.

____________, *The Papers of James Madison, Presidential Series,* edited by Robert A. Rutland, J. C. A. Stagg, et al., Charlottesville: University of Virginia Press, 1984---.

____________, *The Writings of James Madison,* edited by Gaillard Hunt, 9 volumes, New York: G. P. Putnam's Sons, 1900-1910.

____________, *Madison Writings,* edited by Jack N. Rakove, New York: Literary Classics of the United States, 1999.

McCoy, Drew R., *The Last of the Fathers: James Madison and the Republican Legacy,* New York: Cambridge University Press, 1989.

Mahon, John K., *The War of 1812,* Gainesville: The University of Florida, 1972.

Meriwether, Robert .L. ed., *The Papers of John C. Calhoun,* 10 volumes, Columbia: University of South Carolina Press, 1959-2003.

Miller, Robert S. and Donald O. Dewey, "The Congressional Salary Amendment," *Glendale Law Review,* X (1991), pp. 98-109.

Molotsky, Irvin, *The Flag, the Poet, & the Song, The Story of the Star-Spangled Banner,* New York: Dutton, 2001.

Morgan, Henry J., *Sketches of Celebrated Canadians and Persons Connected to Canada,* London: Hunter, Rose, 1934.

Morris, Richard Brandon, *The War of 1812,* Minneapolis: Lerner Publications, Co., 1985.

Mosteller, Frederick and Daniel P. Wallace, *Inference and Disputed Authorship: The Federalist,* Middleton, CT: Wesleyan University Press, 1961.

Nardo, Don, *The War of 1812,* San Diego: Lucent Books, 2000.

National Archives in Washington, D.C., Record Group 107.

National Intelligencer, Washington, D.C. newspaper 1801-1815.

Niles' Register, Baltimore, MD newspaper 1811-1815.

Nursey, Walter R., *The Story of Isaac Brock: Hero, Defender and Savior of Upper Canada, 1812,* Toronto: William Briggs, 1909, republished 2006.

Perkins, Bradford, "George Canning, Great Britain, and the United States, 1807-1809," *American Historical Review* LXIII (1957), pp. 1-22.

________________, *Prologue to War: England and the United States, 1805-1812,* Berkeley: University of California Press, 1961.

Peterson, Barbara Bennett, *George Washington, America's Moral Exemplar,* New York: Nova Science Publishers, 2006.

______________________, "Benjamin Franklin," in Gregory Fremont-Barnes and Richard A. Ryerson, eds., *Encyclopedia of the American Revolutionary War, A Political, Social, and Military History,* ABC-CLIO Publishers, Santa Barbara, CA and Oxford, UK, 2006.

______________________, "Joseph Bonaparte," in Gregory-Fremont-Barnes, ed., *The French Revolution and Napoleonic Wars,* Vol. One, Santa Barbara, CA and Oxford, UK: ABC-CLIO, 2006, pp. 159-162.

______________________, "Sir Edward Pakenham," in Gregory-Fremont Barnes, ed., *The French Revolution and Napoleonic Wars,* Vol. Two, Santa Barbara, CA and Oxford, UK: ABC-CLIO, 2006, pp. 733-734.

______________________, "Joseph Galloway," in Gregory Fremont-Barnes ed., *Encyclopedia of the Age of Political Revolutions and New Ideologies,* Westport, CT: Greenwood Press, 2007.

______________________, "John Hancock," Gregory Fremont-Barnes, ed., *Encyclopedia of the Age of Political Revolutions and New Ideologies,* Westport, CT: Greenwood Press, 2007.

______________________, "Patrick Henry," Gregory Fremont-Barnes, ed., *Encyclopedia of the Age of Political Revolutions and New Ideologies,* Westport, CT: Greenwood Press, 2007.

Peterson, Merrill D., *The Founding Fathers: James Madison, A Biography in His Own Words,* New York: Newsweek Book Division, 1974.

Pitch, Anthony S., *The Burning of Washington, The British Invasion of 1814,* Annapolis: Naval Institute Press, 1998.

Purcell, L. Edward, ed., *The Vice Presidents: A Biographical Dictionary,* New York: Facts on File, 1998.

Queen, Mary Jane Child, *William Henry Harrison, General and President,* New York: Nova Science Publishers, 2006.

Rakove, Jack N., *James Madison and the Creation of the American Republic,* Glenview, IL: Scott, Foresman, 1993.

____________________, ed., *James Madison Writings,* New York: The Library of America, 1999.

____________________, *James Madison,* New York: Longman, 2002.

Read, D.B., *The Lieutenant-Governors of Upper Canada and Ontario, 1792-1899,* Toronto: William Briggs, 1900.

Reeder, Red, *The Story of the War of 1812,* New York: Duell, Sloan and Pearce, 1960.

Richardson, James D., ed., *A Compilation of the Messages and Papers of the Presidents,* New York: Bureau of National Literature, 1897.

Rives, William C. and Philip R. Kendall, eds., *Letters and Other Writings of James Madison,* 4 volumes, Philadelphia: J. B. Lippincott, 1865.

Roosevelt, Theodore, *The Naval War of 1812,* New York: Modern Library, revised edition, 1999.

Rutland, Robert A., and J. C. A. Stagg, et al., eds., *The Papers of James Madison, Presidential Series,* Charlottesville: University of Virginia Press, 1986---.

_____________, *James Madison The Founding Father,* New York: Macmillan, 1987.

_______________, *Madison's Alternatives: The Jeffersonian Republicans and the Coming of War, 1805-1812,* Philadelphia, Lippincott, 1975.

_______________, *The Presidency of James Madison,* Lawrence: University of Kansas Press, 1990.

_______________, *James Madison and the American Nation, 1751-1836, An Encyclopedia,* New York: Simon & Schuster, 1994.

Schultz, Harold S., *James Madison,* New York: Twayne Publishers, 1970.

Schultz, Randy, *Washington Ablaze: The War of 1812,* Vero Beach, FL: Rourke Publishers, 2007.

Severance, Frank H., ed., "Documents Relating to the War of 1812: The Letter-book of General Roger Hale Sheaffe," Buffalo Historical Society Publications, Buffalo, NY: 1913, Vol. 17, pp. 271-381.

Shalhope, Robert E., *John Taylor of Caroline: Pastoral Republican,* Columbia: University of South Carolina Press, 1980.

Skeen, C. Edward, *Citizen Soldiers in the War of 1812,* Lexington: University of Kentucky Press, 1999.

_______________, "James Wilkinson," in Robert A. Rutland, ed., *James Madison and the American Nation 1751-1836, An Encyclopedia,* New York: Simon & Schuster, 1994, pp. 449-451.

Stacey, C.P., *The Battle of Little York,* Toronto: Toronto Historical Board, revised edition, 1977.

Stagg, J.C.A., *Mr. Madison's War: Politics, Diplomacy, and Warfare in the Early Republic, 1783-1830,* Princeton: Princeton University Press, 1983.

Staudenraus, P.J., *The African Colonial Movement, 1816-1865,* New York: Columbia University Press, 1961.

Story, Joseph, *Commentaries on the Constitution of the United States,* 4th ed., Boston: Little Brown, 1873.

Syrett, Harold, et al., eds., *The Papers of Alexander Hamilton,* 10 volumes, *New* York: Columbia University Press, 1961-1987.

Taylor, G.R., "Agrarian Discontent in the Mississippi Valley Preceding the War of 1812," *Journal of Political Economy* XXXIX (1931): 471-505.

Teed, Paul E., *John Quincy Adams: Yankee Nationalist,* New York: Nova Science Publishers, 2006.

Todd, Anne, *The War of 1812,* Mankato, MN: Capstone Books, 2001.

Walch, Timothy, ed., *At the President's Side: The Vice Presidency in the Twentieth Century,* Columbia: University of Missouri Press, 1997.

Waldman, Steven, *Founding Faith: Providence, Politics, and the Birth of Religious Freedom in America,* New York: Random House, 2008.

Webster's Biographical Dictionary, Springfield, MA: G. & C. Merriam Co., 1959.

Westcott, Alan, "Stephen Decatur," in Allen Johnson and Dumas Malone, eds., *Dictionary of American Biography,* New York: Charles Scribner's Sons, 1946.

White, Leonard D., *The Jeffersonians: A Study in Administrative History, 1801-1829,* New York: Macmillan Co., 1951.

Wills, Gary, *James Madison,* Lawrence: University of Kansas Press, 2007.

Zall, Paul M., *Dolley Madison,* New York: Nova Science Publishers, 2001.

Zarcher, Alfred J., *Trial and Triumph: Presidential Power in the Second Term,* Fort Wayne, Indiana: Presidential Press, 1996.

INDEX

A

B

D

E

F

G

H

I

J

K

N

O

P

Q

R

S

T

W

Y

Z